An American Vision for the Middle East

Bruce Abramson, Ph.D., J.D.
Senior Fellow, the London Center for Policy Research
VP & Director of Policy, the Iron Dome Alliance
bdabramson@gmail.com
October 2016*

Introduction by Jeff Ballabon

I feel privileged to offer an introductory note to this brilliant contribution to American foreign policy written by my colleague, collaborator and friend, Dr. Bruce Abramson, Esq.

An American Vision for the Middle East is articulate, compelling, and in many ways revolutionary for its clarity. *An American Vision for the Middle East* makes order out of chaos and sets forth lucid, comprehensive goals and strategies for the pursuit of America's interests in one of the most troubled and consequential regions on the planet.

The politics and real trajectory of the Middle East are obscured behind a host of labels, theories, projections and prejudices. In this seminal monograph, Dr. Abramson's ability to analyze, interpret, extrapolate, predict and diagnose large, seemingly chaotic and disparate data sets is on brilliant display. As compelling as it is from a cold-eyed realpolitik perspective, *An American Vision for the Middle East* is no less a document of great moral clarity and a vigorous assertion of American Exceptionalism and the restoration of America to its proper - and direly needed - role as the global superpower and bulwark of Western Civilization and liberal values.

I have spent the last 25 years dealing with the nitty gritty of American policy in numerous arenas, first as a US Senate professional committee staffer and legislative counsel, then as a strategist, tactician, lawyer, and lobbyist. But it is this one area—America's role in the Middle East—that has been the common thread throughout. It has been a passion, even a compulsion, as I saw the terrible devastation not only to America's strategic ally Israel, but to the Jewish people, as well as the horrible human suffering throughout the region that stemmed as often from the confusion of friends as from the ill will of foes. Here, in Bruce's book, is the way out of that terrible darkness.

As a director of the London Center for Policy Research, it also was my pleasure to introduce Bruce to its founder and chairman, Dr. Herbert London. Herb, seeing Bruce's genius. promptly enlisted him as a Senior Fellow—where Bruce joined other London Center fellows, including National Security Advisor General Michael Flynn and Secretary of Defense-designate General James Mattis. Herb is not only an exceptional spotter of talent and policy genius, he is a luminary who has earned a level of genuine admiration and affection rarely seen in the contentious worlds of academia, politics, policy and public affairs. In its few years of existence, the London Center has quickly garnered a reputation similar to that of its namesake for its openness, intellectual honesty and seriousness of purpose in translating important American ideas into actionable policy. Herb's support for this book gives it an imprimatur far beyond my ability.

While many in the think tank world sniffed, Bruce and I worked happily and productively with Donald Trump's outstanding advisors on Israel policy, and we actively supported his campaign. We are persuaded that President Trump represents an extraordinary pivot away from the groupthink, mythologies, counterproductive pieties, and entrenched interests that have so plagued America's foreign policy. It is our hope that the policies contained in this book make their way to the Trump Administration because we believe they are the best way to achieve stability in the Middle East and fully aligned with Donald Trump's sincere goal to Make America Great Again.

Jeff Ballabon, January 2017

Introduction by Herbert I. London

The pathway to peace, or more sensibly stability, in the Middle East is paved with pathologies, i.e. ethnic hatred, ancient territorial claims, colonial imposition. It is also saddled with conventional ideas that repudiate the present reality, ideas either anachronistic or wrongheaded.

In the middle of this cauldron is a small nation of seven million people that defies regional reality. At least 75 million Arabs want to destroy this island of prosperity, Israel. In fact, missiles are assembled from Lebanon to Gaza with only one goal in mind – the destruction of this land of Jews.

To make matters more acute, many in the U.S. State Department and European officials are sympathetic to the hostile neighbors of Israel. Fortunately, the evolution of events have converted Israel and the so-called Palestinian issue onto the backburner as an ISIS army has conquered huge swaths of Iraq and Syria – and has metastasized into Libya, Pakistan and Afghanistan – and an Iranian force seeking a Shia Crescent throughout the Middle East is attempting to create the Persian Empire redux.

Making sense of these conditions is no small task. Many have attempted to so but few have been successful. Bruce Abramson, however, has launched into this murky landscape and produced a book that is clear, interesting and filled with appropriate prescriptions. He not only provides background and analysis; he offers guidance to the policy maker. *An American Vision for The Middle East* is an ideological map for those seeking a way out of the present maze. Not everyone will agree with Dr. Abramson, but no one can ignore his profound analysis.

HIL, December 2016

Contents

Journey to the Center of the Conflict

Chapter 1. A Confusing Place

The Middle East is a confusing place. It seems that no matter what we try to do, no matter how we set U.S. policy, things just keep getting worse. Pick a President—pick your favorite President—and consider his legacy in the Middle East.

Most recently, Barack Obama alienated our allies, slept through the birth of ISIS, helped replace stable dictators with genocidal Islamists, and handed Iran respectability, cash, and a clear path to nuclear weapons and a missile delivery system. George W. Bush diverted resources from Afghanistan before rooting out al Qaeda and the Taliban, expected post-Saddam Iraq to fall neatly into democracy, waited too long before trying to correct that error, and encouraged Israel to create a power vacuum that quickly became the terror statelet of Gaza.

Before that, Bill Clinton trusted Yasir Arafat and ignored Osama bin Laden, creating near-perfect conditions for them to nurture the leading terrorist movements of the twenty-first century. George H.W. Bush started strong in Iraq, let Saddam slaughter Shiites and Kurds while hoping that they could end his totalitarian regime by themselves, then mired our military in a lengthy stalemate—while handing Lebanon to Syria, enabling a refugee flow that almost destabilized Jordan, and challenging Israel's future as a secure Jewish state. Ronald Reagan sent the Marines into Lebanon, watched them get shot, then retreated—and for good measure opposed Israel's destruction of Saddam's nuclear weapons program. Jimmy Carter favored the Ayatollah Khomeini over the Shah, then stood like a deer in the headlights while fifty-two Americans spent 444 days as Iranian hostages. Gerald Ford watched crises engulf Cyprus and Lebanon, alienated Turkey, Greece, and Israel, and cozied up to Saddam Hussein in Iraq.

I could continue, but you get the point. If past performance is any guide, we can rule out intervention, withdrawal, economic engagement, aid, limited war, and diplomacy, as the bases of a viable American approach to the region. Which leaves us with...what, exactly?

So if you've ever found the Middle East confusing, you're in good company. By all evidence, and no matter how capable they may be in other areas, our finest political, military, academic, and journalistic experts consistently get the region wrong.

This essay starts with a simple hypothesis: *Maybe they're missing something.*

I'll go further. Maybe our finest accredited experts on the Middle East are missing something big, something foundational. Maybe some of the most common assumptions they internalize on day one of their training are so backwards that they doom smart, hard-working scholars and pundits to lengthy careers of distinguished failure. Maybe the goal of contemporary Middle Eastern studies is currying favor among other Middle Eastern scholars rather than explaining the region's recent history, understanding its current trends, or helping the U.S. devise policies capable of stabilizing the region and improving the lives of its people.

Perhaps it's time to take a step backwards, to drop some long held beliefs and preconceived notions, to question conventional wisdom, and to see if we can figure out what they've been missing.

Think of the pages that follow as a journey to various corners of the Middle East, at various moments of its history, with a particular focus on the past century. We will meet the region's people, watch its leaders, and listen to its thinkers. We will also keep an eye on American—and at times, broader Western—policy, particularly since the end of the Cold War. We will remind ourselves of our own leaders' stated goals and our most accomplished experts' most confident predictions. Then we will assess their performance in light of history's outcomes.

We will also undertake a few side excursions into analytic methodology so that we can appreciate why the (numerous) failures and (occasional) successes of American policy unfolded as they did. On those side trips, we will consider the relationship among observable evidence, explanations, predictions, and recommendations—dipping our toes lightly into political science, psychology, philosophy, economics, logic, statistics, and the sociology of science. (I promise: No math).

Our journey may be uncomfortable. For those who have paid the region scant attention in the past, the panorama should be clear but much of the action may bewilder. For others, the action will be familiar, but past preconceptions may obscure the view. Only those willing to concede that conventional wisdom may—just may—incorporate far more conventionality than wisdom should join us.

Though all are welcome, this trip will not accommodate all needs, desires, or tastes:

If you believe that our accredited, recognized, Middle East "experts" have done a fine job explaining the region's nuances, while amassing an admirable track record predicting the course of regional events, I have little to offer. If, for example, you swear by the gospel according to Thomas Friedman, whose breathless faith in the transformative effects of social media (that he punctuates with occasional open letters to dictators) defines the sunny era about to dawn, you would do far better sticking to the *New York Times* than reading any further.

If you believe that the population of the Middle East is disproportionately comprised of insane, violent, irrational sociopaths, you already have your answer. Prediction and forecasting are forms of logical extrapolation; they assume that the forces shaping the future will be similar to those that shaped the recent past. Such an assumption is horribly misplaced among the insane, whose behavior can whipsaw quickly in unforeseeable directions. Navigating an asylum requires prophecy or clairvoyance—hardly skills abundant among America's punditry, scholarly, or political classes. Widespread insanity explains everything fully—and thus nothing usefully. If you believe in it, however, stop trying to understand the region, reason with its people, or treat them with compassion; only the heartless tyranny of a Nurse Ratched can bring order to an asylum.

If you believe that the people of the Middle East are hapless victims, robbed of their own agency and minimally responsible for the consequences of their actions, studying the region and its history is pointless. Perhaps Hillary Clinton expressed this view best, in her testimony to Congress about the terrorist attack on the American Consulate in Benghazi and the consequent loss of American lives: "What difference does it make"[1] whether the trigger was Islamism or a YouTube video? When victims nursing longstanding grievances lash out, they're rarely responding to a single, specific event. Whatever straw may have broken the camel's back broke it only because of the weight that the camel was already carrying. If the Arab/Islamic psyche has been so badly damaged that it is unfair to expect basic decency, rationality, or proportionality from Arabs or Muslims, the only safe thing to do is to hold them all at arm's length until they have recovered their rational faculties. Any encounter with them will end badly—and violently. Detailed policy analysis and inquiries into specifics—precisely our goals on this journey—are misplaced. Those who take this view of Middle Easterners are thus unlikely to enjoy the trip.

Similarly, if you believe that U.S. policy—and Western intervention in general—can do little to guide the region and less to affect the balance among indigenous forces, this exercise is likely a waste of your time. You too know what needs to be done: Batten down the hatches while the victims work through a violent adolescence, then argue about the balance between hands-off containment and humanitarian intervention as the brutality intensifies and spreads. Take pride in knowing that the millions of dead and millions more suffering bear no Western fingerprints—and certainly not yours.

If you believe that "we all want the same things," you're welcome to join us but you're likely to be disappointed. While this particular platitude might sound friendly and hopeful, in reality it is neither. When you think about it, the insistence that other people must want the same things you want is really rather aggressive and insulting. Most Americans these days are happy to acknowledge that Republicans and Democrats—who share language, culture, history, religious traditions, and a political system—can rarely find common ground on questions of morality, belief, attitude, value, or perception of human nature. Astoundingly, many of these same Americans who disdain half of their own countrymen look over at the Middle East, see people possessing entirely distinct languages, cultures, histories, religions, and political traditions, and proclaim that they want the same things "we" do (rarely bothering to wonder whether the "we" they emulate are Democrats or Republicans). Far too many Americans speak and act as if all of the world's great cultures and civilizations share Western morals, beliefs, attitudes, values, preferences, views of history, notions of justice, definitions of honor, and balances between material and spiritual fulfillment. A touch of humility might suggest the greater wisdom in first wondering whether there is any basis for such a belief. So if you're on this journey, please stop pretending that *your* values shape *their* desires or goals. Otherwise, I can almost guarantee that you won't like what we find.

For those who do choose to join us, I ask—at least for the duration of this journey—that you maintain a healthy respect for the people of the Middle East. Remember at all times that they are proud people, confident in their own identities, with a deep attachment to their ethnic, religious, tribal, or national affiliations *as they themselves define them*. Their attachments to designations that outsiders have created to shoehorn them into the global state system is far, far weaker. Middle Easterners are neither insane, nor hapless victims, nor reflections of frustrated, misunderstood Westerners, but rather highly rational actors attempting to improve both the world at large and their own localities. The key to understanding their behavior is to recall that "improvement" is inherently subjective; they seek improvement vis-à-vis their own values, not ours. As with anyone, if we seek to understand those values and the actions to which they lead, we must be prepared to look past mere words to actual, demonstrated choices. After all, words often represent ideals to which people aspire, or marketing ploys designed to sell something that no one who knew the truth would consider buying. Only actions can reveal the actor's true preferences and values.

Beyond that, for the journey to prove worthwhile, it is also important to believe that American intervention *can and should* improve the region's future. And while we can concede that improvement is indeed subjective, we can't be bashful about standing for our own values—or their roots in the Judeo-Christian tradition as refined through classical eighteenth century liberalism. So let's be clear: our goal on this journey is to find ways to infuse the region with liberal ideals including tolerance and coexistence, the dignity and freedom of the individual (explicitly including women), respect for the rule of law, the self-determination of unique and distinct nations, and mutual respect among neighboring states.

We must admit from the outset that not everyone we encounter in the region is likely to share those goals. In fact, many of the region's key players, movements, and groups have been fighting actively against the incursion of these ideas—ideas that we consider universal, but that we concede arose first in the West—into their cultures and lives. We must thus understand the distribution of values and dreams throughout the region—those animating our friends and our enemies alike.

This journey is thus intended for those who want to understand the values and beliefs driving the Middle East. It is intended for those who want to help inspire and ally ourselves with the Middle Easterners whose values are closest to our own, and to defeat those—now ascendant—whose beliefs, values, and actions run in strongly illiberal directions. It is intended for those who fear that the value-driven brutality emanating from the Middle East's most illiberal corners threatens the Western world, the prevailing global order—itself an outgrowth of eighteenth century liberalism—and any hope for a peaceful, prosperous twenty-first century. Most of all, it is intended for those who want the U.S., classic liberalism, and Western civilization to prevail in the long war against radical Islamists seeking to restructure the world according to their own notions of God's will.

With those thoughts in mind, we may jettison the proven misconceptions that pervade conventional wisdom. We may begin our trek towards obtaining a clearer view of the region, and devising a policy framework that will serve American interests and further liberal values. At the risk of spoiling the adventure, however, it is only fair to tell you where we are heading. We will discover that the key to the region's problems is imperialism; the key to their resolution is minority self-determination. And the operative definition of "minority" hinges on the ways that the people of the region see themselves—not on categories that Western powers or international organizations have created on their behalf.

That focus creates a very different starting point from the one that we have heard repeated ad infinitum for nearly eight decades—despite overwhelming evidence that while it might sound reasonable in theory, it is, in fact, grounded in fantasy. Conventional wisdom often places the "Two-State Solution" to the Arab/Israeli conflict as the first critical stepping-stone towards a more stable region. As the plan's label itself suggests, there are two components to this approach: a new state of Palestine, and a solution to the conflict. Those who like to go further typically describe the solution as Jewish and Arab states living side-by-side in peace and security. Particularly ambitious advocates of this approach like to throw in a mixture of wonderful spiritual and material goals, such as dignity, tolerance, freedom of religion, prosperity, and the ability to focus on human capital development. Conventional wisdom then ignores the glorious benefits that such a solution would bring, and focuses entirely on the creation of an independent State of Palestine simply for the sake of creating an independent State of Palestine.

In contemporary political discourse, few advocates for Palestine even bother pretending that its independence would stabilize the region or resolve the conflict between Arabs and Jews. They are, of course, free to take that position if they so choose, but truth in advertising compels them to stop falsely calling it a two-state solution, stop pretending that it would solve anything other than the absence of a state called Palestine, and concede that peace and stability are not among their goals. Those who advocate for a State of Palestine do so simply because, in their view, justice requires the international community to establish a twenty-second Arab state, racked from the outset with civil war, terrorism, cronyism, and corruption; dismissive of human rights; genocidal; anti-Jewish and anti-Christian; and incapable of economic sustainability without massive foreign aid. Honesty, however, might induce observers of good faith to wonder precisely where these advocates obtained their sense of "justice."

We thus embark upon our journey with an unconventional view of the "Two-State Solution." We neither accept it as a necessity nor reject it out of hand. We recognize that millions of people are moving around the Middle East, that states and governments are falling, and that the map drawn in the wake of the first World War is not sacred. The Arab/Islamic claims for a State of Palestine are just that—claims. We will try to understand the context in which they arose, and evaluate them using the same principles we apply to the many conflicting and overlapping claims that contribute to the region's instability. By the end of our journey, we will advocate U.S. policies favoring the establishment, security, and growth of states likely to help stabilize the region—and only states likely to stabilize the region.

We are thus prepared to ask: might those who see the "Two-State Solution" as the key to a better Middle East be missing something? If so, what? Their core observation—that it is best to divide intertwined populations who aspire to incompatible goals—is sound. Winston Churchill said much the same thing while trying to stabilize postwar Europe.[2] History has shown that conflicts among such peoples will continue until one of three things occurs. First, intermarriage and commerce could knit the groups together into something new. Second, one side could win a decisive victory. Third, a much larger power could enter the area and scramble the chessboard so completely that few hints of its previous conflict remained. In today's Middle East, intermarriage and commerce seem unlikely to fuse multiple ethnicities together. Such a development appears unlikely not only among Arabs and Jews, but also among Sunnis, Shiites, Turks, Persians, Kurds, Druze, Alawites, and others. A great-power war could indeed remake the region—possibly, once the dust settled, for the better—but the cost in human suffering seems worth avoiding.

That leaves two basic possibilities: The world can either let the bloodletting continue until the various local factions reach decisive battles. Or the world—under American leadership—can help disentangle the populations. Disentanglement is neither easy nor painless, and it is unachievable without at least some coercion. As the many advocates for the Two-State Solution have noted repeatedly, such coercion is regrettable—but worth the price if it can indeed usher in an era of regional stability, mutual respect, and development. What they have missed, however, is that they invariably want to put the cart before the horse. The critical component of the Two-State Solution is *the solution*, not the new state.

On our journey, we will adopt such regional stability as our primary goal, and the regrettably coercive disentangling of populations as the least-bad way to get there. We will not, however, fall prey to the monomaniacal focus on a State of Palestine—a country that history has never known for a people who see themselves as an integral part of the larger Arab/Islamic world. We will, as promised, look to the people of the region to see how they identify themselves and whom they claim as kin. And in particular, rather than looking to the non-existent Palestine as the paradigm of things that should exist in some theoretical fantasy universe, we will look to Israel as the paradigm of things that do work in the real world.

As the region's sole truly successful exercise in indigenous ethnic minority self-determination, Israel is a model worthy of emulation—not, as conventional wisdom teaches, a problem in need of management. Fortunately, we will not be the first to notice Israel's success, even within the region. Neighboring minorities like the Druze and the Kurds appear to have come to appreciate the Israeli model; they reportedly seek closer ties, assistance, and support from the successful Jewish State. And even some of Israel's Sunni Arab neighbors—including Saudi Arabia and the UAE as well as Egypt and Jordan—are beginning to recognize the benefits of a stable, quiet neighbor making no claims against their territories or people. As we will see, Israel is a proven solution in need of expansion: It is the first successful demonstration of what will become a Multi-State Solution to the Middle East's many overlapping crises.

Before we embark, however, I feel that one note about timing is in order. I have been developing the ideas in this essay since the late 1980s, and laid out many of its major themes in blog posts between about 2005 and 2007. Throughout those years, I have followed closely as our most prestigious experts and most beloved pundits have issued explanation after explanation, and prediction after prediction, about the Middle East. I have watched our political leaders follow their guidance. I have seen many American policies appear to yield positive results, recalibrated my beliefs in their wake, then watched them crumble into the failures that I had originally considered inevitable. But the costs of getting the Middle East wrong continue to mount as the manifest flaws in the stories we like to tell ourselves about the region and its people deviate further from the truth.

I began the project of arranging this tour towards the end of 2015, as the country geared up for the race to succeed Barack Obama. I am nailing it down in final form in the last few weeks before the 2016 election. This race is critical, and like many Americans I have clear and strong preferences not only about the next occupant of the Oval Office, but more broadly about the configuration of the entire federal government come 2017. Those preferences, however, derive from the likelihood I place on solid policies emerging from each configuration—on issues far beyond those that we will encounter here. The nation's needs, the realities of the Middle East, and the importance of getting our relationship with that critical region will not change on November 9, 2016. The election may change the likelihood that American policy will move in the right direction before it's too late. It may play a critical role in determining the outcome of the clash between Western civilization and the liberal international order on the one hand, and radical, violent, illiberal Islamism on the other. It will not, however, alter the steps that the West must take if it is to prevail in that clash. Our goal on this journey is to internalize a course towards victory. Whether our new leadership chooses to join us is another matter entirely.

With that, we may embark.

The Empires

Chapter 2. The Caliphate Reborn

Let's start with the obvious: It's important to see things clearly. When it comes to the Middle East, we Westerners have lacked clarity for a long, long time. The consequences of viewing the region through a warped lens have always been troubling, but they've become increasingly dire since the end of the Cold War—and even more so since 9/11. Our inability to see the people, the faith and ethnic groups, and the movements of the Middle East clearly is—quite literally—killing us. Western civilization itself hangs in the balance.

The distortion dates back more than a century, from the time that France and Britain—the European powers who defeated the Ottoman Empire—took charge of the region. These fading imperial powers, in the waning days of European imperialism, were conflicted: Did they want to add their new conquests to their empires? Or did they see the region's future as an exercise in post-colonial self-determination? Rather than confronting the psychodramas then altering the ways that Europeans viewed non-Europeans, the French and British issued a series of partial plans, tentative maps, and conflicting promises and pronouncements. What emerged was incoherent. Still, selected indigenous players, Westerners, and international organizations gained a vested interest in that incoherence. From that moment forward, they invested heavily in a series of myths capable of justifying that status quo—and their positions within it. Many of those myths seem at least plausible when taken in isolation, but viewed as a whole, the myth system of the modern Middle East makes no sense at all—*and it never did.*

The elephant in the room somehow remained invisible for a century, despite inflicting precisely the sort of damage one might expect from an invisible elephant. With each elephantine gyration, the keepers of the myth system invented a new story blaming the damage on other players or causes. Finally, over the past few years, a regional actor damaging enough and vocal enough to paint the elephant grey has arisen. Its presence is now indisputable. The Islamic State and its declaration of a Caliphate have laid bare the gargantuan, if previously invisible, truth: The primary force buffeting the modern Middle East has been the drive to reconstruct an empire of the sort that governed the region from the Romans to the Ottomans—this time in the hands of the region's largest ethnic group, the Sunni Arabs.

Let that explanation sink in for a minute. It's important. It's straightforward. It's clear. And it's radical. For years, we've been told that the region's major stories are distinct, and to the extent that there is a lynchpin to the region's problems, it lies in the still-disputed portions of Mandatory Palestine. I'm hardly the first to notice the inherent absurdity of this formulation. The notion that the primary story shaping an immense region that Sunni Arabs dominate is something other than the internal conflict defining Sunni Arab identity would seem laughable were it not entrenched so widely in conventional wisdom. Yet until the recent rise of the Islamic State's Caliphate, there was no central story more capable of capturing the public imagination than the Arab/Israeli conflict.

The reborn Caliphate thus helps to clarify what conventional wisdom has long obscured. All of the region's major stories of the past century—Nasser's pan-Arabism, Khomeini's revolutionary Shiism, the Arab/Israeli conflict, the rise of OPEC, the Iran/Iraq War, Saddam's invasion of Kuwait, Islamist terrorism, and the Arab Spring, to name but a few—have been either parts of or reactions to the Sunni Arab imperial drive. Mainstream Western thinking has mistakenly seen each of these matters as distinct. This clear failure to extract the region's dominant theme has hamstrung Middle Eastern development in ways that have served neither American interests nor the region's people.

So let's take a bold stand here: Sunni Arabs, as the ethnic group that dominates the Middle East, have also dominated the events that have shaped the modern Middle East. Much of that dominance has come from an internal rift among the Sunni Arabs. Religion, history, and culture have convinced the Sunni Arabs that they should be leading a unified empire across the entire region. Reality, on the other hand, has created a class of Sunni Arab elites that have done quite well for themselves within the status quo of a region divided into nation-states. Sunni Arab leaders thus work hard to avoid unification while insisting that they are working towards it. Their people grow increasingly frustrated with the lack of progress.

The many other ethnic groups who share the region with the Sunni Arabs have to tiptoe around their dominant neighbor's internal struggle. They have responded and reacted in different ways. Revolutionary Shiism, the most important reaction to Sunni imperialism, has redefined the region's second largest ethnic group, the Shiites (both Iranian and Arab). Sunni imperialism and revolutionary Shiism have a great deal in common. They are equally deadly, equally opposed to American interests and the rule-based liberal international order, and equally crippling to the human capital development of the people whose lives they dominate. They also both target for extermination or exile the region's smaller ethnic groups: Jews, Christians, Kurds, Druze, Alawites, Baha'i, Yazidi, and others. Revolutionary Shiism, however, remains a reaction—albeit a reaction moving quickly towards nuclear weapons and missile delivery systems. The central story of the past century has been the Sunni Arab quest for empire—and its overriding belief that only such an empire can restore the region's natural order.

Their belief about the imperial nature of regional order is grounded in a solid understanding of history. Imperial roots run deep in the Middle East. The vast region between Egypt and Persia— consisting of the Arabian Peninsula (the six members of the Gulf Cooperation Council (GCC)—Saudi Arabia, Kuwait, Qatar, Bahrain, the UAE, and Oman—plus Yemen) and the Levant (or its Arabic equivalent, the *Mashreq*, consisting of contemporary Iraq, Syria, Lebanon, Jordan, and Israel)—has spent most of the past 2700-plus years as part of one empire or another, more often than not as an imperial hinterland.

The region's age of rarely-broken imperial rule dates back to Biblical times—as does the Levant's role as conquered territory, subject to empires whose roots lay elsewhere. Mesopotamians, Persians, Greeks, Romans, Arabs, Turks, and Europeans have all arrived as conquerors, and given birth to empires intending to inculcate their own cultures. Some ruled from abroad, others moved their capitals into the region. Their success at reshaping regional demographics, linguistics, philosophies, and faiths varied greatly. At the end of the day though, the exceptions of autonomous self-rule were few and far between. If we are to understand the modern Middle East, if we are to appreciate the salience of the Sunni Arab imperial drive, we must first detour through the imperial history of the Middle East.

Chapter 3. From the Bible through Rome

In ancient times, long before the rise of Greece, two great power centers dominated the Eastern Mediterranean: Mesopotamia and Egypt. Archaeology confirms that much of the Levant spent millennia torn between the two: It was essentially a trade route and a battleground.[3] Its people belonged to small tribes, and lived as nomads, farmers, or in fortified cities. With a few exceptions, those tribes were typically poor—whether independent or subjects of one of the two great empires. Most of the Bible, from Moses to Jeconiah, unfolded during one of the region's lengthier stints of independence. Canaanites, Israelites, Jebusites, Edomites, Moabites, Philistines, and others fought numerous wars among themselves, with the Israelites eventually emerging as the strongest of the local groups. At its peak, during the eighty-year reign of Kings David and Solomon in the early Iron Age (tenth century B.C.E.), the Israelites held a medium-sized empire of their own, turning Jerusalem into a respectable imperial capital, complete with palaces, a grand temple, and a tradition of thrice-yearly pilgrimages.[4] At the end of that golden era, the Israelite kingdom split in two—reportedly over tax policy.[5] The northern Kingdom of Israel (or Samaria) fell to Sennacherib's fierce Assyrian Empire in 720 B.C.E.; the southern Kingdom of Judah remained until Nebuchadnezzar's Babylonians arrived in 586 B.C.E.[6]

The Assyrians and Babylonians may have been brutal, but they were not fools. They understood a great deal about the psychology of conquest. They knew that the nations they conquered retained a deep attachment to "their own" land, and would never recognize it as a rightful part of the empire. A people living in its own home would never accept a conquering Emperor as its rightful overlord, and would never acknowledge the inherent superiority of the victorious invaders. A people living in its own home would inevitably resent the conquest, recall the glories (possibly real, possibly invented) of pre-invasion days, and long for the moment that it could expel the invaders to reclaim its independence.

These ancient empires adopted a strategy brilliant in its psychological insight though often devastating in its implementation.[7] Once their soldiers had had their fill of destruction, rape, and pillage, taken their pick of slaves and concubines, and claimed the spoils of war, they moved the remaining conquered population to a different part of the Empire. In one fell swoop, the relocation turned the tales of glory and independence, the memories of the beautiful homeland, the attachment to the local god, and the misery of conquest, destruction, and exile, into legends that broken grandparents would tell future generations who knew only life in the lands that the Emperor had granted them.

The strategy usually worked. Ten tribes of Israel notoriously faded into the imperial ether, along with most of the region's other ancient nations. Only the Judeans—for whatever reason—refused to relinquish their connection to their homeland and their God, passing their desire for a return undiminished from one generation to the next. Seventy years later, when the Babylonian Empire had fallen to the Persians, Cyrus the Great permitted a limited Judean restoration: He allowed the people to return home, rebuild their temple, and reconnect with their God. He did not, however, grant them sovereignty or independence; the Judeans and Judea remained integral parts of the Persian Empire.[8]

In the fourth century B.C.E., Alexander the Great swept down from Macedonia to defeat the Persians. Upon the young king's death, his generals divided his empire. Egypt fell to the Ptolemys, while the Seleucid Empire spread from southern Anatolia, through the Levant, and into Persia.[9] In the second century B.C.E., the Judeans finally reclaimed their full independence from the Selucids—a status they held for only a few decades before encountering the might of Rome.[10]

The tension between Judea and Rome persisted until 136 C.E., when the Romans finally decided to uproot this stubborn culture. Following what was likely the single most disruptive rebellion in the Roman Empire's long history, the Romans finally decided that they had had enough of the Judeans. They took numerous steps intended to end Judean culture once and for all: They banned Judeans from their homeland, renamed the entire province Syria-Palestina, completed their destruction of Jerusalem by building the new city of Aelia Capitolina over its rubble, and erected a statue of Jupiter on the

Temple Mount—precisely on the site of the Judeans' Holiest of Holies.[11]

Yet once again, the obstinate Judeans—soon to become better known as the Jews—proved the exception to these time-tested tricks of imperial conquest. Rome's best efforts and the passage of time notwithstanding, the Jewish connection to the Judean homeland, to Jerusalem, and to the Temple Mount never dimmed. In fact, over the course of the next two centuries, the followers of a Judean temple reformer named Jesus fused elements of Judean culture onto the Empire, turning pagan Rome into Christian Byzantium—and giving birth to a distinctive "Western" culture that would soon dominate Europe. Western persecution of those vowing fidelity to the original, unreformed, Judean creed and rites persisted for centuries; though it suppressed their population, it never terminated their sense of nationhood, their commitment to their God, their connection to their land, or their desire to rebuild Jerusalem.

Meanwhile, however, from the Roman conquest on forward, with only a few short-lived exceptions such as some Crusader city-states, the Middle East knew only empires. In 330, the newly Christian Roman Emperor Constantine split his Empire in two, and moved his capital to Constantinople. For the next few centuries, the Middle East was split between two great monotheistic empires: the Roman Empire in the East, better known as Christian Byzantium, ruled along the Mediterranean; the Zoroastrian Sassanid Empire grew west from Persia. Only the inhospitable Arabian desert escaped imperial rule.[12]

Chapter 4. The Islamic Empires

Contemporary scholarship has raised numerous questions about the historical validity of the traditional accounts of Islam's early years—much as it has for Judaism and Christianity.[13] These questions are critical in many ways. Given that the goal of our journey is an understanding of contemporary Middle Eastern politics, however, historical and theological accuracy is of secondary importance. People respond to the world as they perceive it to be, or as they believe it to be, rather than as it is. Political behavior throughout the Middle East, and in particular the theologically based political movement known as Islamism, is thus an artifact of what the believers believe. Furthermore—and for obvious reasons—the historical record of the politics of Islam's first few centuries is far more detailed, and far more likely to be accurate, than is the record of its theological development throughout that same period. Still, the very existence of critical scholarship challenging accepted beliefs about Muhammad and his early followers is likely to rankle the traditionally faithful. And though this critical scholarship may not be well known in the Islamic world, its Western origins—Germany in the 1880s—seem likely to fuel resentment among the few traditionalists who are aware of it.[14]

The traditional account is well known, but always worth reviewing: In 610, in the Arabian Peninsula's coastal region (the *Hejaz*), the prophecies of Muhammad ibn 'Abdullāh ibn Abdul-Muttalib ibn Hashim gave rise to a new faith.[15] Muhammad began building his flock (the *ummah*) slowly, through persuasion, as a peaceful preacher in Mecca—facing precisely the opposition one might expect to a prophet seeking to restructure society to conform to God's newly-revealed will. He fled to nearby Medina, where he became a fierce warrior preaching a far less tolerant message.[16] By the time of his death in 632, he had unified most of the Peninsula's tribes beneath the banner—and perhaps more importantly, beneath the sword—of Islam.[17]

Leadership of the fledgling *ummah* passed to the four "righteous" (*Rashidun*) Caliphs, who founded an explicitly theocratic empire known as the Caliphate. The first three *Rashidun* Caliphs— Abu Bakr, Umar, and Uthman—had been Mohammed's closest friends, allies, and earliest followers. The fourth, Ali, was Mohammed's cousin and son-in-law. The *Rashidun* Caliphs launched a remarkably successful military campaign to spread their new faith; within thirty years they had expanded it from the Arabian Peninsula through the Levant, to encompass Egypt, Persia, and the southern Transcaucasus.[18]

From the outset, however, the relationship between Mohammed's family and his allies was tense. Uthman's assassination in 656 set the stage for the young faith's first rift (*fitna*): As Uthman's initially reluctant successor, Ali failed to apprehend the assassins— generating ill will and suspicion among the members of Uthman's powerful Umayyad tribe. Believing that Ali had conspired in Uthman's death, Muawiyah of the Umayyad seized control of the Levant and declared the Umayyad Empire, or Caliphate.[19]

Following Ali's own assassination in 661, the *fitna* exploded into a full-blown civil war, pitting Muawiyah's Damascus-based Umayyad Caliphate against Ali's sons—Hasan and Hussein—and their "Party of Ali" (*Shiat Ali*).[20] The *fitna*, however, was ideological as well as political. The *Shiat Ali* contended that the selection of a Caliph belonged to God alone, that a familial relation to Mohammed was a prerequisite for a Caliph, and that Ali had been the Prophet's true successor. Rallying behind the Umayyads—and the legitimacy of Abu Bakr, Umar, and Uthman—were Muslims who put far greater stock in the collected reports of Muhammad's words and deeds (the *sunna*), and who believed that it was the province of the *ummah* to elect a new Caliph.[21]

The political dimension resolved itself in 680, when Hussein fell at the Battle of Karbala. Muawiyah's son Yazid, who had become the Umayyad Caliph earlier that year following his father's death, consolidated his authority; the Damascus-based Umayyad Empire ruled until 750. The ideological dimension of the rift continues to this day: The Umayyads' ideological successors are today's Sunni Muslims; Ali's followers are the Shiites.[22]

Those early Shiites were hardly the only imperial subjects

unhappy about Umayyad rule. The Umayyads, who saw themselves as Arabs in the traditional sense (i.e., residents of the Arabian Peninsula), rather than in the broader contemporary sense (i.e., nearly all native Arabic speakers), were hardcore Arab supremacists. They saw their majority non-Arab imperial subjects (including Muslims), as well as their majority non-Muslim subjects, as second-class citizens. Eventually, the Umayyad's mistreatment of Shiites, non-Muslims, and non-Arab Muslims motivated all three groups to set aside their internal differences and rebel against the Empire. The consequent Abbasid Revolution ended the Umayyad Caliphate and proclaimed the Baghdad-based Abbasid Caliphate in 750.[23]

The Abbasids were far more cosmopolitan than the Umayyads, and it was during their long reign—the Abbasid Caliphate stood for five centuries, until encountering the Mongols in 1258—that the traditional structure of Islamic-run societies took firm hold. The governing supremacism expanded from Arabs to incorporate all Sunni Muslims (including non-Arabs) on the top rung—though those closest to power by familial or ethnic relation always remained first-among-equals. Selected other faiths, notably but not exclusively Judaism and Christianity, were granted measures of autonomy while subject to increasingly discriminatory legislation—essentially tolerated as second-class imperial citizens as long as they knew their place.[24]

The centuries of Abbasid rule also included some other important social developments. First, though the Caliphate remained intact, the balance between temporal and clerical leadership tipped progressively away from the Caliph and towards the Sultan. By the time the Abbasids fell, the Sultan wielded nearly all real power—though the Caliph continued to provide legitimacy to the imperial claims of governance in God's name.[25] Second, Islamic thought and jurisprudence flourished. Philosophical and theological debate ensued.[26] Heresies rose and (mostly) fell. A t least two of the "heretical" Islamic offshoots that never fell completely, however, remain key contributors to the ethnic mosaic of today's Middle East: the Alawites who emerged in the ninth century, and the Druze who arose in the eleventh.[27] Third, in the ninth century, a caste of non-Arab (again, in the traditional sense) Muslim military slaves, the Mamluk, began to evolve into the Islamic counterpart of Christendom's chivalric knights. Mamluk warriors played a key role in defending Islam during the Crusades, and when the Abbasid Caliphate fell to the Mongols, the Mamluk Caliphate arose in Cairo.[28]

During the years of Mamluk rule, the Ottoman Turks completed their march westward from Central Asia to Anatolia. They arrived initially to join Islam's battles against the Christian Byzantine Empire, but soon took leadership of that fight. Their ultimate victory came in 1453, when they sacked the Byzantine capital of Constantinople, and quickly went about converting it from the center of Orthodox Christianity to the capital of Islam. They defeated the Mamluks and moved the Caliphate to Constantinople in 1517, where it remained for four hundred years.[29] During their own long centuries of imperial rule, the Ottomans formalized the discrimination against Jews, Christians, and selected others in a legal framework called the "millet system:" Authorized non-Muslim faiths were allowed to preserve their autonomy, as long as they accepted Muslims as their betters, refrained from prohibited activities and ventures, and paid double taxation for the privilege. This social and governing structure remained more-or-less intact as the Ottoman Empire grew and contracted. It ended only with the Empire's fall during the First World War.[30]

Chapter 5. The Post-Ottoman Century

In 1923, Mustafa Kemal Atatürk declared a secular Turkish nation-state, abolished the Caliphate, and relinquished the vast Ottoman hinterland to the war's victorious allies, Britain and France.[31]   For the first time in Islam's 1300-year history, the *ummah* had to find its way forward without the benefit of either an Emperor or a Caliph. The shock to the Muslim psyche was sharp and clear: The desire to restore the "natural order" burned bright, notwithstanding the often unwelcome incursions of secular thought, modernity, and Westernism throughout the Islamic world.

Whether those incursions included an end to the region's long experience with imperialism was less clear. Britain and France had begun to divvy up their anticipated conquest while the War was still raging. They concluded a series of agreements—the best known of which was probably the Sykes-Picot, or Asia Minor, Agreement—attempting to apply imperial logic to their Levantine conquest.[32] By the time these European powers arrived, however, the age of empires—in the Middle East and around the world—was nearing its end (or at the very least, going out of fashion as part of a trend through which we are still living). The imperial ethos, particularly among the more enlightened, liberal parts of the West, was in decline. Respect for nationalism and the right of self-determination was gaining ground.

The victorious allies thus approached the division of the conquered Ottoman hinterland with conflicting objectives.[33]   One camp, comfortable with traditional imperial and colonial thinking, sought to secure the loyalty of the regional majority by promoting Sunni Arab dominance. They advocated dividing the territory among a handful of powerful Sunni Arab leaders they could control, counting on these local leaders to keep their own people in line while holding down unruly minorities. In the language of international relations, such a relationship is known as "suzerainty," and it was the basic governing strategy that the Ottoman Empire employed to control its various regions. European advocates of this approach thus wanted to keep the region's political relationships more-or-less intact, redrawing selected borders and substituting suzerains in Paris and London for those in Constantinople, but imposing few new ideas about governance.

The second camp favored the enlightened post-colonial cause of self-determination, under which Europe's smaller ethnic groups were then gaining independence while the Continent's empires fell. Advocates of this approach believed that the freedom and dignity that self-determination conferred, and the stability that it enabled, far outweighed the occasional coercion, injustice, and suffering necessary to consolidate ethnic populations into new states— precisely the rational strategy for small nations seeking independent statehood. At various points, their plans included a Jewish state in the Holy Land; a Christian state around Mt. Lebanon; an Alawite state along the northern coast of Syria; a Druze state in the mountains of southern Syria; and an independent Kurdistan in the region's north;[34] with Sunni dominance restricted to Sunni populations.[35] This proposed approach to regional governance was thus a radical departure from anything that the people of the Middle East had ever before encountered. It sought to elevate longstanding second-class citizens to equal dignity with Sunni Muslims, and to eliminate the imperial structure that had dominated the region for nearly three millennia.

The familiar post-Ottoman map incorporated elements from both schools of thought. The cause of self-determination won out most clearly for the Jews, in Israel. The Maronite Christians centered around Mt. Lebanon also succeeded, though somewhat less spectacularly: The French carved out the largest territory they could while maintaining a Christian minority.[36] Lebanon thus arose as an independent "confessional" state, with distinct governmental roles, rights, and responsibilities divided among its Christian, Sunni, Shiite, and Druze citizens—with Christians retaining the most powerful portfolio. Those favoring a de facto Arab empire won a pyrrhic victory everywhere else. The British and French divided the rest of the Levant into the Sunni-led states of Iraq, Jordan, and Syria (where the Alawites seized control fifty years later), attempted to wedge an additional Arab state into the Western portion of its Mandate for

Palestine, and favored powerful Sunni tribes of the Peninsula who turned their Sheikhdoms into states.

This hybrid non-solution—and the entire European imperial experience in the region—proved disappointing to Europeans and Middle Easterners alike. It left behind a number of new states, inventing national identities bearing little relationship to the identities and affiliations that the people of the region used to define themselves.

As a result, by the middle of the twentieth century, the international community comfortably assigned each resident of the region a distinct state-based identity—Israelis, Jordanians, Iraqis, Syrians, Lebanese, or Palestinians—without much wondering whether the people so designated felt any kinship to their newly assigned co-nationals. Aside from the Israelis—whose assigned nationality corresponded to the Jewish identity of their majority—most did not. The others continued to identify as they had long done: Sunni Arabs, Shiite Arabs, Christians, Alawites, Druze, Kurds, and others.

The resulting chasm severed assigned legal identities from felt internal identities. The world may like to talk about "Syrians," "Iraqis," or "Palestinians" as if those designations are meaningful, but overwhelming evidence suggests that they are not. Over the years, that conflict between internalized and assigned identity led to some bizarre linguistic formulations, such as the oft-repeated trope: "Saddam Hussein is the first world leader in modern times to have brutally used chemical weapons against his own people."[37] Those who repeat it rarely seem to notice the inherent contradiction: had Saddam considered Iraqi Kurds "his own people," he never would have gassed them. Furthermore, it is unlikely that anyone in Halabja thought of Saddam as one of their own—or took any solace in knowing the gassing was an internal Iraqi matter, rather than an act of international war.

The fall of the Ottoman Empire thus removed the last of the imperial overlords that had long knit the region together. It freed each of the major ethnic groups to set distinct goals—and to experience the Post-Ottoman century very differently. Their divergent stories, and the often uncomfortable interactions among them, created the confusion, tension, and bloodshed for which the region has become known.

As noted, by far the most important of these stories belongs to the region's dominant ethnic group: the Sunni Arabs. For a century, the Sunni Arab world has been torn between a burning desire for a unified empire and an elite that has done quite well within the state system but is afraid to concede its lack of fidelity to unification. That unspoken tension goes a long way towards explaining why the Islamic State's reborn Caliphate is so popular in some quarters and so threatening to others: As a matter of religious expression, historical practice, and ethnic pride it is the fulfillment of every Sunni Arab dream. But as a matter of practical experience, it will devastate the existing Sunni Arab elite, along with any chance for Sunni Arab coexistence with—or integration into—the broader world. The fate of this new Caliphate—which may well outlive the Islamic State that announced it—is thus central to the region's future.[38] The forces that turned it into a reality provide one key to unlocking the region's confusing, frustrating past; the parallel stories of the region's other ethnic identities provide still others. An understanding of those forces is a minimal prerequisite for devising sound American policy in the Middle East.

Which brings us to the end of our quick detour through the history of Middle Eastern empires. More importantly, it also hands us the key to understanding the confusion that has governed Middle East analysis—and confounded reasonably policy formation—for decades. The newest of the region's true nations are the Druze, who will soon celebrate their first millennium. Jewish, Christian, Sunni Arab, Shiite, Kurdish, Alawite, and Druze identities run deep. People die—and kill—for these nations. Their members have national aspirations and desires, beliefs in their own distinctiveness, ties to their own lands, and pride in their own histories. Analysts and policymakers who have instead focused on the weak bonds tying together members of artificial post-Ottoman states were destined to fail. In line with our key hypothesis, they were indeed missing something fundamental.

Through American Eyes

Chapter 6. American Objectives

To many Americans, for whom 1775 feels pre-historic, our quick excursion through nearly 3000 years of Middle Eastern empires may seem misplaced in a discussion of contemporary politics. Yet this light-speed intro is a critical part of respecting the region on its own terms. Because while dates like 136, 610, 1453, or even 1923 might seem remote, they remain very much alive in the collective consciousness of the Middle East. There are areas in which Middle Easterners of all faiths and ethnicities far outperform Americans—and Westerners in general. For better and for worse, long-term memory is among them. Ethnic ties and ancestral honor play far greater roles in shaping psyches throughout the Middle East than they do in the West. To respect the region is to accept this difference without judging it.

Identities throughout the region remain as they have been for centuries (or longer). The stubborn Judeans—now Jews—never relinquished their claims to their land, their connection to their God, their distinctive culture, or their dreams of return. The Sunnis have never seen themselves as anything other than rightful imperial rulers of the entire region. The Shiites, still grieving Ali's death and Muawiyah's usurpation, challenge the Sunni view directly, though recently, most quietly; they see *themselves* as the rightful inheritors of God's revealed truth, biding their time until messianic deliverance restores divine governance and justice to the world. The Sunni Turks, mostly Sunni Kurds, and Shiite Persians see themselves as heirs to ancient empires, distinct from (and typically more sophisticated than) their Arab co-religionists. The Egyptians, claiming similar ties to historic imperial grandeur, hold themselves out as distinctly superior to other Arabs. The Christians, Zoroastrians, and adherents of other pre-Islamic faiths exist as islands, attempting to retain their identities while remaining safe within the Islamic world. Islamic offshoots like the Druze and the Alawites maintain uneasy relationships with their Islamic neighbors—many of whom would condemn adherents of these localized, closed faiths for the capital crime of apostasy.

Yet with all of those identities, shaped through all of those centuries, it took the Islamic State's declaration of a reborn Caliphate to reveal what should long have been obvious: The twentieth century creation of Levantine nation-states changed nothing. It had minimal effect on how people saw themselves, defined their kinsmen, or related to their neighbors. The story of the twentieth and twenty-first century Middle East is the same as the story of every preceding century: A dominant group claims an empire; the smaller groups react to that claim.

From the moment that the Ottoman Turks began to teeter, the Sunni Arabs have seen themselves as the sole worthy inheritors of the empire—and the Caliphate. The Islamic State did not create this story line; it simply made it explicit. Throughout the twentieth century, Sunni Arabs have sought to convert their demographic dominance into imperial rule—leaving their neighbors little choice but to respond and react. At least one of those neighbors, the Shiites of Iran, responded with an imperial quest of their own—the revolutionary Islamic Republic organized around hastening messianic deliverance. Almost immediately upon taking power, Ayatollah Khomeini's Islamic Republic began to question the propriety of the House of Saud—the Sunnis currently designated as custodians of the Holy Cities of Mecca and Medina—to serve in that role. In recent years, the ensuing cold war has shown increasing signs of heating up; it is likely to play itself out in a very bloody manner before reaching resolution.[39]

While the U.S. may—and almost certainly should—take sides in an overt war between the Sunni state of Saudi Arabia and the Shiite state of Iran, it should oppose the imperial claims of Sunni and Shia with equal fervor. The "traditional" Sunni imperial claim, and the revolutionary apocalyptic Shia imperial claim, are equally toxic ideologies—antithetical to American interests, the rule-based liberal international order, and peaceful coexistence with the region's smaller ethnic and religious groups. The prospects for human capital development under either philosophy is grim. A healthy—or even fully stable—Middle East is impossible as long as either imperial Sunni Arabism or revolutionary Shiism retains its salience to sizable swathes of the region's population. Finessing the distinction between supporting an allied state and endorsing its toxic philosophical underpinnings is a critical challenge of twenty-first century American statesmanship—potentially even greater than the one FDR faced when he aligned the U.S. with Stalinism during the Second World War.

American policy should be simultaneously anti-imperial and anti-revolutionary. The U.S. must identify, promote—and most importantly protect—Sunni and Shiite allies brave enough to stand against their ethnicities' dominant philosophies. The U.S. must also lead an international push to protect the region's minorities, first by creating safe havens for them within the region, and ultimately by helping them work towards autonomy, independence, and full self-determination.

If the U.S. fails to lead the movement towards self-determination and away from revolution and empire, the negative trends of the early twenty-first century will almost certainly intensify. Their reverberations will shake the world, as genocide abounds and refugee flows alter the social fabric of (at least) Europe and (possibly) the U.S. The threat to the rule-based liberal international order, the *Pax Americana* that has brought peace and prosperity to large parts of the globe, is palpable. The Middle East is at a crossroads, and the United States must make some choices. Over the next few decades, the region will experience considerable bloodshed, massive population shifts, and redrawn borders—whether the U.S. chooses to engage fully, to withdraw entirely, or to pursue some intermediate course.

As we noted before embarking on our journey, however, a belief that U.S. policy *can and should* make a difference is necessary. This entire exercise rests upon the assumption that an intelligently engaged America can nudge events in directions that serve American interests and further American values; a disengaged America will watch events unfold from a distance, then react as individual crises arise. To pursue the course of wise engagement, the U.S. will first have to see the region clearly, then move to protect those in need of protection while fighting the two greatest anti-liberal movements of our time. If that assumption is wrong—or if it becomes wrong through American global retreat and military downsizing—the United States, like the rest of the world, will have no choice but to react to events as they occur. It is hard to see how reaction, rather than intelligently engaged proactivity, can help make for a peaceful, prosperous twenty-first century.

Our journey thus moves from the Middle East to points far closer to home. We return to our original hypothesis that conventional wisdom is deeply flawed and that the policy responses it has generated have been consistently inappropriate. We do so to explore the scope of past American failures and to make sense of a perplexing region's seemingly paradoxical recent history. We will propose a strategic vision aligned with both short-term American interests and long-term American values—a vision that begins with an articulation of what should long have been obvious: The Sunni Arabs who dominate the region have played the primary role in shaping its recent history and its current state.

Chapter 7. Visions of the Future

While France and Great Britain were the dominant Western powers in the Middle East throughout the first few post-Ottoman decades, the U.S. moved into the driver's seat there, as elsewhere, at the end of World War II. By 1956—when President Eisenhower disastrously backed Egypt's increasingly pro-Soviet President Nasser over a joint British/French/Israeli force assembled to keep the Suez Canal open—the U.S. had become the region's preeminent Western power player. The U.S. spent the rest of the Cold War trying to minimize Soviet influence in the region.[40]

When the Soviet Union fell, the Middle East assumed a new centrality. Rather than serving as a battleground for outside great powers (as it had through much of its history), the region emerged as important in its own right—as a center of global volatility, awash in oil and seething in local tensions. That emergence exacerbated the negative effects of Western blindness to the region's key story; as the significance of local crises grew, so too did the consequences of misunderstanding their causes and failing to predict their effects. While it has been possible—at times—for the West to undo particularly harmful consequences of the imperial drive without admitting that that's what it was doing, it is simply not possible to address their underlying, unspoken causes while mired in denial.

As a result, the United States amassed a remarkable and consistent record of failure in the post-Cold War Middle East—not despite, but rather because of, the remarkable attention and copious resources devoted to the region. Today's Middle East is the mess that it is in part because of the mythology that Western scholars have created, spread, and used to misinform our political leaders.

America's sustained failure in the region thus tracks directly to our original hypothesis: Western thinkers and American policymakers have missed something fundamental in their approach to the region. What's more, it is possible (though not necessary) that they missed it *intentionally*. The truth, after all, is often inconvenient. Why bother to hire, promote, and fund scholars committed to revealing it when academia can produce a steady stream of scholars committed to making our leadership feel comfortable about its own beliefs and actions? We must thus plunge headfirst into our second historical excursion—this one, in keeping with the timeframes that pass for long-term thinking in the West, dates back about a quarter-century rather than three millennia—to appreciate the consequences of their analytic error.

The end of the Cold War marked a critical turning point in America's regional engagement. The purveyors of the *Pax Americana* that seemed to be blanketing the globe turned their gaze upon the Middle East, hoping to pacify it, as well. Coloring their view of the region were two conflicting visions of the twenty-first century.

The first visionary was Francis Fukuyama, who wrote of the "end of history," the final resolution of the timeless debate about how best to structure society, politics, and economics.[41] The answer was liberal democracy, and the future was about its march across the globe. According to Fukuyama and his devotees, the wisdom of the liberal ideas that had elevated the West from a longstanding civilizational backwater to a position of global dominance in the space of a few centuries was self-evident. As you may have heard, the arc of history supposedly bends towards justice—and progress. In a curious twist, the end-of-history crowd applied the social evolution theories of Hegel and Marx to liberal democracy. The entire world was evolving in our direction; our job was merely to help different corners of the globe move beyond the petty squabbles and parochial concerns that had defined their past so that they could join us in the glorious future.

The second visionary, Samuel Huntington, borrowing a term from Middle East scholar Bernard Lewis, told of a forthcoming "clash of civilizations." He foresaw a twenty-first century of competition between and confrontation among contemporary manifestations of the world's great ethnocultural groups, each extolling a different structural model for society and for the world.[42] Western thinking may have worked well for the West, but the world is not full of failed Westerners. Latin America, Orthodox Christianity, Hinduism, Buddhism, Confucianism, Islam, Sub-Saharan Africa, and a few smaller civilizations possess different values, different priorities, different worldviews, and different hopes for the future than do Westerners. According to Huntington and his devotees, the future was not about harmonious convergence to "justice" as the West idealized it, but rather an uneasy and shifting series of alliances and conflicts among civilizations. At the epicenter of these conflicts, he noted in particular that "Islam has bloody borders."[43] As he explained it, Islam was, in many ways, the most different, the most violent, and the least patient of the world's great civilizations. Tensions within Islam, and between Islam and the other civilizations, would likely become particularly problematic.

Throughout the 1990s, scholars, pundits, and politicians debated the relative merits of these conflicting visions. In the years following 9/11, the truth became clear: Fukuyama's vision had been aspirational; Huntington's descriptive. While it might have been nice to think that humanity's greatest debate will eventually resolve itself in favor of liberal democracy, that day is hardly at hand. Civilizations will continue to clash throughout the foreseeable future. And as adherents of Huntington's vision understood, precisely because the West has dominated the past few centuries of world history, and spent the past few decades apologizing for that dominance and groveling for redemption, the tension between an awakening, bold Islamic civilization and an open, underconfident Western civilization seems destined to define a bloody and troubling century. In stark contrast to the unquestioning optimism of the end-of-history crowd, clash-of-civilization types concede the possibility of Western collapse and a future in which liberal democracy dwindles into insignificance, becoming one more historical footnote as the world returns once again to its traditional authoritarian structures.

Nevertheless, it is Fukuyama's vision that has played the larger role in Western thinking and in shaping American engagement in the Middle East and around the world. Western fidelity to that vision—which even Fukuyama has since repudiated[44]—has impeded its ability to see, much less to respond to, the imperial drive at the heart of the Middle East's numerous crises.

Today's West seems to suffer from an ingrained insistence that having reached the end of history, history's lessons are of little use. The West extolls the virtues of the rule-based liberal international order while doing less and less to ensure that it retains its scope, much less that it expands. Nor, for that matter, have Western liberal democracies done much to make their model attractive. From the press coverage that turned the 2000 election into a circus, through the Bush and Obama presidencies, the 2008 financial crisis, the European debt crisis, the rise in speech codes throughout the West, the resurgence of anti-Semitism and race baiting, the elevation of bureaucratic regulators above elected officials, the acceptance of large numbers of unemployable citizens as part of the new normal, and the U.S. election of 2016, the twenty-first century has provided greater fodder to the enemies of liberal democracy and the rule of law than it has to supporters.[45]

Worse, Western leaders tend to view each new crisis on standalone terms. They attempt to restore something close to the status quo ante, exerting far too little effort wondering whether some underlying cause, if left unchecked, might threaten the entire global architecture. That perspective leaves Western leaders increasingly surprised and frustrated as events fail to unfold as predicted. This frustration is particularly prevalent in addressing Middle East crises, where the dominant if veiled imperial drive is antithetical to the state system, human rights, and many of the rules they embody. But the denial has become visceral; too many prestigious careers and institutions have vested too much of their prestige in supporting an unsupportable view of the Middle East. Our basic hypothesis—that perhaps our finest experts have missed something—rarely even makes it to the table. Which would be fine if those experts were doing a good job. But all available evidence suggests that they are not.

Non-Western civilizations have taken advantage of Western blindness and weakness. The Chinese model combining relatively unrestrained economics with tightly controlled political thought and speech gains popularity around the globe. Russia seems intent on moving back to an era of rules that constrained lesser nations, while the great nations did as they pleased. Islam has evolved from the anarchic terrorism of the PLO, Hezbollah, the Muslim Brotherhood, and al Qaeda to the formation of a Shiite Islamic Republic and a Sunni Caliphate, both committed to global orders that serve the will of God—and a mad race for nuclear weapons to help create them.

Thanks to Western denial and an ingrained if unjustifiable confidence that history moves only "forward" toward an expansion of liberal values, Freedom House reports that global freedom—the quintessential   liberal value—has been declining for at least a decade.[46] This decline is hardly inevitable. It is a consequence of Western retreat—a strategy for which American voters have twice rewarded President Obama. But even if American voters confirm that preference again in 2016, "unforeseeable" events may move Obama's successor in a different direction. The greatest question mark hanging over the American—and global—future is whether the U.S. will reverse course and reassert its leadership before it is too late. That clock will continue ticking no matter how the American electorate reconfigures its government for 2017.

As long as the United States continues on its present course, American strategic policy will devolve to a cycle of retreat-retrench-negotiate-react-repeat. Elements that have long shaped discussions of American strategy, such as vision, understanding, proactivity, and an attempt to shape unfolding events, will fade into the background—becoming as irrelevant to the U.S. over the next few decades as they have become to Europe's once-great powers over the past few. These strategic elements will remain central, however, to an America fighting to preserve its own national interests, ideals, and the global order they have engendered. A strategy that both works in the short term and points in the right direction for the long term will become critical. American leadership will need a coherent strategic vision to operate within the confines of different regions, cultures, and civilizations while promoting a world of relative stability and prosperity, in which the commitment to basic human rights and human development grows—even if glacially—with each passing year. Given such a vision and appropriate resources, significant positive change is possible; the absence of a clear vision can only exacerbate the frittering away of vital American resources to no discernable benefit.

Chapter 8. The Need for Reengagement

If and or when the United States seeks to reverse its recent retreat from its much maligned yet much needed role as "the world's policeman," the best place to start is with the acquisition of corrective lenses. To reengage properly, American policymakers must shed every last vestige of their polyannish end-of-history blinders, and see the world through a clash-of-civilization lens. To do that, they must study each of the world's non-Western civilizations on its own terms. Only then will they be able to discern the values and priorities, successes and failures, ties to the past and hopes for the future, that mark each of these great civilizations as decidedly different from the West.

In none of the world's civilizations is such a reassessment more overdue than the Arab/Islamic Middle East, for none combines as much past failure with as much violent rage. Left unchecked: The violent radicalism of the Islamic State, al Qaeda, the Muslim Brotherhood, Hamas, Fatah, Hezbollah, the Islamic Republic, and other terrorist movements will intensify. Iran will complete both its nuclear weapons program and its missile program capable of reaching at least all of Europe, and possibly the United States—triggering a regional arms race along the way. The anarchy that has already engulfed Iraq and Syria will spread, yielding steady streams of genocide and refugees. The centrality of the region to both global energy and global trade will risk a worldwide economic downturn. And the involvement of major powers with conflicting objectives will create the preconditions for a bloody World War. Given those likely and foreseeable consequences of continued American withdrawal, all decent people had better hope that the U.S. reengages—soon—in a manner capable of checking them. That's why journeys of inquiry like the one we're undertaking are critical.

The time is long past due to concede that the post-Ottoman order that Britain and France imposed in the wake of the First World War has ended. Much of the Middle East has already plunged into anarchy, brutality, and civil war. America's leaders will either accept this degeneration as a fait accompli or work to secure a new regional order. No regional order, of course, will end the bloodletting before it has run its course. But an intelligent approach, intelligent alliances with the region's most forward-looking leaders, and a willingness to nudge these leaders in appropriate directions, can minimize the pain, the dislocation, and the tragedy that is certain to unfold as this volatile region moves fitfully into its next historical era. No positive future for the Middle East can rest upon the platform of failure that has led the region to its current state. It is far past time for the West—with American leadership—to jettison the conventional wisdom that has hamstrung thinking about the Middle East for much of the past century.

Before we take stock of the West's plentiful errors in approaching the region, however, we must concede that failures in the Middle East abound. They begin, of course, with the people of the region; the worst that outsiders have ever done is to compound them by favoring the wrong local players and feeding the worst indigenous instincts. Many of those indigenous instincts are truly deadly to stability, to peace, to coexistence, and to human development. Because while history may be far from ending, it has taught some consistent lessons. A viable society must give direction and purpose to its young men; a prosperous society must educate and empower its young women. Arab/Islamic society has failed dismally on both counts. Its far-too-numerous feral young men are among the most brutal and violent anywhere on the planet; its women are a mass of restrained, degraded, untapped potential.

The best that outsiders can hope to do is to help the best local leaders stabilize the region. Stability will create a platform upon which development is possible, but stability without human capital development will not last. Unless those same local leaders seize the opportunity to rebuild their societies in ways that unleash their peoples' potential, hard-won stability will crumble into a new round of brutal anarchy.

The specifics of that human capital development will thus rest almost entirely with the people of the region. They will have to find ways to give their young men purpose—consistent with the values and ideals of their own cultures. They will have to educate and empower their young women—without destabilizing the existing social fabric and family structures that provide such a central component of both individual and group identity. That work will not be easy, and success is far from guaranteed.

From an American perspective, the need for tough developmental restructuring means that we must avoid the temptation to pack up and go home as soon as the fires stop burning. As the American military presence in Iraq between 2007 and 2011 demonstrated, even when the U.S. is not directly engaged in "nation building," it can fill critical roles as a stabilizer or an arbitrator. President Obama and Secretary Clinton's precipitous withdrawal in 2011 provided a stark illustration of the West's tendency to tackle crises without thinking very much about their underlying causes. Things—including very bad things—happen for a reason. Those who try to fix crises while ignoring their causes invariably waste tremendous time, effort, resources, and lives while accomplishing very little.

Therein lies the tragedy of Western involvement in the Middle East since the fall of the Ottoman Empire. Early on, romantic colonialists saw Arabs as violent peasants, whose shortcomings were endemic to their culture—and thus unavoidable. By the late twentieth century, that view had flipped entirely to become a multiculturalist celebration of Arab authenticity, whose shortcomings have arisen only because they are victims of Western oppression. Western academics and "experts" have fashioned a fable of Arabs and Muslims as victims of outside interference, rather than of their own choices. Because they deny the agency of Arabs and Muslims, these accredited "experts" are incapable of seeing that trends and forces internal to Arabism and Islam have shaped the region to a far greater extent than anything that any outsider has done. From the perspective of regional experts, then, human capital development in the Arab/Islamic world has either been inherently impossible or unachievable only because of Western oppression. Either way, their consistent advice to policymakers has been to address consequences and ignore causes.

Once again then, we return to our original hypothesis. The experts have missed something fundamental. It is the cultural and philosophical shortcomings of the Arab/Islamic world that have doomed the Middle East to a century of slow decline. Western acceptance of that dysfunctionality did not create the region's problems—but it did exacerbate it. American strategists and policymakers—of both the left and the right—have spent decades shielding Middle Easterners from the consequences of their decisions and actions. American policy has twisted itself into a parody of its own values and interests ensuring that Middle Eastern leaders need never face their own internal shortcomings and contradictions—a minimum prerequisite for making fundamentally different choices. Fortunately, our commitment to respecting the people, values, and cultures of the Middle East on their own terms paves the way to a more respectful policy orientation.

The consequences of this American—and Western—failure, and the dismal local instincts that it has empowered, have cascaded to the point of destabilizing the entire region. The luxury of deferred difficult choices has become far too expensive to sustain. The future of the liberal international order rests upon American leadership willing to take a fresh look at the region, to see it through clear and honest eyes, to work towards a stable regional structure, and to push its leaders to make wiser choices. Though it is ultimately the leaders of the Middle East who will have to make those choices, and their people who will feel their direct effects, reverberations from the region will shape the global order of the twenty-first century. Therein lies the case for American attention, action, committed engagement—and clear vision. And therein lies the motivation for the next leg of our journey: a trek through the quarter-century of dismal American performance in the Post-Cold War Middle East.

Chapter 9. A History of Failure

Failure. No single word better summarizes American Middle East policy since the end of the Cold War. In the past quarter-century, four American Presidents have approached the region with four very different strategies. All four have failed. Why? Because all four shared a fatally flawed package of assumptions known as "conventional wisdom."

George H. W. Bush

George H.W. Bush was the first American President to confront a Middle Eastern crisis with minimal risk of escalation. With the Soviet Union on its last legs, Saddam Hussein's 1990 annexation of Kuwait to Iraq provided the United States with an opportunity to view the region on its own terms, rather than as a front in a global Cold War. For guidance through this new Middle East, President Bush and Secretary of State Baker turned to the Saudis. With Saudi blessings, Bush and Baker assembled a broad Arab and international coalition committed to restoring Kuwaiti sovereignty.[47] The international community lauded their skill at coalition building; many still regard it as the pinnacle of American diplomacy.

From a strictly diplomatic perspective, that assessment is probably correct. Bush and Baker were indeed a gifted diplomatic duo. From a strategic perspective, and from the perspective of anyone who cares about the welfare and development of the people of the Middle East, however, their emphasis on forming the broadest possible coalition was a disaster. As is often the case, "broadest possible" means "adhering to the lowest common denominator." And the lowest common denominator cared not one whit for the welfare of Middle Easterners. Its only concern was the ejection of Saddam from Kuwait, and the restoration of the unstable status quo that prevailed prior to the Iraqi invasion.

The most consequential decision of the American team was thus not the successful military campaign itself but rather its approach to coalition. In return for removing a grave threat to the Saudi throne and restoring an illiberal monarchy in Kuwait, the U.S. demanded *nothing* in return: No change in Saudi antipathy towards Israel; no end to Saudi funding of extremist mosques and organizations around the globe; no lessening of Saudi oppression at home; no Kuwaiti liberalization or acceptance of constitutional limitations; and no extension of citizenship anywhere in the Gulf Cooperation Council (GCC) to the many stateless Arabs living in the Gulf. At the behest of the Arab coalition members, the U.S. relinquished all flexibility in deciding how far into Iraq to take the U.S. military, and how many military objectives to achieve. As President Bush and his National Security Advisor, Brent Scowcroft, later explained: "True to the guidelines we had established, when we had achieved our strategic objectives (ejecting Iraqi forces from Kuwait and eroding Saddam's threat to the region) we stopped the fighting."[48]

Secretary Baker was even more forthcoming in explaining how the Administration's solicitude for the Saudis outweighed American strategic interests. While hostilities were ongoing, Baker, Defense Secretary Cheney, and Deputy National Security Adviser Gates all told the American people—and the world—to expect the campaign to end with Saddam's removal.[49] Baker in particular cited the United Nations Security Council resolutions calling for "peace and stability" as an endorsement of Saddam's removal.[50] Yet when push came to shove, Bush halted the military with Saddam still in power. Baker later explained:

> We had promised the entire world in building what was an unprecedented international coalition, that we had no interest in occupying an Arab country. We weren't in this business to occupy Iraq. We were going to do what the United Nations Security Council said we should do, which was unconditionally eject Iraq from Kuwait. That was our war aim. That was our political aim. Would it have been better if Saddam had not survived? You bet. Did our Arab allies and everybody else think he would not survive a defeat of the type that we administered to him? Yes, they did not think he would survive. He did survive... The Arab coalition partners particularly I remember, the Saudis, wanted us to leave as promptly as possible—get our forces out of there after the end of the war—when there was a question of

whether we should occupy some of southern Iraq. There was a clear chance that if we overdid it, that we would lose the coalition or that cracks would begin to develop within the coalition....[51]

Saddam's final twelve years in power, and the need for American troops to return to Iraq in 2003, arose because the George H.W. Bush Administration first elevated the interests of the Arab allies it was saving above those of the United States, and then miscalculated the effects of that elevation.

The decade-plus that Iraqis spent living in a totalitarian state from 1991 to 2003 was hardly the only negative consequence of the Bush/Baker approach to coalition building. In keeping with the spirit of the coalition and the need to attract and retain as many reluctant Arab allies as possible, President Bush left Saddam in power,[52] refused to let Israel protect itself from Saddam's gratuitous missiles,[53] enabled a Syrian takeover of Lebanon,[54] and allowed the returning Kuwaitis to send a flood of refugees into Jordan.[55] Most famously, Bush failed to protect the American-inspired uprisings of southern Iraq's Shia and northern Iraq's Kurds until Saddam had contained both movements and brutalized both populations.[56] Eventually, when the considerations were more humanitarian than military or strategic, Bush did establish no-fly zones over both Iraqi regions—thereby guaranteeing an ongoing American military presence, a perpetuation of Saddam's totalitarian regime, and a new clear focal point for anti-American sentiment throughout the Arab/Islamic world. The forty-plus million people living in Iraq, Jordan, Israel, and Lebanon thus paid steep prices for the grand "success" of international diplomacy.

Meanwhile, following the end of the Soviet threat to Afghanistan, Bush more-or-less lost interest in that country, leaving behind a cache of American weapons, an American-trained mujahedeen militia, a number of squabbling ethnic groups, tribes, and warlords, and no basis for stability or national unity.[57] In short, George H.W. Bush cast the U.S. as the military protector of the Middle East's uncomfortable status quo, working to tamp down crises without addressing their underlying causes. Ten years later, Americans awoke to discover a global terror network based in Afghanistan and bearing clear Saudi fingerprints, an unfinished war in Iraq, and tensions that—if anything—had increased in the duration.

Failure.

Bill Clinton

Bill Clinton did little to alter America's policies vis-à-vis Iraq, the

GCC, Afghanistan, or most of the Arab/Islamic world. His Middle East policy more-or-less rose and fell with the Arab/Israeli conflict, with an occasional glance in the direction of rising Islamist terrorism. On the Arab/Israeli front, Clinton ushered the Oslo Accords to fruition in 1993, culminating in the instantly iconic photo of Yitzchak Rabin and Yasir Arafat shaking hands amidst the President's outstretched arms.[58] He then spent the duration of his term in office attempting to turn a signed agreement into an effective peace.

Clinton had his work cut out for him. To the extent that Arafat had ever had any minimal inclination towards coexistence, he hid it carefully from his people.[59] His newly founded Palestinian Authority (PA)—essentially the terrorist PLO under a new name—promulgated vitriolic Jew hatred, and never opposed anti-Israel terror. Though he moderated his tone in English (and French), his Arabic speeches made clear that he intended to replace every inch of the Jewish State of Israel with a Jew-free State of Palestine—even if he had to do it one inch at a time. As Ephraim Karsh, the noted scholar of Middle Eastern affairs documented, from the very day that "Arafat signed the Oslo Accords, he broadcast to the Palestinians inflammatory anti-Israeli speeches, which invoked the Phased Plan. For the next decade, he continued to go on record with talk of 'liberating' the 'territories of 1948' not 1967 and recapturing the whole of Jerusalem."[60]

The Rabin assassination in November 1995 appeared to free Arafat from any obligation of feigning peaceful intentions that he may once have felt; by 1996, Arafat-inspired terror on the streets of Israel dominated the Israeli elections. Israeli political scientist Gerald Steinberg noted that the assassination had created massive sympathy for Rabin's work, giving Shimon Peres—Rabin's partner and successor at the helm of the Labor Party—an early twenty-five-to-thirty point lead in the polls. The gap closed quickly, however, following four brutal terrorist attacks in late February and early March 1996. "[T]his wave of terrorism led to intense public criticism of the Oslo accords, of Arafat's continued anti-Israeli rhetoric and his failure to take action against the Islamic extremists, such as Hamas, and of the ineffectiveness of the government's responses."[61] Eventually, it led to a Likud victory in the May elections, handing the Premiership to Benjamin Netanyahu—a leader savvy enough to believe Arafat's Arabic rather than his English.

President Clinton, who had demonstrated a clear preference for a Peres victory,[62] developed a far warmer relationship with Arafat than with Netanyahu. Clinton accepted a mild reduction in terror as a sign of the PA's good faith, and avoided pushing it to make any of the tough choices that might have paved the way for actual peace and coexistence.[63]   Of all of the world's dignitaries, Yasir Arafat—an unreformed aging terrorist—was the most frequent guest in the Clinton White House.[64] Clinton's faith in Arafat, which flew in the face of all available evidence, persisted to his very last days in office. But Arafat did not repay Clinton's warm embrace in kind. By the time that Clinton left office, Arafat had rejected precisely the deal that widespread conventional wisdom had long claimed his people both wanted and deserved. He chose instead to launch a long-planned, full-blown wave of militant terrorism in September 2000. As Karsh noted:

> Arafat cleverly used Ariel Sharon's visit to the Temple Mount as a pretext to unleashing a campaign of organized terror against Israel. He opened up the jails, armed the militias, and incited mobs to engage in violence. Months after the outbreak of war, top Palestinian officials like Marwan Barghouti admitted that intense preparations were made long before 2000 to launch a terrorist offensive.[65]

Arafat's terror war, commonly known as the "second *intifada*," should have demonstrated conclusively that the Oslo Accords had always been a sham. His actions aligned perfectly with the PLO's "Phased Plan" of 1974: First, establish an "independent combatant national authority" in any land that the PLO can "liberate." Second, use that "national authority" to attack Israel. Third, provoke an all-out Arab Israeli war.[66] The Oslo Accords had provided Arafat with "liberated" land and a Palestinian Authority per phase one. His *intifada* merely moved the plan into phase two.

This Phased Plan was hardly a secret; the PLO had published it, announced it, broadcast it widely—and never retracted it. Arafat's strategy had been in plain view for nearly two decades prior to the Oslo Accords. Anyone paying attention could have seen him putting his announced strategy into play. Yet the world—and specifically President Clinton—refused to pay attention. Even the launch of Arafat's phase-two terror war couldn't get the world to refocus. As a result, though Arafat had effectively nullified the Oslo Accords in 2000, they persisted in zombie state until September 2015, when Mahmoud Abbas declared to the United Nations General Assembly "that we cannot continue to be bound by these agreements...."[67]

The Palestinian Authority's unilateral withdrawal from Oslo ended a long, sorry chapter in the history of failed U.S. peacemaking (though President Obama and Secretary Kerry emphatically ignored its demise). For all of Clinton's efforts, the only positive lasting contribution of his "peace process" was the 1994 Jordanian/Israeli treaty—something that the leadership of both countries had long wanted to conclude but that the PLO had held hostage until the Oslo Accords freed Jordan's King Hussein to move forward.[68]

The only other noteworthy aspect of Clinton's Middle East policy dealt with terrorism. Al Qaeda's 1993 truck bombing of the World Trade Center made the issue impossible to avoid. The Administration's response, however, more-or-less treated the problem as one of international criminality, rather than as anything resembling war.[69] A 1998 cruise missile attack on an al-Qaeda base in Afghanistan targeting Osama bin Laden missed him by a matter of hours, yet generated few further attempts and little else in the nature of follow-up.[70] Al-Qaeda was clearly not cowed. Its 2000 attack on the USS Cole in the Yemeni port of Aden further heightened U.S. concerns, but led to little in the way of either public education or programmatic response.[71] To the extent that anyone in the Clinton Administration understood the gravity of the challenge, the outgoing team failed to convey that message to either the American public or the incoming President Bush; the 9/11 Commission later reported that "[t]here was no National Intelligence Estimate on terrorism between 1995 and 9/11."[72] The primary effects of Clinton's efforts in the Middle East were thus an increase in the lethality of anti-Israel terrorism and a missed opportunity to educate the American public about the rising threat of Islamist terrorism.

Failure.

George W. Bush

George W. Bush bore the brunt of his two immediate predecessors' failures. By the time he had completed his first year in office, he found himself forced to confront a region in turmoil. Al Qaeda proved itself capable of reaching the American homeland, as its coordinated attacks brought down the Twin Towers and punched a gaping hole in the Pentagon. The Taliban, a brutal, backwards, Islamist movement that had seized control of most of Afghanistan provided al Qaeda with a comfortable home base. American troops remained uneasily in the Arabian desert, locked in an interminable stalemate with Saddam and grating on the nerves of their GCC hosts. The Oslo-born Arab/Israeli "peace process" had collapsed into the phased-plan terror war that Arafat had long planned; much of the world pretended that its negotiations were still viable (or even more bizarrely, blamed Israel for the collapse). Iran was busily courting European businesses and politicians, seeking to moderate its image without altering its behavior—or its longstanding role as the world's foremost state sponsor of terror.

Bush responded boldly to the 9/11 attacks. He inverted large parts of his foreign policy overnight, becoming the nation builder he had derided on the campaign trail less than a year earlier. His Treasury department reversed its position on the rules governing international cash flows in an effort to reduce money laundering. His armed forces launched military campaigns in Afghanistan and Iraq. His state department pressured Iran and Libya. And Bush himself defined a "freedom agenda:" He promised American support to dissidents seeking to overthrow repressive regimes—and insisted upon democratic elections as the *sine qua non* of that freedom. He distanced himself, and the U.S., from those, like Arafat, who had chosen terrorism and war over freedom and development.

Yet despite Bush's poetic proclamation: "All who live in tyranny and hopelessness can know: the United States will not ignore your oppression, or excuse your oppressors. When you stand for your liberty, we will stand with you,"[73] he approached each of those bold moves with inadequate resources and naïve assumptions. His end-of-history blinders led him to overestimate the universal appeal of Western ideals. He never told America what should have been obvious all along—the liberalization of the Arab/Islamic world would be a long, uncertain, high-risk process. The time commitment to Iraq would be at least as great as the fifty-to-sixty years (and counting) that U.S. forces had remained in Germany, Japan, and South Korea. The nature of the engagement would change over time, but if the West were to take the challenge seriously, the grandchildren of the people who lived through 9/11 would probably still be talking about American troops stabilizing the Arab/Islamic world.

Bush's blindness, and his consequent shortage of resources and contingency plans, doomed his elegant freedom agenda to failure. Bush ignored early and repeated warnings from military[74] and political[75] leaders supportive of his war aims that he was allocating insufficient resources to stabilize post-Saddam Iraq. Democratic Senator Joe Lieberman, whose steadfast support for the war came at significant political cost, lamented repeatedly that Bush's insistence on overselling the case for toppling Saddam while undersupplying the war effort was giving "a bad name to a just war:"[76]

> Look, long before George Bush became president, I reached a conclusion that Saddam Hussein was a threat to the US and to the world, and particularly to his own people who he was brutally suppressing. I believe that the war against Saddam was right, and that the world is safer with him gone. I said last fall and then again a month before the war, "Mr. President, here's what you have to do to get ready to secure

post-Saddam Iraq." No planning was done by this administration. I believe it's because this administration divided within itself, and the president as commander in chief has not brought it together.[77]

Bush ignored all such advice for four years.

In the early going, Bush seemed prescient. His approach showed early promise in Iraq,[78] Libya,[79] Lebanon,[80] and according to some accounts even Iran,[81] before crumbling predictably into a bloody sectarian conflict that threatened to split Iraq in three.[82] In March 2006, Congress appointed the "Iraq Study Group," (ISG) a high level, ten-person, bipartisan, commission of respected elder statesmen—most of whom had served at high levels in the (G.H.W.) Bush or Clinton Administrations—charged with assessing the situation in Iraq and recommending a way forward. Their report, issued in December 2006, opened:

> The situation in Iraq is grave and deteriorating…. Our most important recommendations call for new and enhanced diplomatic and political efforts in Iraq and the region, and a change in the primary mission of U.S. forces in Iraq that will enable the United States to begin to move its combat forces out of Iraq responsibly.[83]

In an emphatic reassertion of conventional wisdom, they explicitly linked Iraq's civil war to numerous other regional conflicts, asserting most clearly "[t]he United States will not be able to achieve its goals in the Middle East unless the United States deals directly with the Arab-Israeli conflict."[84] Perhaps unsurprisingly given the group's membership, many of its specific recommendations resurrected moribund diplomatic failures of the 1990s. Analysts could hardly help noticing that the ISG's recommendations had a "back-to-the-future quality," embodying an "analytical leap of faith…that all the key issues in the Middle East are inextricably linked….," even though "there is no evidence to back them up."[85]

Though his missteps in Iraq cost him dearly in the 2006 midterm elections, Bush stood strong and chose to fly in the face of conventional wisdom. He ignored the ISG, and instead increased the American military presence in Iraq[86]—prompting enraged leading Democrats to declare the war "lost," and insisting that it "could not be won by military force."[87] The 2007 counterinsurgency surge, which he and General Petraeus implemented masterfully, represented a rare American victory in the Middle East—as even vociferous critics like Hillary Clinton and Barack Obama later acknowledged.[88] The Bush/Petraeus surge stabilized Iraq and allowed Bush to leave office with the region seemingly and uncharacteristically on the right track.[89]

The effects of Bush's policies vis-à-vis the Arab/Israeli conflict, on the other hand, were far less successful. Unlike most Western leaders, Bush actually approached the conflict in an evenhanded manner, demanding comparable commitments from both sides rather than from just the Israelis.[90] His refusal to ignore Arafat's incitement and terrorism motivated Ariel Sharon to take the enormous political and national security risk of removing *all* Israeli civilian and military presence from Gaza, effectively forcing its Arab residents to choose between development and war with no further reference to an "occupying power."[91] Despite knowing that the power vacuum was likely to turn Gaza into a safe haven for terror, Bush nevertheless supported the disengagement in the name of peace.[92] Unsurprisingly, the Gazans made the wrong choice, acting immediately to uproot the economic infrastructure the Israelis had gifted them,[93] favoring Hamas[94] and smaller, even more radical groups,[95] turning Gaza into a terrorist statelet on the Mediterranean, and threatening both Israel and Egypt.[96]

The challenges of Bush's middle years in office were a harbinger of those that would follow his departure. His confidence that people living in an authoritarian straitjacket would choose peace, coexistence, and development when freed to do so proved naïve in the extreme. His decisions to divert resources from Afghanistan to Iraq before eliminating either al Qaeda or the Taliban, and to topple Saddam without an adequate plan for Iraqi reconstruction, eroded any goodwill that his early successes might have engendered. His overemphasis on elections and the allure of freedom led him to understate the importance of institutions and cultures capable of sustaining a liberal society—and thus to underestimate by orders of magnitude the external resources needed to effect his desired regional transformation. He never prepared the American public for an open-ended, expensive, and likely bloody commitment to liberalizing the Arab/Islamic world. When the unprepared public chose to move on, the George W. Bush freedom agenda met its ultimate—and predictable—demise. Failure.

Barack Obama

Barack Obama, elected with a mandate to reverse Bush's policies wherever possible, took to the freedom agenda—and the broader Middle East—with particular gusto. He announced precise bounds and durational limits on American involvement in Iraq and in Afghanistan,[97] effectively putting enemies and allies alike on notice that the United States would not become a long-term player in their local dramas. In a shocking breach of diplomatic norms, he reached out to Muslims as Muslims rather than as citizens of their respective states[98]—an address every bit as radical as his predecessor's appeal to dissidents around the world.

Obama placed increasing amounts of "daylight" between the U.S. and Israel,[99] an explicit part of a strategy that he insisted would motivate Arab concessions to the moribund "peace process." As a seemingly contradictory part of the same strategy, he rewarded the recalcitrance of the Palestinian Authority and condoned Hamas' military campaign against civilians.[100] But Israel was hardly the sole recipient of Obama's coolness: He also distanced the U.S. from its longstanding allies in Jordan and the GCC,[101] believing that a balance-of-power struggle between Saudi Arabia and Iran better served regional stability. He abandoned the authoritarian but pro-Western regime in Egypt,[102] while coddling the Islamists running Turkey, Qatar, and the Muslim Brotherhood.[103]

Elsewhere in the region, Obama "led from behind" to topple the toothless Qaddafi in Libya, plunging the county into anarchy that Islamists soon exploited.[104] He spearheaded the diplomatic push to reintegrate Iran into the community of nations.[105] He stood idle while Syria collapsed into a bloody civil war.[106] He remained silent while the Islamic Republic crushed a nascent pro-democracy movement.[107] He invited a significant increase in both Russian and Iranian influence throughout the region.[108] And in what he called "the most significant achievement to date in our nation's effort to defeat al Qaeda,"[109] he authorized Navy SEAL Team Six to kill Osama bin Laden, allegedly putting al Qaeda "on the run."[110]

Obama's masterful use of an overly credulous and often clueless press allowed him to take a number of actions in the Middle East— specifically vis-à-vis Israel—that the American public opposed in theory but misunderstood in practice. Obama's advisers took particular pride in their use of the press to mislead the American public on a broad range of issues. One of his key Obamacare advisers noted that: "Lack of transparency is a huge political advantage. And basically, call it the stupidity of the American voter or whatever, but basically that was really really critical for the thing to pass."[111] The situation was no different when it came to foreign policy. The press repeatedly helped the President mislead the American people to minimize protests against his many unpopular positions.[112]

Throughout his eight years in office, President Obama took numerous steps to endanger Israel's security—from delaying necessary arms shipments and halting commercial air traffic during the 2014 Gaza War to cutting a deal that enriched Iran and smoothed its path toward nuclearization—while insisting that he "had Israel's back." He repeatedly insisted—against all available evidence—that he considered the bonds between the countries "unbreakable," and that, indeed, he warranted the honorary status of being America's "first Jewish President."[113]

In other arenas, Obama traded five high-value, recidivist, Taliban leaders for an American deserter—Bowe Bergdahl—whom he then feted as a hero, likely as part of a plan to empty Guantanamo Bay at all costs.[114] When a coordinated, premeditated al Qaeda attack against the U.S. Consulate in Benghazi, Libya killed four Americans, including Ambassador Chris Stevens, on the anniversary of 9/11, the Administration insisted that it was a spontaneous uprising reacting to an obscure YouTube video—despite knowing the truth.[115] In each of these cases, large parts of the press simply related whatever story the Administration asked it to relate.

Finally, following the conclusion of Obama's deal with Iran—the Joint Comprehensive Plan of Action (JCPOA)—the extent to which the Administration had been using the press to propagandize became clear. According to Deputy National Security Adviser for Strategic Communications Ben Rhodes, the Administration point person selling the Iran deal:

> We created an echo chamber... [The press] were saying things that validated what we had given them to say…. In the absence of rational discourse, we are going to discourse the [expletive] out of this…We had test drives to know who was going to be able to carry our message effectively, and how to use outside groups like Ploughshares, the Iran Project and whomever else. So we knew the tactics that worked…We drove the [deal's opponents] crazy….I'd prefer a sober, reasoned public debate, after which members of Congress reflect and take a vote...[b]ut that's impossible.[116]

President Obama took great personal pride in having altered the balance of power and the course of events throughout the Middle East—and even greater pride in having rejected the advice of his advisors while doing so. In speaking specifically about his decision not to enforce his own "red line" of Syrian chemical weapons use, he explained:

> The perception was that my credibility was at stake, that America's credibility was at stake. And so for me to press the pause button at that moment, I knew, would cost me politically. And the fact that I was able to pull back from the immediate pressures and think through in my own mind

what was in America's interest, not only with respect to Syria but also with respect to our democracy, was as tough a decision as I've made—and I believe ultimately it was the right decision to make... There's a playbook in Washington that presidents are supposed to follow. It's a playbook that comes out of the foreign-policy establishment. And the playbook prescribes responses to different events, and these responses tend to be militarized responses. Where America is directly threatened, the playbook works. But the playbook can also be a trap that can lead to bad decisions. In the midst of an international challenge like Syria, you get judged harshly if you don't follow the playbook, even if there are good reasons why it does not apply.[117]

All told, President Obama inverted nearly every aspect of America's longstanding bipartisan approach to the Middle East—not by challenging the underlying conventional wisdom, but rather by switching sides in a number of long-running disputes while insisting that he was doing nothing of the sort. He jettisoned Israel, Saudi Arabia, and Egypt's Mubarak in favor of the Palestinian Authority, Iran, and the Muslim Brotherhood.

The results of Obama's policies through mid-2016 include: resurgent global terror;[118] a Caliphate spreading its tentacles throughout the anarchic regions once known as Iraq, Syria, and Libya;[119] low points in American relations with Israel,[120] Saudi Arabia,[121] and Egypt;[122] the reemergence of Russia as a major regional player;[123] Iran's consolidation of its influence among the Shiite Arabs;[124] genocidal slaughter terminating Christian, Yazidi, and other communities that predated the Arab Conquest by centuries;[125] a new regional arms race likely to culminate in nuclear proliferation;[126] and a flood of refugees threatening to destabilize the EU.[127]

Failure.

American Influence

Twenty-five years, four Presidents, four approaches, four emphases, and not a success among them. Of course, each of these Presidents did oversee some positive achievements on their way to grand strategic failure—the liberation of Kuwait, the Jordan/Israel treaty, the toppling of Saddam, the counterinsurgency surge, and the killing of bin Laden come readily to mind—and each approach still boasts devotees. Numerous experts, analysts, and pundits still stand in support of their preferred President and approach, arguing that it *almost* succeeded, or that it *would have* succeeded but for the inexplicable and unpredictable behavior of some regional actor—or the quirks of the American political system.

None of these arguments is remotely compelling. George H. W. Bush relinquished a strong hand in negotiating with GCC allies in favor of hopes for after-the-fact gratitude, and bequeathed his successors a regional strategy without an end game. Bill Clinton continued Bush's Iraqi mid-game, underestimated the threat of Islamist terror, and banked his own regional strategy on the reformation of an unreformed terrorist whose Arabic statements to his own people never wavered from Jew-hating incitement and calls for war. George W. Bush severely underestimated the complexity of the task he was undertaking—and consequently of the American time, blood, treasure, and other resources necessary to succeed. Barack Obama combined the (G.H.W.) Bush reliance on ex-post gratitude, the Clinton hope in reforming the unreformable, and the longstanding leftist preference for America's traditional adversaries over its traditional allies, to oversee the greatest bloodletting in the modern history of a bloody region. The idea that any of these strategic approaches came close to succeeding would be laughable had the consequences of failure been less tragic.

The region's many unfolding tragedies, which seem to grow only more pronounced over time, lead to a sobering question: Why have so many differing approaches failed to halt the region's downward spiral? Or perhaps even more poignantly, as attention shifts from Obama to America's fifth post-Cold War presidency, how should the U.S. reorient its strategic approach toward the Middle East?

One potential answer is that American (or for that matter, any outside) influence is limited. If enough key regional actors are hell-bent on following Tunisian street vendor Mohamed Bouazizi into self-immolation,[128] there is little that any outsider can do to stem the conflagration. Under such circumstances, no policy could "succeed." The West's only two options would both run counter to its liberal humanitarian tendencies: containment and conquest. Under the former, Western forces would work to contain the fire until *something* emerged from the smoldering ashes; stem its spread by refusing to allow refugees, expatriates, or even business interests out of the area; and decapitate anyone who tried to export the region's problems. Under the latter, Western forces would wreak sufficient destruction upon the region to cow its remaining residents into submission. In the language of bumper stickers, either "Let Them Fight It Out Among Themselves" or "Bomb Them All and Let God Sort Them Out." Neither alternative seems remotely appealing.

A less defeatist—and consequently more attractive—possibility is that the U.S. *can* influence the region's development in positive directions, but only by approaching the problems and players realistically. Fortunately, we incorporated that position into our journey, noting at the outset that very little of our inquiry was meaningful if the U.S. and its Western allies are incapable of bringing positive change to the Middle East. We also, however, recognized that to effect such positive change, American policymakers must be honest about *both* the values that the U.S. would like to promulgate *and* those that already dominate the region.

The failure of George W. Bush's freedom agenda should prove particularly instructive to anyone thinking about American values. A far wiser and humbler approach would deemphasize elections and focus exclusively on the infrastructure necessary to support human freedom—stability, toleration, personal security, labor mobility, education, economic growth, religious pluralism, the enfranchisement of women, and the institutions of civil society—and the first few steps along the long road to that freedom. Elections would enter the mix only where a plausibly liberal infrastructure existed to support them. After all, liberalism of the sort that Americans take for granted did not emerge overnight. The Anglo-American tradition—the earliest of all traditions to embrace philosophical liberalism—required 650 years to evolve from the Magna Carta's concession that there are some rights beyond the control of the Crown to the Thirteenth Amendment's pronouncement that slavery is incompatible with a society in which all men are created equal.[129] A lot can change in 650 years, even in the Middle East.

The American goal at this point should be to help establish a workable foundation and nudge day-to-day developments in the "right" direction—namely the direction most compatible with short-term American interests and long-term liberal values. Long-term stability is a necessary precondition for any other positive development, but it is hardly sufficient. Anything further will require identifying and cultivating local allies eager to accept American guidance—and to adopt at least some core American values.

That realization alone, however, is bug one prerequisite for crafting a forward-looking strategy. It is one thing to understand the consistent failure of American approaches to the Middle East. It is another thing entirely to appreciate the enormity and the pervasiveness of the myth system that underpins that failure. For the next leg of our journey, we must board a magic bus—as we enter a universe that exists only in the seminar rooms of academia and the halls of power. We must learn of a Middle East that differs greatly from the one that exists in reality—a fantasyland of half-truths and full-blown lies crafted with loving care to justify theories of sociology, anthropology, and political science, while disregarding entirely the pain, the suffering, and the death that this storyline has caused. Welcome to the widely accepted, widely believe, wholly fictional False Narrative of the Middle East.

Chapter 10. The False Narrative
Hope vs. Reality

The most compelling question about America's post-2016 approach to the region is not what America wants but rather what the Middle East is. The failure of four distinct American approaches to the region did not stem from a lack of clarity about American desires; it emerged from American misperceptions of Middle Eastern players, movements, motivations, history, and values. After all, *we* may indeed hold certain truths to be self-evident, but even America's own history acknowledges that the very declaration of these self-evident truths can be a radical act. The world is full of people and movements who bristle at the suggestion that "all men are created equal" for reasons unrelated to the gendered subject. The Middle East hosts far more than its fair share of such people.

Americans across the political spectrum persist in a seemingly benign form of hubris: the insistence that "we all want the same things." Because we all want the same things, of course, it should not be hard to build bridges to the Islamist world rooted in common values and desires for the future. Political leaders, most of whom seem incapable of addressing the concerns and passions of nearly half of America's own citizens, make repeated pronouncements about the deepest desires of Islamists, terrorists, totalitarians, tribal leaders, warlords, and the residents of the societies in which they flourish—and then direct American policy accordingly. The misinformation has accelerated since 9/11;[130] our political leaders now issue repeated assurances that the overwhelming majority of Arabs (of all national, tribal, or religious affiliations), Muslims (whether Sunni or Shiite, living anywhere on the globe), and Iranians (both pro- and anti-regime), seek peace, tolerance, coexistence, prosperity, human rights, and most absurdly, religious freedom—all more-or-less as Americans understand those terms.

The sentiment is aspirational, the assertions fictional. They imply, for example, that support for enormously popular terror organizations like Hamas, Hezbollah, al Qaeda, the Muslim Brotherhood, Fatah, and the Islamic State, is weak and inauthentic. They suggest that there is little organic backing for authoritarian leaders like Arafat, Saddam, the Assads, or the Iranian Mullahcracy. And they discount the hordes flocking to radical, violent, hatemongering speakers like Yusuf al-Qaradawi[131] while slandering and exiling those like Ayaan Hirsi Ali, who actually do preach the liberal values of peace, tolerance, coexistence, prosperity, and human rights.[132]

Perhaps most contemptuously, Western leaders expect their publics to buy a convenient contradiction. On the one hand, they ask us to ignore the role of radicalism, misogyny, and anti-Semitism in contemporary Islamic thought when contemplating Muslims who happen to be in Western countries at any particular moment in time; viewing them skeptically because of the shortcomings of the culture to which they belong would be wrong. At the same time, however, they also ask us to excuse radicalism, misogyny, and anti-Semitism inherent in the policies that Muslim majority countries pursue—and that many Islamic organizations and communities in the West embrace—as valid and authentic expressions of their culture and unavoidable given the political realities that Muslim leaders face. It is tempting to say that this preposterous double standard culminated in UNESCO's absurd vote—with Western accession—to deny the historically uncontestable Jewish and Christian ties to Jerusalem, but supremacist Islamic imperialism is impossible to placate; even greater absurdities likely lie in our future.[133]

Little has changed in mainstream Western thinking about Islam since Bernard Lewis, probably the greatest Western scholar of Islam of the post-Ottoman era, described the source of the fallacy in 1976—more than three years before the Iranian revolution of 1979 brought radical Islam to the front pages, seventeen years before the 1993 bombing of the World Trade Center demonstrated its ability to reach the United States, and more than forty years ago:

> Modern Western man, being unable for the most part to assign a dominant and central place to religion in his own affairs, found himself unable to conceive that any other peoples in any other place could have done so, and was therefore impelled to devise other explanations of what

seemed to him only superficially religious phenomena. ... To the modern Western mind, it is not conceivable that men would fight and die in such numbers over mere differences of religion; there have to be some other "genuine" reasons underneath the religious veil.... Even to suggest such a thing is regarded as offensive by liberal opinion, always ready to take protective umbrage on behalf of those whom it regards as its wards. This is reflected in the present inability, political, journalistic, and scholarly alike, to recognize the importance of the factor of religion in the current affairs of the Muslim world and in the consequent recourse to the language of left-wing and right-wing, progressive and conservative, and the rest of the Western terminology, the use of which in explaining Muslim political phenomena is about as accurate and as enlightening as an account of a cricket match by a baseball correspondent.... For the Muslim, religion traditionally was not only universal but also central in the sense that it constituted the essential basis and focus of identity and loyalty. It was religion which distinguished those who belonged to the group and marked them off from those outside the group. A Muslim Iraqi would feel far closer bonds with a non-Iraqi Muslim than with a non-Muslim Iraqi....[134]

The flawed notion that "we all want the same things" is but the starting point for a stunningly false narrative, a set of tales that leading Middle East experts have concocted to serve the interests of academics and diplomats—a narrative so self-evidently inaccurate that only a credentialed expert could propound it. As the narrative moves from general to specific, and as its predictive failures mount, the evidence against it becomes ever clearer. Yet nearly a century after the Ottoman Empire collapsed into the modern Middle East, and five years after the grossly misnamed "Arab Spring" ended that post-Ottoman order, the fatally flawed conventional wisdom that helped bring about the region's current state persists.

To consider but a few specifics, conventional wisdom teaches that:

- The Arab/Israeli conflict is the region's most critical problem;[135]
- There is an Israeli/Palestinian conflict distinct from the Arab/Israeli conflict;[136]
- The nation-states of the Middle East embody both real states and real nations;[137]
- There is a clear sense of nationalism among Arab citizenry, particularly among the less tribal communities known as Syrians,

Iraqis, Palestinians and Lebanese;[138]
- The creation of a new State of Palestine west of the Jordan River is the key to regional peace, stability, and development;[139]
- The revolutionary Iran of 1979 has moderated itself to become a "more normal" authoritarian state;[140]
- Saudi Arabia, which has combined a generally *status quo* foreign policy, a preference for low-to-modest oil prices, a repressive theocracy at home, and a massive campaign funding radical Islamic institutions abroad, typically shares American interests;[141]
- Most Arabs want to integrate Israel into the region and share peace and security with their Jewish neighbor;[142]
- Terrorist movements that also provide basic services to their adherents are more interested in economic and social development than in violent conquest;[143]
- Islamism, or the supremacist elevation of Islam above all other forms of political organization, may be compatible with the prevailing liberal international order;[144]
- Until fairly recently and with a few tragic exceptions, minorities across the Middle East have been treated decently;[145]
- Arabs, or at the very least Sunni Arabs, share a certain kinship with and responsibility towards each other;[146]
- Movements like the Islamic State, al Qaeda, Hamas, Hezbollah, the Muslim Brotherhood, and Fatah, combine a small core of dedicated leaders with large numbers of weak supporters easily won away by kinder, gentler alternatives;[147]
- Most of the people living in the Middle East seek the same sorts of opportunities for their children as do liberal westerners, and would welcome the emergence of a more tolerant, open, prosperous society;[148]
- The Middle East is, always has been, and should rightly be, an Arab/Islamic region in which other cultures are illegitimate implants;[149]
- Misery across the Middle East is largely an artifact of a colonial past in which Westerners inflicted grave harm and shame upon the region's residents.[150]

To put the matter bluntly, the evidence does not support *any* of these assertions. In fact, the available evidence suggests strongly that they are *all* false. Yet most Americans believe at least most of them, few leaders question them publicly, academic and diplomatic opinion treats them as gospel, and they consistently underpin American policy. It is hardly a coincidence that the most successful recent American action in the Middle East, George W. Bush's 2007 surge, ran counter to the sober advice of America's most respected elder statesmen.[151]

The durability and popularity of this prevailing narrative is not hard to understand; though false, it is not without its merits. It permits Western leaders to treat Islam and Islamic militancy as unrelated phenomena, freeing them to praise the former while fighting the latter.[152] It confines Western fears to a few small but violent groups living among co-religionists whose support they coerce, rather than wondering whether a community touching a fifth of the world's population remains committed to overturning the liberal international order.[153] It allows Westerners to find hope where hope is dim—such as the absurd hope that a few hundred thousand young Egyptians with Twitter accounts might dominate a nation of eighty million poor, religious, illiterate peasants.[154] It plays off longstanding anti-Jewish stereotypes, and enables social justice warriors to set unachievable standards applicable only to Israel.[155] And it feeds the anti-Westernism that dominates so much of contemporary academic and elite opinion.[156] In short, it is an excellent narrative if the goals are to placate the public, vilify the Jews, denigrate liberalism, oppose U.S. policy, and promote trendy academic theory.

If the goal is to advance American interests and values in the Middle East, on the other hand, the prevailing narrative is sorely lacking. It provides few insights into the Middle East's arrival at its current state, and it rarely predicts the general flow of events. Because explanation and prediction are the two critical parameters for measuring any model's accuracy and utility,[157] the prevailing "feel good" false narrative is worse than incorrect. It is dangerous.

Falsehood in Practice

A narrative is more than a mere story; it is a model designed to simplify reality, an outlook, a worldview, or a policy framework fleshed out with a story. A good narrative provides the lens through which policymakers view and contextualize individual developments as they arise. It describes an understanding of history, explains why things happen the way they do, provides insights into current events, predicts future developments, and recommends actions likely to nudge that future in a desirable direction. In the absence of a reasonable narrative, both individual citizens and government policymakers misconstrue events, miss opportunities for positive change, and pursue expensive, painful dead ends to failure. The four failed post-Cold War approaches to the Middle East have had a cascading effect. Whether through strategic missteps, lack of resolve, misallocation of resources, delaying the inevitable until it was too late, or the poor selection of regional partners, the years since 9/11 have witnessed inordinate American investment in the region with strongly negative returns.

The explanatory and predictive failure of the prevailing Middle East narrative is hardly new. It has been a constant at least throughout the post-WWII period. Most news emanating from the region has long seemed inexplicable, at times even nonsensical. What has changed in the twenty-first century is the centrality of the region to American consciousness. Throughout the latter half of the twentieth century, Americans with a particular interest in Israel, oil, Islam, or American foreign policy followed the region intently, while most others tuned in only during the all-too-frequent crises. Since 9/11, the Middle East has been unavoidable. The region's emergence from seminar rooms—where false narratives metastasize—into living rooms has increased the criticality of understanding the various forces and influences buffeting the region. The track record of recent failure has been remarkable—and bipartisan.

During the Bush years, Americans: Watched the Palestinian Authority repeatedly reject the independent state it supposedly seeks.[158] We learned that the Saudis—though longstanding reliable American allies in selected areas of foreign policy—have long funded the world's largest network of anti-Western, anti-liberal indoctrination institutes.[159] We observed a Lebanese government, finally free of Syrian occupation, content to leave in place a heavily-armed Hezbollah running a mini-state blessed with its own foreign and defense policies—a mini-state that got the entire Lebanon into several wars with Israel that few Lebanese other than Hezbollah wanted.[160] We saw the "moderating" Islamic Republic of Iran lurch backwards into an aggressive, expansionist, revolutionary mode promulgating Jew-hatred, Holocaust denial, and genocide.[161] We squirmed as Islamic countries condoned the wholesale slaughter of black Sudanese Muslims at the hands of Arab Sudanese Muslims.[162] We stood stunned as a civil war tore apart the post-Saddam Iraq.[163] We subsidized the Gazans' drive to capitalize on Israel's complete withdrawal by turning the territory into an armed terrorist camp rather than a functioning polity.[164] Meanwhile, the international community reaffirmed its fecklessness at holding Arabs to even the most basic levels of decent behavior, as the world concluded that Israel was the source of the region's greatest problems. For all of Bush's involvement in the region, the only policy that produced its desired result was the 2007 counterinsurgency surge to reestablish the Iraqi central government—a policy that ran counter to the advice of America's most respected elder statesmen.[165]

During the Obama years, Americans: Watched a self-immolating Tunisian street vendor bring down the post-Ottoman order without warning.[166] We placed daylight between the U.S. and Israel to secure Arab overtures that were never forthcoming.[167] We saw Bashar Assad, the man whom John Kerry, Nancy Pelosi, and Vogue Magazine all touted as the great Syrian "reformer," slide into barbarism and cruelty.[168] Our President abandoned a longstanding ally in Egypt in favor of an Islamist successor who oversaw attacks on Christians at home and Jews across the border,[169] representing but one small part in his overall attempts at cozying up to the Muslim Brotherhood and the Islamic Republic of Iran at the expense of traditional Arab and Israeli allies.[170] The U.S. also abandoned a weakly unified Iraq, pushing it back into bloody civil war.[171] America showed the world that the only redlines that it is willing to enforce[172] are those condemning Jews who chose to live in Israeli neighborhoods and villages of which our enlightened leadership disapproved.[173] The Obama team worked overtime to provide Iran with an enormous cash infusion while legitimizing its nuclear program.[174] For good measure, America's leaders also sat silently as Iran expanded its influence into Iraq, Syria, and Yemen,[175] and invited Russia back into the Middle East.[176] Thanks to the Obama national security team, the U.S. toppled Libya's dictator in favor of Islamist anarchy;[177] asserted a strongly liberal future for a region in which Facebook and Twitter were more important than Islam and the military;[178] and slept through the rise of an anti-state Caliphate that draws recruits from around the globe and now controls parts of several countries.[179]

And that's just a quick review of selected headlines. In every case, America's leaders, pundits, and experts told the public what to expect—and in almost every case, the opposite occurred. (*L'oeuvre de* Thomas Friedman comes immediately to mind).[180] Did these experts and leaders believe their own predictions? Odds are they did, because they remain mired in a false narrative whose leftist and rightist versions share numerous fundamental and irretrievable flaws.

As more and more Americans turned their attention toward the Middle East, they came to discover a region in which none of the proffered narratives explains either the major or the minor stories. The only predictions that ever seem prophetic are those promising that the situation will degrade with time. Americans are finally getting more than just an occasional glimpse of a region that has been in steady slow decline since its last hegemonic ruler, the Ottoman Empire, slipped into history's dustbin with the Treaties of

Sèvres and Lausanne in the early 1920s.[181] Since then, Western powers seeking "stability" have helped to ensure that no battle was ever decisive and that no issue was ever resolved. The region exists in a seemingly perpetual cycle of crisis; cries to restore the status quo; grudging restoration of something resembling that status quo; inattention to the issues that created the crisis; and the inevitable next, bloodier, crisis. Americans have never been more justified in tweeting: *WTF?*[182]

U.S. Middle East policy has failed precisely because four Presidents grounded it in a fable rather than in reality—and in many ways, in a fable that inverts reality. The aggregate effect of those failures is leading to a stark choice: either withdraw entirely, allow the liberal international order to decline, and watch a new order, incompatible with American ideals and far less amenable to American interests, arise in its place; or develop a new engagement strategy, attuned to both American ideals and American interests, grounded firmly in reality. If President Obama's successor is to break free of the trap, to craft a Middle Eastern policy with a hope of restoring stability, to pave the way towards tolerance and coexistence, and to nudge the region's leaders to take the first necessary steps down the road to a free society, America's policymakers must first see the prevailing narrative for the falsehood that it is. They must replace it with one that explains past facts and predicts future events with some semblance of accuracy. And they must ground America's regional policy accordingly.

Returning once again to our original hypothesis, the evidence is overwhelming that conventional wisdom—and our finest experts who have helped make it conventional—have missed something fundamental. Our next question, which defines the next part of our journey, involves understanding how we can do better.

Beyond Conventional Wisdom

Chapter 11. The Fog of Expertise
Revolutionary Thinking

Incredulous queries born of widespread predictive failure tend to suggest that the time has come to return to first principles. Middle East experts share some common foundational assumptions under the rubric of conventional wisdom. These assumptions, embedded deeply in the way that academic institutions approach the region and train generation after generation of experts, define the orthodoxy of the field. Those who reject them are summarily dismissed as unserious or biased.

The existence of such an orthodoxy is hardly unique unto those who study the Middle East—or international affairs. Nor, for that matter, is the astounding amount of time and evidence necessary before the very expert we trust to know better discard a flawed orthodoxy. Trained professional experts can cling tenaciously to their beliefs long after any rational digestion of the data has disproved them. But flaws in foundational assumptions necessarily lead to unfulfilled predictions, inappropriate actions, and misallocated resources. As empirical data of such predictive failures mount so too should the challenges to conventional wisdom. Yet inertia and the intransigence of experts who have built careers upon foundational myths of questionable veracity combine to keep conventional wisdom conventional far longer than the data can support its wisdom. When the orthodoxy governing a field fails to deliver the expected results, the psychic damage to the experts who own it can be significant. More often than not they double down, head into deep denial, and insist that the problem lies not with their theories but rather with a real world that refuses to conform.

Thomas Kuhn's analysis of the structure of scientific revolutions describes the ways in which mounting empirical data eventually overcome flawed conventional wisdom in the sciences, and lead to fundamentally new foundational stories consistent with empiricism.[183] Scientific—or perhaps more broadly, disciplinary—revolutions are at least as much a property of the institutions that study, teach, and promote them as they are of the disciplines themselves. Academia, media, and government all play critical roles in promoting the orthodoxies—or at times a small number of competing orthodoxies resting upon some shared assumptions—that set the parameters for acceptable experimentation within a discipline. Funding, prestige, and careers hinge on fidelity to that orthodoxy. Junior entrants are evaluated in large part on their adherence to orthodox thinking, and on their eagerness to burnish the credentials of their field's luminaries. Those standing atop this pyramid—the most prestigious professors at the most prestigious institutions—cling to power as tenaciously as do other despots, in their case the power to define the appropriate direction for their disciplines and promote junior colleagues who canonize their work rather than challenge it. Such leaders are ill equipped to address revolutionary possibilities: *What if the conventional wisdom to which all recognized experts subscribe, upon which all prestigious research rests, and on which the most prominent leaders have based their careers, is wrong?*

Such questions need not imply that everything that the experts believe is wrong. The questioning simply acknowledges that conventional training has taught generations of students to overlook (or at times to deny quite emphatically, or to "teach away from") a foundational element that caused many seeming anomalies to arise. Bold innovators within the scientific community propose heretical models—and as Copernicus and Galileo can attest, often receive the treatment reserved for heretics. Eventually, however, evidence overwhelms entrenched institutional interests and the new models become "revolutionary" rather than heretical. New orthodoxies lead to new textbooks, often recasting the old orthodoxy (and thus the careers of the still-prestigious scientists who had clung to it most tenaciously) as an important building block of the post-revolutionary field, rather than as the impediment it truly had been. In modern science, atoms, germs, genes, DNA, relativity, and uncertainty have all played such revolutionary roles. When the luminaries of the revolutionized fields finally embraced them, the redefined disciplines retained the previously recorded empirical data, swept aside the increasingly implausible explanations for "anomalies," and replaced them with simple elegant explanations blessed with first explanatory and then predictive power.

Though Kuhn wrote explicitly about the natural sciences, the institutional imperatives entrenching theories inconsistent with observed data are even stronger in the social sciences—in part because the corrective empiricism is far clearer in the natural world than in the social one. The time has come for a structural revolution in thinking about the Middle East. It is blindingly clear that something has been missing from conventional discourse—precisely as we first hypothesized. People take actions and events unfold for a reason. Contrary to popular opinion, residents of the Middle East are no less rational than are residents of other regions—they simply approach decision-making with different underlying beliefs, attitudes, values, and perceptions. If their behavior seems impervious to common sense, the flaw likely lies with the definition of common sense, not with their behavior.

We Don't All Want the Same Thing

To pick a stark example of such seemingly paradoxical behavior, it is astounding how much Western discourse observes young folks— and in particular, young Westerners—drawn to the Islamic State and asks: What drove these kids there? What sort of terrible childhood traumas must they have experienced to behave in such a depraved manner? How marginalized these children must have felt growing as Muslims in the West! Surely, they must have been driven out of their minds to pursue this irrational, immoral course! Some combination of past discrimination, deprivation, and victimization at the hands of their host countries—or Westerners blundering into their ancestral homes—is surely to blame. Had they received decent treatment, their rational faculties would have pointed them in more productive, and less barbaric, directions.

Journalists studying the question have received variants of this framing from numerous "experts." Excerpts from *The Atlantic*, CNN, and *Time* are illustrative:

> On the one side are those, including British officials, who portray ISIS recruits as "vulnerable" or impressionable youth who, despite their murderous intentions or actions, are actually victims. On the other side are those, often academics and human-rights activists, who similarly argue that ISIS recruits are victims, but of oppressive government policies and actions rather than sinister jihadist groomers.[184]

> The recruits are often young -- sometimes disillusioned teenagers trying to find purpose and make their mark. For

many, it boils down to a lack of a sense of identity or belonging...The general picture provided by foreign fighters of their lives in Syria suggests camaraderie, good morale and purposeful activity, all mixed in with a sense of understated heroism, designed to attract their friends as well as to boost their own self-esteem.[185]

For many people who are lacking a strong sense of identity and purpose, their violent radical global narrative provides easy answers and solutions: it can be very powerful message for people who are looking for answers.... Their online material shows capturing territory, establishing states, beheading enemies: they show that they are the sexiest jihadi group on the block.[186]

Such analyses, entirely logical given the conventional notion that "we all want the same things," ask exactly the wrong questions; "they deny the agency of those who join ISIS, and obscure the religious idealism that motivates them."[187]   Nothing happened to drive the recruits there, and none of them set off to become depraved. In fact, it's a safe bet that few if any Islamic State recruits consider YouTube beheadings or brothels filled with sex slaves depraved if they are done in the service of the Caliph. To the contrary; to those who answer the Caliph's call to *jihad*, such actions are noble, perhaps even sanctified.

A far better line of questioning—one designed to yield useful insights—would begin: *What sorts of values and beliefs might lead young people to see this sort of behavior as noble?* Western misdeeds have not created the young monsters who set off seeking sex, adventure, and the celebrity of beheading infidels on YouTube. It is the recruits' own rejection of liberal values—or more accurately, their adoption of a contrary set of decidedly illiberal values—that makes them appear monstrous to liberal Western eyes. Previous Islamist recruiting efforts glorified suicide bombers, martyrdom, and a highly sexualized afterlife. Many in the target market cheered the glorification, but preferred to leave the honor of martyrdom to others. The current recruiting efforts promise social media stardom and a steady stream of sex slaves—a far more attractive offering whose far greater success is not hard to fathom. The only requirements are an inversion of liberal values and a taste for adventure (though a certain amount of sexual dysfunction doesn't hurt).[188]

Canadian journalist Graeme Wood, in his powerful attempt to awaken the West to the true nature of the Caliphate, makes clear just how anti-liberal its values and aspirations are:

> Baghdadi has spoken on camera only once. But his address, and the Islamic State's countless other propaganda videos and encyclicals, are online, and the caliphate's supporters have toiled mightily to make their project knowable. We can gather that their state rejects peace as a matter of principle; that it hungers for genocide; that its religious views make it constitutionally incapable of certain types of change, even if that change might ensure its survival; and that it considers itself a harbinger of—and headline player in—the imminent end of the world…. Its rise to power is less like the triumph of the Muslim Brotherhood in Egypt (a group whose leaders the Islamic State considers apostates) than like the realization of a dystopian alternate reality in which David Koresh or Jim Jones survived to wield absolute power over not just a few hundred people, but some 8 million.[189]

Wood discussed the new Caliphate with prominent—and well-informed—supporters living in Australia and England who were effusive in extolling its virtues:

> [One of them] explained the joy he felt when Baghdadi was declared the caliph on June 29—and the sudden, magnetic attraction that Mesopotamia began to exert on him and his friends. "I was in a hotel [in the Philippines], and I saw the declaration on television," he told me. "And I was just amazed, and I'm like, *Why am I stuck here in this bloody room?*"… The caliphate, [he] told me, is not just a political entity but also a vehicle for salvation…. [T]he Muslim who acknowledges one omnipotent god and prays, but who dies without pledging himself to a valid caliph and incurring the obligations of that oath, has failed to live a fully Islamic life… "I would go so far as to say that Islam has been reestablished" by the caliphate…
>
> After Baghdadi's July sermon, a stream of jihadists began flowing daily into Syria with renewed motivation…ready to give up everything at home for a shot at paradise in the worst place on Earth…. [T]hey regard[] the caliphate as the only righteous government on Earth…. Before the caliphate, "maybe 85 percent of the Sharia was absent from our lives," [another] told me. "These laws are in abeyance until we have *khilafa*"—a caliphate— "and now we have one."… In theory, all Muslims are obliged to immigrate to the territory where the caliph is applying

these laws…."The problem," he explained, "is that when places like Saudi Arabia just implement the penal code, and don't provide the social and economic justice of the Sharia—the whole package—they simply engender hatred toward the Sharia." That whole package, he said, would include free housing, food, and clothing for all, though of course anyone who wished to enrich himself with work could do so…. [I]ts social-welfare program is, at least in some aspects, progressive to a degree that would please an MSNBC pundit. Health care, he said, is free. ("Isn't it free in Britain, too?," I asked. "Not really," he said. "Some procedures aren't covered, such as vision.") This provision of social welfare was not, he said, a policy choice of the Islamic State, but a policy *obligation* inherent in God's law.[190]

Few reading Wood's interviews could doubt that the Caliphate's anti-liberal values are a critical part of its attraction—particularly to Western recruits. Within these recruits' own value system, their behavior is indeed noble. Laying the blame on some combination of material poverty, abuse, and weak psyches attempts to exonerate the culpable individuals and the subculture to which they belong, pretending that it does not *really* embrace values antithetical to liberalism. The Caliphate sees the people that it kills, enslaves, brutalizes, torments, and rapes as subhuman—much as the very illiberal but very Western Nazis saw their own victims.[191] The conflict between the West and Islamists is emphatically one of values. If the West cannot stand strong against those who invert the very values that define liberal humanity, dignity, and decency, it cannot hope to prevail. These recruits are not victims of Western failure; they have simply embraced an anti-liberal value system.

To the extent that there is any Western culpability at issue, it stems from indifference and complacency in the face of a new, rising, Islamic supremacist movement, not in its victimization of fragile Muslim minorities. Muslims who do not share the Islamists' radical, anti-liberal values may be front-line victims, but they are also the West's first line of defense. Rather than coddling them out of fear that they are perpetually one insult or one sermon away from radicalization, Western leadership must push them to take a side and clarify their values. Muslims who share Western notions of tolerance and acceptance should be the most visible, vocal leaders of the campaign against Islamism. Those who attempt to excuse or explain Islamist brutality, or who try to deflect blame outside the *ummah* and onto the West, are parts of the problem, not parts of the solution. Conventional wisdom gets it exactly backwards.

Revolutionary thinking begins with a recognition of the obvious: These recruits choose to join the Caliphate—or before it, to support al Qaeda, Hamas, Hezbollah, Saddam, or Arafat—because they share the values that those organizations or despots espouse. Liberalism cannot "win them back" with sensitivity and compassion. Western overtures, if any, must begin with full cognizance of the values that Islamic supremacists hold dear. As long as Westerners pretend otherwise, liberalism is operating at a clear disadvantage. Islamists understand the values that drive Western action, and they exploit that understanding fully; their increasing use of civilian human shields provides a particularly poignant example.[192] Western liberalism owes itself, its friends in the Middle East, and above all its enemies, the respect of recognizing the starkly incompatible values to which Islamists and other terror supporters adhere—whether those supporters originated in the Arab/Islamic world, the West, or elsewhere.

Beyond this small example of the dangers of conventional wisdom, revolutionary thinking is necessary if the Middle East is—finally—to make sense. A useful narrative must accept that Middle Eastern values and perspectives—not those of the liberal West—shape calculations across the Middle East. A useful narrative must review post-Ottoman history, explain its events, predict future occurrences, and lay the groundwork for a potentially successful American strategy.

Where can such a narrative begin? Occam's Razor, a well-known problem-solving paradigm, teaches that the simplest explanation is likely correct. In a region that Sunni Arabs dominate, the most important storyline should lie within the Sunni Arab community—an origination point that conventional wisdom has oddly chosen to ignore. The dominant desire driving that community for more than a century has been an inchoate imperialism: the frustrated desire for a unified Sunni Arab superstate, of which the Islamic State's Caliphate is merely the most recent manifestation. That then, is our next stop on our journey through the region: An appreciation of the inchoate imperialism at the heart of the Sunni Arab world, and an understanding of the way that this heartfelt goal to which all Sunni Arabs must subscribe would devastate the elite leadership of the Sunni Arab world.

Chapter 12. Inchoate Imperialism

Nations and States

Perhaps the single best guide to understanding this sense of "inchoate imperialism" is Hannah Arendt's *The Origins of Totalitarianism*.[193] While Arendt espoused many opinions that I do not share, her analyses of the trends leading to European totalitarianism are insightful. They are also useful in understanding how similar trends in the Middle East have been responsible for many of that region's current problems. Writing in the stretch between Hitler's defeat and Stalin's death, Arendt extracted the characteristics of nineteenth and early twentieth century European history that made the twin monstrosities of Hitlerism and Stalinism inevitable. In particular, she focused on two critical precursor movements—anti-Semitism and imperialism—both of which now play central roles in Arab/Islamic thinking. She showed how their toxic combination created a glide path to totalitarian states. Of particular relevance, Arendt saw nation building (to use a contemporary term) as the primary objective of nineteenth century Europeans.

Every "nation state" combines two dissimilar components: a state and a nation. "Statehood" is an artifact of the international system. An entity is a state if enough other states admit it to their statehood clubs. States are relatively easy to create; lines drawn on a map do the trick. If the "governments" on both sides of the line consolidate power on their own side and relinquish claims to the other, the states emerge and gain international recognition. "Nations," on the other hand, are properties of individual people. If a group of people feel a certain kinship among themselves that they do not share with others, they define a distinct nation. Some nations predated the modern nation-state system by thousands of years: the Jews, the Japanese, the Persians, the Greeks, and the Chinese all come readily to mind. Others are artifacts of the modern nation-state system; someone had to create them.

Creating nations is tough work. It requires the governments leading these new states to convince the people living within their boundaries that they share some common notion of nationhood that differentiates them from those living in other states—or at a bare minimum, that a critical number of them share that "nationhood." Most references to "failed states" are actually directed towards failed nations—states in which the recognized government failed to instill a sense of nationhood to supplant or augment older tribal, ethnic, or religious identities.

Consolidating pre-existing nations within state boundaries can be just as difficult—though the challenges are very different. Israel and Greece are examples of modern nation-states that began with the nation, defined a state around it, then consolidated its nationals within the newly drawn boundaries. In both cases, this approach aligned well with history and personal identity, but generated lengthy conflicts between the new ethnically and historically meaningful nation-states and their far larger and more powerful neighbors who saw ethnic minority independence as an infringement of their imperial rights. (In the case of modern Greece, the Turks were the primary source of tension; in Israel's case it has been the Sunni Arabs). To some extent, these conflicts are predictable and likely inevitable. Historic homelands tend to overlap, and small nations tend to live on lands that their larger neighbors also claim.

Taken together, it is hardly surprising that the spread of the nation-state, from its birth in Europe in the mid-seventeenth century to its global dominance three hundred years later, has generated multi-generational regional conflicts in each part of the globe it reached. Neither the state-first approach nor the nation-first approach are organic outgrowths of world history. Whether they require the imposition of state lines and the consolidation of national populations across what had been a multi-ethnic empire, or the imposition of shared national identity among people who previously felt little or no shared kinship, the formation of a stable nation-state necessarily embodies coercion.

For better or for worse—and there are impressive arguments supporting the idea that it has been for the better—the decision to divide the world into nation-states defines the modern world. The coercion necessary for stability has been baked into that decision as a recognized cost. The world will not finish paying that cost until every nation-state, and every regional collection of nation-states, has stabilized fully. Perhaps the reason that history has clearly not yet ended is that the day of such global stability appears to lie in some very distant future—if indeed it is achievable at all.

These inherent problems, and the human suffering that they engender, have been known throughout much of the nation-state era. The German philosopher Johann Gottlieb Fichte, for example, articulated the nation-first approach—and its potential for conflict between small and large nations—in 1806. He addressed his speech "To the German Nation" in French-occupied Berlin, then part of Napoleon's Empire rather than (as it is today) the capital of a unified, independent German state:

> Those who speak the same language are joined to each other by a multitude of invisible bonds by nature herself, long before any human art begins; they understand each other and have the power of continuing to make themselves understood more and more clearly; they belong together and are by nature one and an inseparable whole. Such a whole, if it wishes to absorb and mingle with itself any other people of different descent and language, cannot do so without itself becoming confused, in the beginning at any rate, and violently disturbing the even progress of its culture.[194]

As a matter of simple logic, a linguistically defined nation seeking to create a state has only two options: it can consolidate its people within the recognized boundaries of a state, or it can conquer the territory in which its people happen to live. Perhaps unsurprisingly, small nations—like the Jews or the Greeks—living as minorities among much larger neighbors tended towards the more peaceful option of consolidating their people into a portion of their historic homelands. Larger nations typically prefer conquest and empire. As Arendt showed, it was precisely this expansionist drive that led Hitler to his theory of *lebensraum*—his need to clear Europe of its "lesser" people to create room for its superior Aryans—and that continues to justify the territorial expansion of large ethnic powers into their minority neighbors' lands well into the twenty-first century.[195] Russia's claims on parts of the Ukraine, China's hold on Tibet, Turkey's long occupation of Northern Cyprus, and the Arab claims against Israel are all contemporary cases in point.

The state-first approach requires a very different sort of effort. The key to building a nation within state boundaries is education— or as some might call it, propaganda. European thinkers have understood the connection between nationalist education and nation building for millennia, at the very least from Aristotle:

> Of all the things that I have mentioned that which contributes most to the permanence of constitutions is the adaptation of education to the form of government. . . . That education should be regulated by law and should be an affair of the state is not to be denied. The citizen should be molded to suit the form of government under which he lives.[196]

to Napoleon:

> There cannot be a firmly established political state unless there is a teaching body with definitely recognized principles. If the child is not taught from infancy that he ought to be a republican or a monarchist, a Catholic or a free-thinker, the state will not constitute a nation; it will rest on uncertain and shifting foundations; and it will be constantly exposed to disorder and change.[197]

France put this theory into practice with great success in the nineteenth century, as it sought to unify the language and historical sense of once-warring fiefdoms.[198] The United States did the same in the early twentieth century, as it integrated record numbers of immigrants from numerous cultures in history's most successful melting pot—a bold experiment in unifying a nation around ideas rather than bloodlines.[199] Few of the artificially drawn post-colonial states of Africa or Asia have followed suit; the constant turmoil in which many of them find themselves is a predictable consequence of that failure.

Empires and Nation-States

Arendt provided a framework for understanding the challenges of nationalism, transnationalism, and statelessness—whether in nineteenth century Europe or across the modern Middle East. By the nineteenth century Europe boasted many nationless states whose governments worked hard to construct national identities. At the same time, however, Europe also boasted many stateless nations. Some of these nations occupied small plots of land that eventually achieved statehood (e.g., the Irish, the Czechs, the Lithuanians); some are still fighting for states today, mostly half-heartedly (e.g., the Basque, the Corsicans, the Scots).[200] Two of them, however, posed a particular challenge: the Jews and the Gypsies were pan-European stateless nations. Their insistence upon maintaining their own identities exacerbated a problem that was among the greatest causes of social instability in nineteenth century Europe: that of permanently stateless people.

Perhaps more significantly, those identities complicated the

European social experiment in nation building. In 1789, with revolutionary fervor defining a new France, Count Clermont-Tonnerre famously proclaimed: "We must refuse everything to the Jews as a nation and accord everything to Jews as individuals."[201] He sought to emancipate France's Jews by insisting that they relinquish their ancient Jewishness in favor of newborn Frenchness.

A century later, as France's Third Republic tore itself apart in the anti-Semitic witch hunt known as "the Dreyfus Affair,"[202] the Jews came to appreciate that Tonnerre's individualized, assimilationist approach to building a revolutionary French nation represented the very best deal that they might receive as the Old World restructured itself into ethnically-, religiously-, or linguistically-defined nation-states. A young assimilated Jew, an Austrian journalist covering the Dreyfus trial named Theodor Herzl, drew the obvious conclusion: In the era of the nation-state, the continued national integrity of the Jewish nation required a Jewish state in the historic Jewish homeland. Zionism arose as the nineteenth century, state-centric, nationalist movement of the ancient nation known as the Israelites, the Judeans, and eventually the Jews—a classic effort of a small preexisting nation seeking to transition into the era of the nation-state.[203] The absence of a corresponding nationalist movement from the similarly pan-European Gypsies has hardly served that community well.

Jews and Gypsies were not the only continent-wide nations whose membership confounded state boundaries. Arendt identified two much larger and more important groups whose nationhood and statehood seemed misaligned: Germans and Slavs. This misalignment gave birth to pan-Germanic and pan-Slavic movements of "Continental Imperialism" (to use her term). One key element to take from her analysis of these "movements" when contemplating the modern Middle East is that they shifted over time. Bismarck and Hitler were both pan-Germanic leaders who sought to unify the Germanic Volk into a single state in an attempt to reconcile the notions of Germanic nationhood and German statehood—as Fichte had foreshadowed.[204] Czarism and Stalinism took similar views about the Slavic people and the Russian state. In both cases, the notion of unifying two of Europe's largest nations into states served as an undercurrent for numerous movements—royalist, socialist, authoritarian, totalitarian, and otherwise. Different factions within these "pan" movements may have hated—and attacked—each other, but they shared the bedrock concern with unification. Different factions also showed differing levels of tolerance of smaller (or "lesser") nations living within the boundaries of the putative unified state. Even the most tolerant and liberal among them, however, rejected the notion that any of these minorities had a "right" to a state of their own—or at the very least, a right as strong as that of the majority Germans or Slavs. Minority rights and ethnic self-determination are anathema to all imperialists, continental or otherwise.

The twentieth century Middle East raised a parallel set of issues. At the end of WWI, the demise of the Ottoman Empire left behind a vast undifferentiated expanse, sweeping from Aden to Turkey and from the Mediterranean to Persia. Though a majority of its residents was Sunni Arab, thriving Jewish, Christian, Shiite, Kurdish, Druze, and other communities also called it home. Crisscrossed by barely-livable deserts, the region had no history of either nationalism or statehood. The people identified with their village or tribe, with their ethnic group, with their faith community, or with the larger causes of Arabism or Islam.

As we noted, the victorious allies were conflicted between their authoritarian desire to let the Sunni Arabs form their "Empire" subject to European oversight, and their romantic attachment to the notion of minority self-determination.[205] The resulting (and now familiar) map tried to split the baby. Minority self-determination won out for the two indigenous ethnic groups with whom Europeans were familiar: the Jews (in a Jewish Israel) and the Maronite Christians (in a confessional Lebanon). The inchoate imperial drive of the Sunni Arabs defeated the claims of the region's other minorities—none of whom could boast counterparts or kinsmen in Europe. The British and French handed control to the Sunni Arabs in the newly drawn states of Iraq, Jordan, and Syria (where the Alawites seized control fifty years later), and favored powerful Sunni tribes throughout the Peninsula. As expected, the exercise of drawing lines through the desert sands to create a collection of new states gave birth to the need for nationalist education campaigns.

The track record of the Sunni Arab elites appointed to run these new states at launching such programs has been dismal. Jordan's King Abdullah II launched a "Jordan First" initiative in 2002—eighty years after Jordan became a state—to "promote the concept of a modern democratic state,...consolidate the spirit of belonging among citizens,...affirm[ing] the primacy of Jordanian interests above other interests,...[and] strengthen[ing] the concepts of parliamentary democracy, rule of law, public freedom, accountability, transparency, justice and equal rights."[206] Lebanon, designed as a confessional state, fell into a civil war in the 1970s that has never fully healed, leaving its various ethnic groups (primarily Christian, Sunni, Shiite, and Druze) in constant tension and rendering any feeling of national unity impossible.[207] To the extent that any Palestinian identity may have emerged even in the absence of a state, it too is mired in a civil war pitting Hamas Islamists (who deny the existence of national identities within Islam) against Fatah warlords, with ample factionalism further subdividing both sides.[208]

Most recently, events have demonstrated the ongoing weakness (verging on nonexistence) of the Syrian and Iraqi nations. The cross-border civil war roiling the territory assigned to both artificial states shows quite clearly that most residents of that territory continue to identify with tribal, ethnic, or religious affiliations rather as "Syrians" or "Iraqis." In short, there is no indication that either the Sunni Arab majority dominating the Ottoman hinterland or any of the minorities living in their midst—other than the Jews—have embraced the new identities that the state system assigned them.

Across the broader region, in Iran, Turkey, and Egypt (as in Israel) nationhood preceded the modern states by centuries, if not millennia.   In others, notably the Sheikhdoms of the Arabian Peninsula, "tribes with flags" cast themselves as states without broadening tribal membership to embrace the full concept of citizenry central to modern nationhood.   But among the Arab populations grouped in ways least capable of claiming attachment to either historic or tribal affiliations—those resident in the post-Ottoman Mandates for Mesopotamia, Syria, and Palestine and their successor states—the sense of national identity never gelled.   It remains weak-to-nonexistent throughout the region.

Finally, to round out the parallels with Arendt's description of the rise of totalitarianism in Europe, expressions of the "pan" movements seem to come and go, some in the guise of pan-Arabism, others in the guise of pan-Islamism. Stateless people abound—some as fourth-generation "refugees."[209] Their numbers grow larger with each new crisis; hundreds of thousands are now clamoring for entry into Europe, and that wave has likely not yet crested.

In the Wake of the Ottoman Empire

How can we—or any outsiders—understand this morass? Arendt's analysis points the way. The Sunni Arabs are the proper starting point. The region's remaining ethnicities, and their interactions with Sunni Arabs, tell the rest of the story. The relevant "Pan" movement—Sunni Arab Imperialism—is far broader than the movement known as Pan-Arabism. For the past century, the Sunni Arabs' imperial drive has been the most important force in the modern Middle East, even as its expression has shifted among ideologies. The centrality of this Sunni sense of entitlement is hardly coincidental; Sunnism has always been Islam's dominant branch. It governed almost the entire Islamic world from the Battle of Karbala in 680 until the Safavid Dynasty converted Persia to Shiism in the sixteenth century.[210] Beyond Persia, there have been few if any Shiite rulers of note.[211]

From the fifteenth century through the end of WWI, the Asian lands west of Persia were parts of the Ottoman Empire, in which Sunni Turks ruled and citizens of different faiths assumed the lesser legal and social status of *dhimmitude.* *Dhimmis* faced numerous restrictions, making it clear that they were second-class citizens and far from the equal of Muslims. Neither synagogues nor churches could be taller than nearby mosques, *dhimmis* had to pray *sotto voce* to avoid offending Muslims, and *dhimmi* houses could not be higher than those of their Muslim neighbors. *Dhimmis* deferred to their Muslim betters by yielding the middle of the road, and acknowledged their debt to the Muslims by paying far higher taxes. They were prohibited from bearing arms, riding horses or camels, serving in the military, holding public office, or testifying in court against a Muslim—rendering the *dhimmi* unlikely to prevail in any dispute with a Muslim.[212] As one contemporaneous observer—the British Vice Consul in Mosul in 1909—described the situation, "The attitude of the Muslims toward the Christians and the Jews is that of a master towards slaves, whom he treats with a certain lordly tolerance so long as they keep their place. Any sign of pretension to equality is promptly repressed."[213] While this "millet system" may have been less oppressive than many of the indignities heaped upon minorities over the past millennium, it was hardly a bastion of enlightened equality and ethnic harmony.[214] In American terms, it was most closely akin to Jim Crow.

When the Ottoman Empire fell, Mustafa Kemal Atatürk abolished the Caliphate and attempted to pull the Turks out of the Islamic world and push them into a modern, secular, European state.[215] His success more-or-less minimized Turkish influence on the broader region for the rest of the twentieth century. Turkey's recent return to regional significance has been part of the effort of the country's current leader, Recep Tayyip Erdoğan, to replace Kemalist secularism with Islamism—effectively making twenty-first century Turkey a more belligerent, less tolerant, less free, and "more Middle Eastern" place.[216] Aided by the studied indifference of Western leaders, Erdoğan's efforts appear poised to succeed, likely making Turkey a far greater player in the region's future than it has been in its recent past. Through much of the post-Ottoman order, however,

Turkey has been something of an outsider to the broad currents of regional history. It is thus perhaps unsurprising that Erdoğan's program has earned the label "neo-Ottomanism."[217]

With the Turkish abdication at the end of WWI, the Sunni Arabs—the largest single ethnic group in an ethnically diverse region—saw themselves as the obvious inheritors of the Empire.[218] They believed that Sunni Arabs should rule everywhere, from the straits of Gibraltar to the Shatt-al-Arab.[219] Members of other ethnic groups living within that territory were to become second-class citizens (if not exiles or corpses).

Perhaps the earliest indication of Arab plans to inherit the Empire came in the Hussein-McMahon Correspondence of 1915-16, a series of letters between Sharif Hussein, the Emir of Mecca, and Sir Henry McMahon, the British High Commissioner in Egypt.[220] Hussein, as a member of the Hashemite clan, was a direct descendent of the Prophet.[221] As Emir of Mecca, he was responsible for the Holy cities of Mecca and Medina—including logistical management of the Hajj, the annual pilgrimage to Islam's holiest shrine. Though the Sublime Porte (i.e., the rulers of the Ottoman Empire) granted him a great deal of autonomy, his appointment was nevertheless conditional on his fealty to his imperial overlords. When tensions between them arose, Hussein reached out to the British, seeking support for his goal of enshrining himself as the head of a hereditary dynasty.[222] The Arab Empire he sought to build would likely have preserved the basic Ottoman social structure, once again relegating minorities to *dhimmitude*, where they could live in relative safety as long as they knew their place.

Hussein first wrote to McMahon in July 1915, claiming to represent all Arabic-speaking people, and seeking to extend his realm to include all Arabic-speaking lands east of Egypt. McMahon's attempts to accept Hussein's claims in principle while placing practical limitations on their territorial scope led to ambiguity, confusion, and tension in the 1920s—most significantly over its apparent conflict with both the Balfour Declaration's commitment to an independent Jewish homeland in Palestine and the Sykes-Picot Agreement between England and France dividing responsibility for the Ottoman hinterland. Nevertheless, the vague Hussein/McMahon Correspondence likely marked the high point in agreement between European imperialists and Arab imperialists to form a unified Arab Empire.

The San Remo Peace Conference of April 1920 resolved the ambiguities in favor of the Balfour Declaration as a matter of international law[223]—but not in the minds of many Sunni Arabs, who persist to this day in believing that the non-binding and vague Hussein-McMahon letters granted them unquestioned sovereignty over the entire region.[224] Though often overlooked in discussions of the many international settlements that followed WWI, the San Remo Conference remains critical to understanding the modern Middle East. Having conquered the Ottoman Empire, the victorious allies met at San Remo to do what every victorious conqueror had done throughout recorded history: redraw the map and reassign legal rights. Key among their decisions at San Remo—and as the League of Nations confirmed two years later—was the creation of a "Mandate" system, under which European powers would administer the conquered Ottoman territories on behalf of the international community and the residents of those territories.[225]

As we have noted, the French administered the Mandate for Syria, while the British administered the Mandates for Mesopotamia and Palestine—all subject to approved guidelines. When it came to Syria and Mesopotamia, the territories were "provisionally recognized as independent States, subject to the rendering of administrative advice and assistance by a mandatory until such time as they are able to stand alone."[226] As to Palestine:

> The Mandatory will be responsible for putting into effect the [Balfour] declaration originally made on November 8, 1917, by the British Government, and adopted by the other Allied Powers, in favour of the establishment in Palestine of a national home for the Jewish people, it being clearly understood that nothing shall be done which may prejudice the civil and religious rights of existing non-Jewish communities in Palestine, or the rights and political status enjoyed by Jews in any other country. [227]

Though international law always explicitly rejected the Arab interpretation of the Hussein/McMahon Correspondence, the agreements they reached proved significant in the history of the region: Hussein's alliance with the British allowed him to take control of the Hejaz, the Peninsula's coastal region, in 1916. Unfortunately for Hussein, his putative empire faced greater difficulties than ambiguous drafting. Between 1919 and 1925, in a series of wars pitting the Hashemite Hejaz against the Saudi clan of the Nejd—the Peninsula's vast desert interior—Abd al-Aziz ibn Saud led his forces to victory. The unified Hejaz and Nejd became the Kingdom of Saudi Arabia (also aligned with the British),[228] and Hussein fled to Cyprus.

Ibn Saud's victory, and the subsequent discovery of oil, turned his tribe's puritanical, austere form of Islam—Wahhabism—from a minor movement inconsequential outside the Nejd to a major factor in post-Ottoman Islamic thought. In particular, its belief in the invalidity of all competing interpretations of Islam has led to significant tension with adherents of other schools of thought—notably though hardly exclusively the Shiites (whom Wahhabis view as idolators).[229] As a result, contemporary Islam differs in many ways from the dominant Islam that people practiced throughout the long centuries of the Ottoman Empire.[230]

Meanwhile, the British, seeking to retain the allegiance of both royal clans, helped the Hashemites move north. Hussein's son Faisal declared himself King of Syria, but lasted in that role only briefly before the French drove him out of the Mandatory lands they administered. The British installed him instead as King of the newly created Iraq, in the Mandate for Mesopotamia; his monarchy fell to a military coup in a 1958.[231] The British also installed a second son, Abdullah, as King of the newly created Transjordan, to which they assigned the majority of the Mandate for Palestine in direct contravention to the charter. Abdullah ruled until his assassination in 1951, for the crime of appearing too conciliatory towards Israel.[232] His Hashemite dynasty lives on, however; his great-grandson is now King Abdullah II of Jordan.

Pan-Arabism

Sharif Hussein proved to be the only Arab leader of his time capable of establishing even a colorable claim to the imperial throne. His inability to consolidate his power led to an immediate fragmentation among Arab leaders and thinkers. They responded with a series of distinct rationalizations for imperial dominance of the entire region.

The simultaneous end of the Ottoman Empire and the Caliphate, and the rise of even nominal Arab nation-states in their wake, however, also awoke the long-suffering *dhimmis*, who saw—for the first time since the Arab conquest—the possibility of living on equal footing with their Muslim neighbors. A group of secular, liberal, intellectual Arabs seized the opportunity. They sought to create a new "Arab" identity, and an enabling Pan-Arab ideology, that explicitly placed Christian Arabs on equal footing with Muslims.[233] George Antonius, a Cambridge-trained Orthodox Christian Arab, was particularly influential in adapting European nationalist thought to the peculiarities of the Arabic speaking world.[234]

Antonius was no devotee of Fichte's German nationalism. He rejected the idea that a nation was some inherent property into which people fell through use of a common language. Instead, Antonius adhered to the French understanding that a nation is a voluntary association of individuals. He thus sought to Arabize the nationalism that began with Rousseau's social contract and rose to prominence during the French revolution.[235]

Antonius's inclusive approach to nationalism, however, had a clear limit. It reflected his own Christian community's desire for acceptance as the equals of Muslims in a secularizing, westernizing Arab nation—while rejecting the desire of the Jewish community for voluntary disassociation and self-determination.[236] Though fully aware that the San Remo Conference had rejected the broad Arab claims drawn from the Hussein-McMahon Correspondence, incorporated the Balfour Declaration explicitly, and enshrined Jewish self-determination in Palestine as a matter of international law, (making Israel the only post-colonial nation to bear such a pedigree),[237] Antonius nevertheless insisted that Hussein-McMahon was binding. The liberal Antonius was thus willing to extend to Jews the same liberation that he desired for Christians—but not to recognize that community's own voluntary self-definition and deepest desires:

> There seems to be no valid reason why Palestine should not be constituted into an independent Arab state in which as many Jews as the country can hold without prejudice to its political and economic freedom would live in peace, security and dignity, and would enjoy full rights of citizenship. Such an Arab state would...ensur[e] the safety and inviolability of the Holy Places of all faiths, for the protection of all minorities and minority rights, and for affording the Jewish community the widest freedom in the pursuit of their spiritual and cultural ideals.[238]

Antonius's simultaneous affirmation of Jewish rights within an Arab state and denial of the Jewish desire for self-determination poses a stark contrast to Arab positions that have since become commonplace—from the exile of the Jewish communities from most Arab states in the 1950s through Mahmoud Abbas' proclamation that the independent Palestine he seeks would be *judenrein*.[239] It thus serves as a poignant reminder of just how far Arab thought has deviated from anything that might once have qualified as liberalism.

The Arab flirtation with liberalism, in fact, was rather brief. By the 1940s, exposure to Nazi Germany—and even closer exposure to the French Mandatory authorities answerable to Vichy—had moved Arab nationalism in a very different direction.[240] Sati' al-Husri, an influential secular Arab nationalist of Muslim descent, could have been channeling Fichte when he insisted:

> Every person who speaks Arabic is an Arab. Everyone

who is affiliated with these people is an Arab. If he does not know this or if he does not cherish his Arabism, then we must study the reasons for his position. It may be the result of ignorance — then we must teach him the truth. It may be because he is unaware or deceived — then we must awaken him and reassure him. It may be a result of selfishness — then we must work to limit his selfishness.[241]

Al-Husri was also explicit about where this view of Arabism as inherent rather than voluntary led. "[T]he system to which we should direct our hopes and aspirations is a Fascist system, not a Bolshevik system."[242]

Aspirational fascism became a reality with the founding of the Baath,[243] an explicitly fascist Pan-Arab political party that eventually seized control of both Syria and Iraq (though not before splitting into two factions that made the two neighboring Baathist regimes bitter enemies for decades). The Baath Party's 1947 Constitution declares the Arab Homeland (defined to coincide roughly with the twenty-plus Arabic speaking states of North Africa and West Asia)[244] "an indivisible political and economic entity... All differences among its natives are casual and fake. They can be removed by the awakening of the Arab conscience."[245] It defines nationalism as "a living immortal fact," Pan-Arab nationalism as a "sacred feeling" and "the will of the Arab people to liberate and unify themselves."[246] The Baath Party itself is "revolutionary and believes that its main objectives in the resurrection of Pan-Arab Nationalism and the establishment of Socialism can not be fulfilled but through the road of revolution and struggle."[247]

One of the great challenges facing any out-of-power fascist movement, however, is the need for a charismatic leader strong enough to articulate the national interest on behalf of the nation. This shortcoming led to factionalism within the Baath Party, and ultimately to a clear antagonistic division between its Syrian and Iraqi wings.[248] Hafez al-Assad eventually assumed control in Syria and Saddam Hussein in Iraq. Notwithstanding the assertions of Arab unity, both leaders deployed their Baath Parties as mechanisms of ethnic dominance. Assad's Baath allowed Syria's Alawite minority to suppress its Sunni majority.[249] Saddam's Baath exerted minority Sunni Arab dominance over a Shia majority and a sizable Kurdish population.[250] The grand fascist experiment in crafting an overarching "Arab" identity thus devolved into little more than sectarian conflict, effectively maintaining traditional identities trapped within Western-drawn state lines.

The fascist Baath Party's failure to define a new Arab identity was only part of the Pan-Arabism story. The Bolshevism that al-Husri had sought to avoid appeared in the other important strain of Pan-Arabism, namely Nasserism. Though more a personality cult centered on Egypt's Gamal-Abdul Nasser than a distinct ideology, Nasser's National Charter for Arab socialism spoke with decidedly Marxist overtones. It declared that "the major economic and social problems confronting our people at present must be resolved on a scientific basis" and articulated an "immediate aim…to do away with exploitation, and to make possible the exercise of the natural right to have an equal opportunity, to dissolve class distinctions and to end the domination of one class…by eliminating the exploiting class, to dissolve peacefully class distinctions…"[251] Coupled with the close relationship between Nasser's Egypt and the Soviet Union, Nasserism hewed closer to a Marxist model of socialism than to the National Socialism of the Baath—though as Arendt had noted when comparing Stalin's Marxism to Hitler's National Socialism, the distinctions were subtle.

Nasserism was the most successful of the Pan-Arab movements.[252] Its United Arab Republic, the short-lived political union of Egypt and Syria, was the "pinnacle of pan-Arab success."[253] But a personality cult requires a truly charismatic personality, an individual "set apart from ordinary men and treated as though endowed with supernatural, superhuman or, at least, specifically exceptional qualities."[254] Nasser's charismatic connection to the Arab masses could not survive his defeat at Israel's hands in 1967's Six Day War. He "was shattered with the defeat… He would stay in power not as a confident, vibrant hero, but as a tragic figure, a symbol of better days, an indication of the will to resist."[255] In the words of his successor Anwar el-Sadat, Nasser became a "living corpse,"[256] hardly able to inspire anyone. Nasser's deflation more-or-less marked the end of the Pan-Arab experiment in defining a new Arab nation.[257] Left in its wake were the traditional identities and affiliations of faith and tribe that remained strong, and the new offerings of individual nationalities that—as in post-Communist Yugoslavia—seemed sustainable only when an authoritarian prevented them from splintering to reflect actual identities.

Islamism

Perhaps unsurprisingly, the secular desire to import European nationalism and create an Arab identity distinct from faith engendered significant pushback from those who believed that the future of the Arabs (and the world) lay with a recommitment to Islam. The rise and fall of Pan-Arabism coincided with the birth of modern

Islamism—a movement with far deeper and far more authentic local roots than nationalism.[258] Islamism began with its own charismatic leader, Hasan al-Bana, a former schoolteacher who founded the Muslim Brotherhood in Egypt in 1928. At the time, Islam—and faith in general—was considered a personal matter. Al-Bana's innovation was to politicize it, setting the restoration of the recently terminated Caliphate as his goal.[259]

The Brotherhood soon forged an alliance with Nazi Germany and took a leading role in calling for massacres of Jews and Christians;[260] its hatred of, and brutality towards, adherents of other faiths persists to this day.[261] At the end of the Second World War, with the Egyptian monarchy teetering, the Brotherhood organized a terrorist organization focused in Egypt. It also organized a volunteer army (which counted Yasir Arafat among its soldiers) intended to fight the Jews in Palestine. Its goal was simple: to govern Egypt and Palestine subject to their strict Islamist interpretation of *sharia*, or Islamic law.[262] Both efforts failed. Nasser's Officers Rebellion toppled the monarchy, seized control of Egypt in the name of Pan-Arabism—and set the stage for an overt conflict between the nationalists and the Islamists. The nationalists won. The Muslim Brotherhood went underground and into exile.[263]

Saudi funding helped the Brotherhood build an international structure during Nasser's crackdown; in particular, it developed a strong presence among European Muslims in a period of significant Islamic immigration to Europe.[264] In Egypt, much of the Brotherhood's leadership found itself in jail, including the most influential thinker the organization has ever produced: Sayyid Qutb, the "godfather of Islamism."[265] Qutb was executed in 1966, in large part for his radical notion that nominally Islamic societies were not, in fact, Islamic—implying that *jihad* against the regimes governing such societies is permissible.[266] This doctrine ran counter to the classic Sunni Muslim tradition of obedience to the ruler and the state. It posed a particular and very specific threat to Nasser. Having challenged the Brotherhood, promoted secular (largely socialist) ideals, and jailed Qutb, there could be little doubt that Nasser ran afoul of Qutb's radical new distinction.[267]

The Brotherhood's leadership ultimately rejected many of Qutb's more radical ideas, though it did adopt his strategy of proceeding in stages.[268] Qutb had understood that revolutions do not always happen overnight. He urged patience, believing that time was on the Islamist side, and that slow incremental gains would ultimately deliver victory to the Islamist vision—and more importantly, God's vision as the Islamists saw it. Through its long and difficult years underground, the Brotherhood learned the benefits of operating as a legal, reform-oriented group focused on social change rather than the immediate seizure of power.[269] That strategy has served the Brotherhood well. It became an extremely disciplined organization, willing to bide its time for decades while awaiting its opportunity to assume control—an opportunity that arose during the brief Presidency of Mohammed Morsi in 2012-13.[270]

While that opportunity was nearing, many of the commentators who saw Egypt's Arab Spring as a "Facebook Revolution"[271] also began to extol the authentic virtues of the Muslim Brotherhood. Barry Rubin, the prominent scholar of radical Middle Eastern movements explained their fallacy—and predicted the negative consequences that the Brotherhood's governance would bring:

> [The Brotherhood's] political strategy is based on the two-stage notion: the stage of *dawa* and the stage of political action, and they would always say patience, patience. And then because they saw Mubarak was faltering and they didn't want him to hand over to his son, they saw the son as weak, they changed gears....[T]he Muslim Brotherhood is not a moderate group.[272]

True to form, during Morsi's year in power, the Brotherhood began to flex its Nazi-inspired authoritarian muscles, once again promoting attacks on Christians and Jews while fomenting terror in Sinai and Gaza.[273] Morsi's fall returned the Brotherhood to opposition status. Whether it has retained or recalibrated its strategic forbearance remains to be seen; the past few years have witnessed previously uncharacteristic levels of violence and terror coming from the Brotherhood.[274]

Over the decades, however, the Brotherhood's prudence led some of its less patient members to follow Qutb's radical theories to their logical conclusion, and to branch out on their own. Every significant Sunni Arab terrorist group of the past half-century—including the PLO, Hamas, al Qaeda, and the Islamic State—can trace its roots back to the Muslim Brotherhood: Yasir Arafat and Ayman al-Zawahiri were former affiliates and Hamas is the Brotherhood's Gaza chapter.[275] Their point of departure from the parent organization (for those who do depart) is invariably Qutb. Al-Zawahiri often quotes Qutb in his writings,[276] and the 9/11 Commission cited the Qutb as a primary influence on Osama bin Laden:

> Bin Ladin also relies heavily on the Egyptian writer Sayyid Qutb... Sent by the Egyptian government to study the United States in the late 1940s, Qutb returned with an enormous loathing of Western society and history... Three basic themes

emerge from Qutb's writings. First, he claimed that the world was beset with barbarism, licentiousness, and unbelief (a condition he called *jahiliyya*, the religious term for the period of ignorance prior to the revelations given to the prophet Mohammed). Qutb argued that humans can choose only between Islam and *jahiliyya*. Second, he warned that more people, including Muslims, were attracted to *jahiliyya* and its material comforts than to his view of Islam; *jahiliyya* could therefore triumph over Islam. Third, no middle ground exists in what Qutb conceived as a struggle between God and Satan. All Muslims—as he defined them—therefore must take up arms in this fight. Any Muslim who rejects his ideas is just one more nonbeliever worthy of destruction.[277]

The Islamic State's self-proclaimed Caliph Baghdadi was also once a member of the Brotherhood. That affiliation did not last for much the same reason: too much talk, not enough action for Baghdadi's taste.[278]

The direct influence of Qutb and the Brotherhood on the Islamic State's current thought (and practice), however, is a matter of some debate. The Saudis contend that the Islamic State is a direct offshoot of the Muslim Brotherhood;[279] others see it as a Salafist movement much closer to Saudi Wahhabism.[280] That finger pointing is hardly a new phenomenon. Wahhabi fingerprints on Islamic terror groups are as abundant as are those of the Brotherhood, and notwithstanding the Saudi funding that kept the Brotherhood afloat during Nasser's crackdown, their relationship has always been rocky; it is currently near a low point.[281] Saudi Arabia declared the Muslim Brotherhood a terrorist group in 2014,[282] and fell relatively silent during that summer's Gaza War—at times appearing more supportive of Israel than of Hamas.[283] Yet a year later, reports began to surface that the Saudis were deliberating whether the Brotherhood might make a viable ally against Iran, various Shiite militias, and the Islamic State.[284] Rumored deliberations notwithstanding, the Saudis continue to provide generous funding to Egyptian President al-Sisi, who deposed Morsi and who has since cracked down on the Brotherhood.[285]

The causes of the rift between these two grand Islamist groups may appear subtle to outsiders, but as with adherents of most extreme philosophies, seemingly small differences in doctrine and in strategy can generate considerable antagonism. Saudi Wahhabism is an outgrowth of a far older movement known as Salafism, a conviction that Mohammed's earliest followers provide the proper role models for Islamic society, and that any difficulties befalling the *ummah* have arisen because of a failure to follow their lead.[286] While Salafism is not necessarily political, some Salafis gravitate towards radical medieval Sunni scholars whose work makes it political. Perhaps the most prominent among them was Taqi ad-Din Ahmed ibn Taymiyyah, who—like Qutb, five centuries later—advocated *jihad* not only against infidels, but also against insufficiently pure Muslim rulers.[287] Ibn Taymiyyah thus laid the groundwork for an intensely political movement that is Salafi, Islamist, puritanical, and anti-modern. For centuries, his radical teachings remained of marginal significance.[288] Today, they are among the most influential ideas in all of Islam.

The turning point came with Muhammad ibn 'Abd al-Wahhab, an eighteenth century Salafi follower of Ibn Taymiyyah who lived in the Nejd.[289] Muhammad ibn Saud, the ambitious leader of the Nejdi al-Saud tribe, was an early convert to his movement, Wahhabism. The two formed a theological/military partnership in 1744 that persists to this day.[290] The fierce puritanical commitment of Wahhabism justified Ibn Saud's conquest of nearby Shiites and insufficiently pious Sunni tribes to form the first Saudi Kingdom— which fell in 1818—and the resumption of Saudi conquests to form the modern Kingdom of Saudi Arabia in 1932.[291] The partnership has remained strong for over 250 years, though tension between the ruling al Saud and elements of the Wahhabi clerisy has boiled over into overt tension at least twice, in the late 1920s and late 1970s;[292] some observers see tensions rising again today.[293]

The official Wahhabi theology of Saudi Arabia is thus a rigid fundamentalism proud of its draconian enforcement methods, boasting an extreme intolerance for any behavior that violates its puritanical norms. Thanks to Saudi oil money flowing to Muslim communities, organizations, and mosques around the world, Salafism—and even Wahhabism—is now a mainstream Islamic movement.[294] Though the Muslim Brotherhood sees itself as Salafi, many other Salafis—including the Wahhabis—disagree.[295] The key difference is tactical, and it derives from Qutb's writings: The Brotherhood, as a reform movement, engages fully with modernity. This tactical dispute has a clear stylistic component. Salafis tend to keep to themselves, to retain their traditional dress, and to convey the impression of a focus on personal religious piety. The Brotherhood, on the other hand, has gotten quite skilled at playing to its audience and at integrating itself into modern society.[296]

Mutual antipathy notwithstanding, the similarities between the Muslim Brotherhood and the Wahhabis are more important than their differences (at least to outsiders). Both of these Sunni Islamist movements believe that their mission is to reshape the world according to God's will. While they may not be "imperial" in the sense of the state-based European empires of the past few centuries, they are imperial in the far more important tradition of Islamic (and pre-Islamic) empires. They seek to conquer the world in God's name, setting themselves—the true believers—as sole arbiters of God's governing will.

The Empire

Every major intellectual trend to hit the Arab/Islamic Middle East over the past century—liberalism, fascism, Marxism, and Islamism—has led to the same fundamental belief: There is a single dominant people destined to rule the entire realm as a unified empire. The role foreseen for minorities in this empire differed by ideology. In some, the minorities could (at least in theory) blend into the majority—and possibly (as in the Syrian Baathists), even usurp power. In others, minorities were worthy of destruction. In none, however, were minorities allowed to retain their own full identities, secede from the empire, or exercise self-determination. The Sunni imperialists thus showed, at best, the same disdain that Count Clermont-Tonnerre had reserved for the Jews of revolutionary France: acceptance of minorities only if they jettison their distinctness to blend into the national whole.[297]

None of the secular approaches to empire made it to the end of the twentieth century. The hole that the demise of Pan-Arabism left in Arab thinking is hard to underestimate. Writing of that demise in the late 1970s, the Arab-American scholar Fouad Ajami called it "an idea that has dominated the political consciousness of modern Arabs...the *Umma Arabiyya Wahida Dhat Risala Khalida*, 'the one Arab nation with an immortal mission.'"[298] The secular manifestations of the imperial drive, however, were but variants on a theme that lives on. In the twenty-first century, there is only Islamism—and its domination of the region's political consciousness is growing.

Whether secular or Islamist, however, the imperial drive is the same—much as German imperialism survived the move from Bismarck to Hitler, and Russian imperialism the move from the Czars to the Commissars. In Arendt's terms, the Sunni Arabs have developed precisely the sort of continental imperialism that that led the Pan-Germanic and Pan-Slavic movements to slide inexorably into totalitarianism after experimenting with various less extreme approaches. In Huntington's terms, this "Pan" movement's desire for a Sunni Arab Empire defines the organizational model of Arab/Islamic civilization—a model that is obviously incompatible with a liberal, rule-based, international order. In its own terms, as the proudly pan-Arabist scholar Walid Khalidi expressed them around the same time that Ajami wrote of their demise:

> The Arab states' system is first and foremost a "Pan" system. It postulates the existence of a single Arab Nation behind the facade of a multiplicity of sovereign states. In pan-Arab ideology, this Nation is actual, not potential. It is a present reality, not a distant goal. The manifest failure even to approximate unity does not negate the empirical reality of the Arab Nation. It merely adds normative and prescriptive dimensions to the ideology of pan-Arabism. The Arab Nation both is, and should be, one..[299]

Fortunately for the U.S., the West, and all who have benefited from the existing world order, this empire remains largely inchoate. That is not to say, however, that the imperial drive has been without effect. The Arab League[300] is a club of Sunni governments whose primary purpose is to preserve the integrity of the empire while its various factions vie for supremacy. Arab League rules require unanimity before action.[301] This organizational structure ensures that the hardest-line voices will always prevail—precluding any part of the empire from making binding concessions to outsiders. For the League's first few decades, Egypt possessed that voice. When Anwar el-Sadat made peace with Israel, the Arab League ejected Egypt,[302] readmitting it only when Saddam Hussein began threatening Iraq's neighbors in the aftermath of his war with Iran and the smaller Arab states needed Egypt's heft for balance.[303]

The Arab League notwithstanding, the Sunni Arab world is hardly unified. It boasts numerous strongmen and royal families, none of whom would willingly cede control to another for the sake of unity. The struggle for supremacy among Sunni Arabs accounts for most of the wars, much of the tension, and many of the most important collaborations in post-Ottoman Middle Eastern history.[304]

The deceptive unity that the Arab League suggests to casual observers helped hide decades of inter-Sunni conflict from Western conventional wisdom. The Yemeni Civil War of 1962-70 (now forgotten to most Westerners), for example, was actually a proxy war between Egypt and Saudi Arabia, pitting pan-Arab nationalists seeking to expand the Nasserite Empire against Arab royalists hoping to retain their own thrones.[305] In a similar vein, Iraq's longstanding desire for Kuwait and Syria's longstanding desire for Lebanon strike most Sunni Arabs as little more than *anschluss*;[306] whether they favor or oppose such annexations at any given moment depends on the politics of day rather than on any fundamental commitment to the sanctity of state borders. After all, eventual unification is necessary if the Empire is ever to become whole.

Few but students of the region would know the extent of the intra-Sunni rivalry, however, because few of these wars have generated much interest beyond the region; inter-ethnic conflicts yield many more headlines than do intra-ethnic ones. Furthermore, many of the region's leading states belong to an organization far more consequential than the Arab League, an organization representing yet another subtle expression of Sunni Arab imperialism.

OPEC, founded in 1960 against strong Western resistance, was the brainchild of Venezuelan Oil Minister Juan Pablo Pérez Alfonso and Sheikh Abdullah al-Tariki, Saudi Arabia's first Oil Minister—and uncharacteristically (for a Saudi) a devotee of Nasser.[307] Tariki, who pushed at different times for Arab control of oil prices and outright nationalization of oil industries, famously called oil "the strongest of weapons the Arabs wield."[308] In 1967, having long since been exiled to Lebanon for his pan-Arabism and for backing the losing side in a palace struggle, Tariki clarified his plans for deploying this weapon in the imperial cause:

> [T]he Arab nation lives in penury with Arab oil enriching the civilization of other nations... The Arab nation cannot hope to realize its aims of unity, freedom and socialism without the nationalization of the oil industry in the Arab world and the eviction of the oil companies who are the instruments of neo-imperialism... Nationalization requires collective effort by all Arab forces and a common confrontation of foreign domination.[309]

Saudi dominance of OPEC turned out to be Tariki's longstanding gift to the regime that exiled him—and perhaps the most successful vehicle to date at exercising the Sunni Arabs' imperial power: Saudi-led OPEC deployed the oil weapon to brutal effect in 1973, when "Oil Diplomacy" designed to punish those (like the United States) who had allowed Israel to rearm during the Yom Kippur war, triggered a worldwide economic crisis. This flexing of powerful Arab muscles on behalf of the Arab imperial cause, perhaps more than any other single event, drove the reality of decolonization home for the Western powers.[310]

The Empire's significant limitations notwithstanding, however, it has gone a long way towards purging its realm of ethnic minorities. North Africa—the part of *dar-al-Islam* that the Muslims had lost to Europeans long before WWI—though fragmented into several states, boasts only Sunni Arab governments.[311] Shiites were always a small minority, and they remain so today.[312] Black Africans, whether Islamic or not, were marked for genocide.[313] Tens of millions of the mostly-Sunni Berbers, spread from Morocco through Libya, live as an oppressed minority with a language and culture granted no official status—much like the Kurds of Turkey, Iraq, Iran, and Syria.[314] Egypt's Coptic Christians similarly remain in sizable numbers, though as the brief recent reign of the Muslim Brotherhood highlighted, their position has become precarious.[315] North Africa's Sunni Arabs have been quite successful at securing their dominance. Both there and in most of the Arab states of West Asia, the large historic communities of Jews and Christians faced exile or fled to Israel, Europe, or the United States, reducing their representation to the lowest levels since the early days of the Roman Empire.[316] Recent events suggest that the Christian presence in the Arab world will soon dwindle even further;[317] its Jews have already been all but eliminated.

Unified or not, inchoate or not, secular or religious, the Sunni Arab imperial drive has been moving inexorably forward for more than a century. Its most recent manifestation, which President Obama could mistake as a junior varsity terrorist group as recently as 2014,[318] is the Islamic State's Caliphate. Perhaps better than any other movement, the Islamic State demonstrates both Sunni Arabism and imperialism—notwithstanding its Islamic designation. Its stated goal is the eradication of all states within the *dar-al-Islam*, and their replacement with an Empire stretching from Portugal to India known as the reborn Caliphate—run, of course, by Sunni Arabs.[319] The absence of the term "Arab" from its mission statement notwithstanding, it is hard to miss the explicitly Sunni nature of its Islam, the Arab roots of its leaders and members, or its focus on the Arab world.

So far, the Islamic State has effectively eradicated the border between Syria and Iraq—meaning that at least at the moment, neither of these states meets one of the minimal requirements for continued statehood—and made a beachhead in Libya. It is thus hardly a stretch to see the Caliphate (an explicitly imperial term) as little more than the current expression of Sunni Arab Imperialism.

Chapter 13.   The Permanent Crises

Our newfound insights into the region's largest and most important ethnic group, the Sunni Arabs, frees us to tour its various minority communities: Jewish, Christian, Kurd, Druze, Alawite, and Shiite. The inchoate Sunni Arab empire is critical to understanding their stories as well, because most of the Middle East's inter-ethnic conflicts have pitted Sunni Arabs against their putative imperial subjects. The centrality of the Sunni Arabs to the fabric of life across the region is hardly surprising. As the dominant ethnic group, they should feature prominently in most regional affairs. What is surprising, however, is how often this simple and obvious observation seems to evade analysis—and how little importance conventional wisdom seems to place on it. Once again, the feeling that our finest accredited Middle East analysts are missing something seems inescapable.

Sunni Arab Imperialism and reactions to it explain many of the region's most vexing problems: the unremitting hostility toward Israel; the establishment of the Arabs of western Palestine as the world's only multi-generational refugees; the general ambivalence toward Lebanon; the resistance to the partition of Iraq; the factional civil wars sweeping Iraq, Syria, Yemen, and often Lebanon; the antipathy between the Sunni Arabs and Shiite Iran; and Syria's curious position as odd man out, staunchest anti-Zionist, and Teheran's man in Arab politics. In many ways, inchoate imperialism guarantees a region in permanent crisis.

Israel

Israel is the only successful example of genuine minority ethnic self-determination in all of West Asia. As such, Israel is a model worthy of emulation, not—as conventional wisdom seems to believe—a problem in need of management. As a Jewish State in part of the historic Jewish homeland, Israel is thus a singular standout success—under the value system of the liberal West. As a non-Arab, non-Islamic state within the parts of the *dar-al-Islam* most successfully and most completely swallowed during the Arab conquest, however, Israel is a failure of epic proportions—under the value systems of Islamic supremacy and Arab imperialism. In those systems, recognition of Israel's legitimacy simultaneously narrows the putative empire's borders and affirms a concept of minority rights and ethnic self-determination as antithetical to Sunni Arab imperialists as it was to the English, French, German, and Russian imperialists who preceded them.

As Americans and Westerners, we should never feel ashamed of promoting our own values. To the extent that the U.S. retains any voice at all in the Middle East, it must be a voice extolling the virtues of classic Western liberalism and condemning supremacism in all of its forms. We must also remember, however, that many of our values are alien to a region whose history accommodated supremacism and ethnic hierarchies for many centuries.

With those thoughts in mind, it is not hard to see why Israel's fundamental illegitimacy is non-negotiable among those who long for a Sunni Arab empire—or a Caliphate. And "non-negotiable" likely understates the case. The belief is nearly universal. The Arab/Islamic world boasts no dissenting voices capable of speaking for more than the individual uttering them—though over time, a handful of pragmatic voices have come forward. Some Arabs, including some influential Sunni leaders, have recognized that Israel is unlikely to disappear within the foreseeable future, and that accommodations with illegitimacy are occasionally necessary. Jordan's King Abdullah I, Egypt's President Anwar el-Sadat, and Lebanon's President-elect Bashir Gemayel were assassinated for showing such pragmatism; their respective successors learned to put some distance between themselves and Israel. The Saudi-led Arab Peace Initiative—which has returned to the front pages in various forms several times since its initial proposal in 2002—expresses its pragmatism quite clearly; it repeatedly refers to a just and comprehensive peace in the Middle East as a "strategic option," rather than as a moral imperative.[320]

Conventional wisdom often mislabels such views "moderate," though they rest entirely upon pragmatism rather than upon some philosophical moderation.[321] The region's consistent reactions to Israeli concessions drive home the difference between the two. Because every Israeli demonstration of restraint, withdrawal, or vulnerability to international pressure hints at the country's potential impermanence, it also suggests that Arab pragmatism may have been premature. Israeli concessions thus invariably lead to a reduction in Arab "moderation" and an increase in Arab violence, incitement, and terror—often in inverse proportion to the size of the concession—much to the surprise of Western (including some Israeli) observers and prognosticators.[322]   As Israeli Journalist Evelyn Gordon noted glumly:

> [I]n the two-and-a-half years following the Oslo Accords in 1993, when Israel withdrew from most of Gaza and parts of the West Bank, more Israelis were killed by Palestinians than in the entire preceding decade. The second intifada, which erupted in 2000, produced more Israeli casualties in four years than all the terror attacks of the previous 53 years combined. Since 2005, the year in which Israel evacuated every last soldier and settler from Gaza, Palestinians there have fired over 16,000 rockets and mortars at Israel's civilian population.[323]

Were Arab restraint born of actual moderation, reciprocal concessions should have followed instead,[324] at a bare minimum in increased security cooperation between Israel and the moderate Arabs against Arab extremists and in a reduction in anti-Jewish incitement from the moderates.[325]   Political theorists have shown that such concessions tend to drive a wedge between the "moderate" revolutionary factions who negotiate them and do indeed increase their cooperation with the authorities, and their more radical revolutionary allies who increase their incitement and violence.[326] The absence of anything more than occasional fleeting cooperation from the PA, and its demonstrated preference for reconciliation with its radicals over coexistence with Israel, suggest that Arab moderation is indeed in short supply.

Of perhaps greater significance, however, even the pragmatists seem incapable of acknowledging the pressing need to resettle the region's permanently stateless people among ethnic kin in places likely to promote, rather than to erode, regional stability. The Arab Peace Initiative, for example, pointedly failed to abandon a "right of return,"[327] a perpetual claim on behalf of every Arab whose ancestors lived in the Mandate for Palestine between 1946 and 1948 to "return" to Israel.[328] The purpose of this claim is straightforward: it is to erode the Jewish character of the Jewish state, thereby weakening and destabilizing Israel to better enable its destruction. The insistence upon keeping this "right" alive simultaneously absolves the Arab states of responsibility for adopting and resettling the stateless Arabs about whose welfare they claim to care, and keeps a sword drawn over Israel's head. It is a significant and needless contributor to the instability of a region—a region that threatens to export instability around the globe. It is also a manifestly unjust claim that ignores a key demographic movement of the mid-twentieth century, and that fosters the misconception that Israel's Jewish population is not indigenous to the Middle East.

Setting aside longstanding historical claims and bonds to the land, and looking back only a few generations, a majority of today's Israeli Jews had ancestors living in the Middle East or North Africa in the early twentieth century.[329] The Arab insistence on a right to "return" to Israel, rather than on a right to some form of compensation for property lost or abandoned during a series of wars, refugee flows, and population exchanges, is a smokescreen intended to hide the actual demographics and demographic movements that allowed Israel to become a flourishing Jewish State.[330] As recently as the late 1940s, over 850,000 Jews lived in the territory comprising today's Arab League.[331] Parts of it, such as the Iraqi Jewish community, could trace its history to the Babylonian exile, more than 2500 years ago.[332] The New Testament and the Koran, as well as numerous histories written over the centuries, speak of these Jewish communities; no one ever doubted that Jews were an important and indigenous part of the Middle East.

The competing theories of the Arab world that emerged in the early twentieth century saw these Jews in different ways. As we noted, Antonius's liberal (French-inspired) nationalism was willing to recognize these Jews as Arabs if and only if they were willing to relinquish all claims to self-determination.[333] Al-Husri's fascist (German-inspired) nationalism, based heavily in linguistic definition, noted that the region's autonomous Jewish communities spoke their own language and dialects, typically using Arabic only when dealing with Muslims or governments; he thus saw them as inherent outsiders.[334] Islamists, of course, continued to see the Jews as *dhimmis* at best, and with increasing frequency as suitable targets for massacres and pogroms.

By the time of Israel's independence in 1948, the situation of Jews living in the Arab world had become precarious. Shortly before the UN voted to partition the remaining portion of the Mandate for Palestine in 1947, Heykal Pasha, an Egyptian delegate, cautioned the General Assembly not to

> lose sight of the fact that the proposed solution might endanger a million Jews living in the Moslem countries.
> Partition of Palestine might create in those countries an anti-

Semitism even more difficult to root out than the anti-Semitism which the Allies were trying to eradicate in Germany. . . If the United Nations decides to partition Palestine, it might be responsible for the massacre of a large number of Jews.[335]

Iraqi Foreign Minister Jamali echoed the Egyptian warning four days later:

The masses in the Arab world cannot be restrained. The Arab-Jewish relationship in the Arab world will greatly deteriorate. . . . Harmony prevails among Muslims, Christians and Jews [in Iraq]. But any injustice imposed upon the Arabs of Palestine will disturb the harmony among Jews and non-Jews in Iraq; it will breed interreligious prejudice and hatred.[336]

Similar threats arose throughout the Arab world, as did coordinated campaigns to turn them into reality. Jews throughout the broader Middle East were stripped of citizenship rights and subject to various forms of discrimination and violence. By mid-May 1948, *The New York Times* warned that Jews were "in grave danger in all Moslem lands."

Reports from the Middle East: make it clear that there is serious tension in all Arab countries. The Jewish populations there are gravely worried at the prospect that an Arab-Jewish war may break out suddenly at any moment.... Already in some Moslem states such as Syria and Lebanon there is a tendency to regard all Jews as Zionist agents and "fifth columnists." There have been violent incidents with feeling running high. There are indications that the stage is being set for a tragedy of incalculable proportions.[337]

Over the next few years, the situation worsened to include the widespread expropriation of Jewish property and the exile of Jews from the lands of their birth.[338] Ironically, the only Arabs to complain about this plan to render the Arab world *Judenrein* were those with direct claims against Israel,[339] who understood that the population exchange underway would render hollow any claims to a "right of return" they might later wish to forward. In 1975, Sabri Jiryis, director of the Institute of Palestine Studies in Beirut, noted that the Arab states had expelled the Jews "in a most ugly fashion, and after confiscating their possessions or taking control thereof at the lowest price."[340] These expulsions led to

the reinforcement of Israel, its strengthening and fortification to the degree we see it as present. . . . There is no need to say that the problem of those Jews and their passage to Israel is not merely theoretical, at least from the viewpoint of the Palestinian problem. Clearly, Israel will raise the question in all serious negotiation that may in time be conducted over the rights of the Palestinians. . . . Israel's arguments take approximately the following form: "It is true that we Israelis brought about the exodus of the Arabs from their land in the war of 1948 . . . and that we took control of their property. In return however you Arabs caused the expulsion of a like number of Jews from Arab countries since 1948 until today. Most of these went to Israel after you seized control of their property in one way or another. What happened, therefore, is merely a kind of 'population and property transfer,' the consequences of which both sides have to bear. Thus Israel gathers in the Jews from Arab countries and the Arab countries are obliged in turn to settle the Palestinians within their own borders and work towards a solution of the problem." Israel will undoubtedly advance these claims in the first real debate over the Palestinian problem.[341]

Though Jiryis may have derided this view, he articulated it because he saw it as a clear concern. His concern was warranted; his derision was not. The first half of the population exchange he hoped the world would continue to ignore occurred precisely as he described it: Jewish communities throughout the Middle East were uprooted and consolidated as Israel. Following the population exchange through to its logical completion accords fully with general historical practice, long-term notions of justice, and the imperative of moving forward to reestablish stability in the wake of war and dislocation.

While it is likely that justice also demands that some balancing compensation flow in one direction or the other (which direction, and in what amount, remains debated), Jiryis's candor highlights the imbalance between the sides. Israel resettled its refugee kinsmen to build a flourishing Jewish state. The Arabs preserved their refugee status to better preserve their imperial claims—and to better ensure that the Jewish State would spend its entire existence in a state of permanent crisis. The "right of return" thus highlights both the absence of actual Arab moderation and highlights the central role of inchoate imperialism in Middle Eastern tension and instability; it has never been more than an unjust and transparent ploy to eviscerate the Jewish character of the Jewish state.

Palestinianism

The twentieth century witnessed far too many refugee crises. Many of these refugees were fortunate enough to land among ethnic kinsmen whose governments—despite abject poverty and extremely limited resources—embraced their newly arrived brothers and sisters. These governments elevated the integration of their kin above all other priorities. This welcoming behavior cut across many different cultures and political regimes; Greece,[342] Turkey,[343] Israel,[344] India,[345] Pakistan,[346] and Germany[347] all did their best. In the entire Arab world, only Jordan has even made an effort.[348]

The establishment of a permanent UN agency, the United Nations Relief and Works Agency (UNRWA), dedicated to preserving the refugee status of the "Palestine refugees" and their descendants remains one of the great humanitarian scandals of the modern era. UNRWA concedes that it is

> unique in terms of its long-standing commitment to one group of refugees.... Palestine refugees, defined as "persons whose normal place of residence was Palestine during the period 1 June 1946 to 15 May 1948, and who lost both home and means of livelihood as a result of the 1948 conflict." The descendants of Palestine refugee males, including legally adopted children, are also eligible for registration....When the Agency began operations in 1950, it was responding to the needs of about 750,000 Palestine refugees. Today, some 5 million Palestine refugees are eligible for UNRWA services.[349]

A 667% increase in the number of "refugees," the concept of hereditary refugee status, and refugee camps nearing their seventieth birthdays, are indeed "unique." They do not, and never have, existed anywhere other than in UNRWA's warm embrace, and they have never applied to anyone other than "Palestine refugees." In any parallel situation, the more professional United Nations Commissioner for Refugees (UNHCR) would have worked to find a durable solution to the refugee crisis, most obviously "local integration" into ethnically related and culturally similar host societies—the numerous Arab states.[350]

Fouad Ajami, the Arab-American scholar born into a small Shiite village in southern Lebanon, within the sight lines of the Israeli border,[351] saw the effects of this tragic mistreatment of the refugees quite clearly. On the sixtieth anniversary of Israel's independence, he wrote:

In their utterances, the Arabs were bound by a code of brotherhood, and the "restoration" of Palestinian rights was the creed of their political world. But in the mirror, Arabs could see their fratricide, the chasm between what they said and what they did. The rulers who professed fidelity to Palestine helped themselves to the fragments of Palestine unclaimed by the Zionists. The Arabs who bemoaned the loss of Palestine were in truth made uneasy by the Palestinian refugees. It would have been the humane thing to tell the refugees that huge historical verdicts are never overturned. But it was safer to offer a steady diet of evasion and escapism.

Israel's 60th anniversary suggests what might have been. In those days of battle, when history was fluid, partition of Palestine was the way out—a Jewish state and an Arab state, side by side. The Zionists opted for moderation and rescue; they would take a state, said their legendary leader Chaim Weizmann, even if it were the size of a tablecloth. The Palestinians held out for the whole thing....[352]

As Ajami implied, the Sunni world's steadfast refusal to extend the basic decency of resettlement and integration to refugees that it recognizes at its own makes sense only within the context of an imperial drive, the compulsion to control "the whole thing." One of the biggest misconceptions—and the source of numerous policy errors—about the Middle East is that these Arab "Palestine Refugees" are part of the story of Israel. They are not. They are part of the story of Sunni Arab Imperialism—a movement that has deployed these people as human weapons. Israel is little more than the intended target. The refugees themselves are little more than hapless foot soldiers who serve the putative Emperor well as permanent refugees—no matter who that Emperor might turn out to be. They shine a perpetual light on the illegitimacy of the tiny ethnic Jewish state in the midst of the Empire's rightful land. They also deter the sort of regional stability that might lock the state system—including Israel—in place, precluding the eventual emergence of a unified Empire.

Ironically, these very people, deemed expendable detritus by their Sunni Arab kinsmen, have given rise to a unique and important ideology of their own: Palestinianism. Though history has never known a State of Palestine and Palestinian nation building has been even less successful than the demonstrably failed attempts to build the nations of Syria and Iraq, Palestinianism is a real and important ideology.

Palestinianism refers to the notion that a historic Palestinian people seeks self-determination in the historic state of Palestine. Yet aside from the lack of historic basis to this claim, the very definitions of both the people and the state hinged on what they *were not* rather than from who they *were*. During the early twentieth century, when emerging Pan-Arabism, Islamism, and tribalism competed for hearts and minds throughout the Arab world, the new notion of a "Palestinian" arose to describe the people living in the historic Jewish homeland in which Zionists hoped to build a Jewish state.[353] Initially, the term referred primarily to the Jews; it was Jewish institutions— bank, post office, newspaper, tourism office, etc.—that used the label "Palestine," and the flag featured a Jewish star on a field of blue and white.[354] The minute the Zionist dream became a reality, however, the Jews were written out of "Palestine." The term came to connote, instead, the Arabs who happened to live among those Jews.

The concept of "Palestine," and the Arabs that the Jewish State supposedly dispossessed, was always malleable; it was consistently coterminous with whatever parts of the historic Jewish homeland the Zionists saw as the future Jewish State. The Thirteenth Zionist Congress of August 1923, for example, adopted the San Remo definition that the League of Nations had enshrined the previous year. In keeping with the League's instructions to the British to administer the Palestine Mandate with the specific goal of ushering a Jewish state to fruition, the Zionist Congress recognized "that eastern and western Palestine are in reality and *de facto* one unit historically, geographically, and economically, the Congress expresses its expectation that the future of Transjordan shall be determined in accordance with the legitimate demands of the Jewish people."[355]

Yet when the Zionists relinquished the legitimate historical and legal Jewish claim to lands along the East Bank of the Jordan River as part of the planned Jewish state, so too did the "Palestinians." The PLO Charter, first written in 1964 and reaffirmed in July 1968, proclaimed that "Palestine, with the boundaries it had during the British Mandate, is an indivisible territorial unit,"[356] apparently unconcerned about the overwhelming majority of the Mandatory lands that Jordan claimed—or the Gaza strip under occupation by the PLO's Egyptian patron.[357] In point of fact, Egypt and the Soviet Union sponsored the PLO's founding three years before Israel liberated Judea and Samaria. The PLO's job was always to push the Jews out of the parts of "Palestine" west of the 1949 armistice lines (i.e., the "Green Line").[358] Today, the Palestinian Authority distributes maps that omit Israel entirely.[359] "Palestine" is once again defined as precisely the parts of the historic Jewish homeland in which a Jewish

State is possible.

The PLO Charter defines "Palestinians" as "those Arab nationals who, until 1947, normally resided in Palestine regardless of whether they were evicted from it or have stayed there. Anyone born, after that date, of a Palestinian father -whether inside Palestine or outside it - is also a Palestinian."[360] Though this definition appears similar to UNRWA's, it provides less specificity about dates of residence or arrival. That difference is critical, and telling; census figures and demographic analyses suggest that many if not most "Palestinian" Arab families arrived in the area from Syria or Egypt during the decades between the declaration of the Zionist goal of self-determination and the declaration of the State of Israel.[361] Their primary attraction to the region appears to have been the Jewish economic development that the early Zionists undertook as part of their work towards independence and self-determination.[362]

Prior to those Jewish investments, the area had spent centuries as an impoverished part of the Ottoman hinterland. In the words of Mark Twain, who visited the region shortly before Zionist investment began:

> The population of Jerusalem is composed of Moslems, Jews, Greeks, Latins, Armenians, Syrians, Copts, Abyssinians, Greek Catholics, and a handful of Protestants. One hundred of the latter sect are all that dwell now in this birthplace of Christianity. The nice shades of nationality comprised in the above list, and the languages spoken by them, are altogether too numerous to mention. It seems to me that all the races and colors and tongues of the earth must be represented among the fourteen thousand souls that dwell in Jerusalem. Rags, wretchedness, poverty and dirt, those signs and symbols that indicate the presence of Moslem rule more surely than the crescent-flag itself, abound. Lepers, cripples, the blind, and the idiotic, assail you on every hand, and they know but one word of but one language apparently—the eternal "bucksheesh." To see the numbers of maimed, malformed and diseased humanity that throng the holy places and obstruct the gates, one might suppose that the ancient days had come again, and that the angel of the Lord was expected to descend at any moment to stir the waters of Bethesda. Jerusalem is mournful, and dreary, and lifeless.[363]

The shallowness of most "Palestinian" roots effectively undermines the PLO Charter's entire claim that "[t]he Palestinian identity is a genuine, essential, and inherent characteristic,"[364] or that "there is a Palestinian community and that it has material, spiritual, and historical connection with Palestine."[365]

Finally, as if to confirm both the imperial and the supremacist nature of the Arab claims to all of West Asia, the PLO Charter helpfully explains that "Judaism, being a religion, is not an independent nationality. Nor do Jews constitute a single nation with an identity of its own; they are citizens of the states to which they belong."[366] By way of contrast, "Palestinians" are simultaneously a distinct nation and an essential part of the Arab nation; indeed, "[t]he destiny of the Arab nation, and indeed Arab existence itself, depend upon the destiny of the Palestine cause...."[367]

> The Palestinian people believe in Arab unity. In order to contribute their share toward the attainment of that objective, however, they must, at the present stage of their struggle, safeguard their Palestinian identity and develop their consciousness of that identity, and oppose any plan that may dissolve or impair it.[368]

> Arab unity and the liberation of Palestine are two complementary objectives, the attainment of either of which facilitates the attainment of the other. Thus, Arab unity leads to the liberation of Palestine, the liberation of Palestine leads to Arab unity; and work toward the realization of one objective proceeds side by side with work toward the realization of the other.[369]

> The liberation of Palestine, from an Arab viewpoint, is a national (*qawmi*) duty and it attempts to repel the Zionist and imperialist aggression against the Arab homeland, and aims at the elimination of Zionism in Palestine. Absolute responsibility for this falls upon the Arab nation - peoples and governments - with the Arab people of Palestine in the vanguard....[370]

These definitions—most of which were developed with Nazi and Soviet input decades before the PLO charter enshrined them and all of which predate the Six Day War of June, 1967—highlight the true nature of Palestinianism. The movement arose precisely to counter Zionism and to defeat the cause of Jewish self-determination in the ancient Jewish homeland. Palestinianism, properly understood, was founded as an expression of Arab continental imperialism and as a classic anti-Jewish hate movement.[371]

Throughout its first few decades, Palestinianism was comfortable in that role. Its most prominent leader, Haj Amin al-Husseini, the Grand Mufti of Jerusalem, allied himself happily with Hitler and the Nazis—enjoying the warm embrace of the world's largest and most powerful anti-Jewish hate group, and collaborating on plans to export the Final Solution to the Middle East.[372] Thus, the Arab rejection of the 1947 partition plan, which Western conventional wisdom still sees as a perplexing miscalculation that worked against the cause of Palestinian self-determination, was nothing of the sort. None of the Arabs living in the western sliver of the Palestine Mandate subject to partition ever had any interest in building either a nation or a state; their interest lay entirely in squelching the Jewish state. Partition at that point (or even today) would have conceded failure. As late as 1968, the PLO Charter (never amended) deemed the partition plan "illegal."[373]

Twenty years and three Arab/Israeli wars later, however, the situation had changed—at least from the all-important public relations perspective. While elite Western opinion of the 1960s and 70s deemed anti-Jewish hate groups unacceptable, it welcomed movements of indigenous self-determination. Yasir Arafat, with significant Soviet assistance, *recast* Palestinianism as a nationalist movement,[374] complete with its own national charter.[375] He did not, however, *restructure* it as a nationalist movement, complete with institutions of civil society and a government in exile.

Arafat's sleight of hand persuaded large parts of the world to accept Palestinianism as a legitimate movement of national self-determination. It even led the Israeli government to concede—in the Oslo Accords of 1993—that the myth was likely irreversible. Events of the twenty-first century, however, have undermined the entire context in which the distinct nature of a "Palestinian" nation seemed to make sense. That context was the division of the post-Ottoman hinterland into the distinct nation-states of Syria, Iraq, Jordan, Lebanon, and Israel, and the still-disputed territories of Judea, Samaria, and Gaza. Within that framework, with national identities assigned neatly to most of the region's residents, the Arabs who fled Israel or who resided in the disputed territories seemed to demand a national label of their own—hence, "Palestinian." As a nation without an existing state, the claim for self-determination seemingly followed as a matter of course.

Recent events, however, have demonstrated conclusively that the region's various national labels are meaningless. Though the international community may have designated the region's people Syrians, Iraqis, Jordanians, Lebanese, or Palestinians, the people so designated never internalized those assigned identities. Even today, nearly a century after the initial assignments, the people living in these states clearly identify more closely with their faith group, ethnicity, or tribe than with their assigned nationality. The number of Iraqis or Syrians fighting to preserve national unity in the face of crumbling central authority—articulating a stronger bond with fellow citizens of different ethnicities or faiths than with co-religionists or fellow ethnics of different nationalities—is vanishingly small. The Lebanese Civil War that raged from the mid-1970s through the early 1990s, and that continues to simmer, taught a similar lesson about Lebanese nationalism. The persistent and growing popularity of Islamism, from the Muslim Brotherhood in Egypt and its Gaza chapter, Hamas, to the new cross-border Islamic State Caliphate represent a wholesale rejection of nationalist labels and identities in favor of fealty to Islam. The message is consistent and clear: the international community may have created post-Ottoman states, but there are no post-Ottoman Arab nations.

That the absence of true nationalist feeling among those designated Syrians, Iraqis, or Lebanese applies with at least equal force to those designated Palestinian should be obvious. The Hamas Charter of 1988 (technically "The Covenant of the Islamic Resistance Movement"), which repeatedly rejects the propriety of a "Palestinian" national identity distinct from Islam, is enormously popular among those bearing the Palestinian label—possibly boasting majority support. The charter makes clear that it sees "Palestine" as an Islamic *waqf*, a trust granted to the entire Islamic *ummah* whose "government" simply administers the land on behalf of Islam as a whole.[376] "It is necessary to instill in the minds of the Moslem generations that the Palestinian problem is a religious problem, and should be dealt with on this basis."[377] The Hamas Charter is also clear that it rejects any movements that attempt to apply the secular notion of nationalism to this *waqf*; it sees the "nationalist movement in the Palestinian area" as fellow travelers, as long as they do not overstep their appropriate boundaries to trample the religious edicts:

> The question of the liberation of Palestine is bound to three circles: the Palestinian circle, the Arab circle and the Islamic circle. Each of these circles has its role in the struggle against Zionism. Each has its duties, and it is a horrible mistake and a sign of deep ignorance to overlook any of these circles. [Because] Palestine is an Islamic land... liberation of Palestine is then an individual duty for very Moslem wherever he may be.[378]

> The Islamic Resistance Movement respects these [nationalist movements in the Palestinian area] and appreciates their circumstances and the conditions surrounding and affecting them. It encourages them as long

as they do not give their allegiance to the Communist East or the Crusading West.... The Movement assures all the nationalist trends operating in the Palestinian arena for the liberation of Palestine, that it is there for their support and assistance. It will never be more than that, both in words and deeds, now and in the future.[379]

[W]ith all our appreciation for the Palestinian Liberation Organization - and what it can develop into - and without belittling its role in the Arab-Israeli conflict, we are unable to exchange the present or future Islamic Palestine with the secular idea. The Islamic nature of Palestine is part of our religion and whoever takes his religion lightly is a loser.[380]

It is thus clear that Hamas's many supporters have not internalized Palestinian nationalism as a core identity any more than have their Syrian, Iraqi, or Lebanese counterparts. Furthermore, whereas the residents of the Syrian, Iraqi, and Lebanese nation-states at least shared a post-Ottoman existence that differentiated them from co-religionists or ethnic kin living elsewhere, not so those designated Palestinian. Even the UNRWA definition restricts their commonality of national experience to a period of less than two years.[381] The Palestinian Authority itself recognizes the absence of a shared national experience of any meaningful duration. Its comprehensive 2006 census,[382] despite incorporating questionable raw population numbers,[383] divides the members of its claimed nation into six distinct categories: those living in Israel west of the Green Line (11.2%), Judea and Samaria (24.6%), Gaza (14.6%), Jordan (27.7%), Other Arab countries (16.2%), and Other countries (5.7%).[384]

While the percentages have fluctuated over time, it is clear that the residents of each of these categories have experienced the period since May 1948 very differently. Most of the 44.6% living in Israel west of the Green Line, Jordan, or other (non-Arab) countries have become citizens and integrated into their countries of residence— defining as many distinct experiences as there are host countries. While some are undoubtedly unhappy with their present circumstances, there is nothing unique about their displeasure; nearly every country around the globe includes citizens who believe that their lives would be better elsewhere, or who wish that their ancestors had faced different opportunities and made different choices. The experience of the 16.2% living in Arab states other than Jordan has largely been that of a minority facing discrimination from their majority hosts—notwithstanding their cultural similarities and claims of kinship. These experiences obviously differed from those of the residents of Gaza, Judea, and Samaria. There too, from 1948 to 1967 Gaza was effectively a large Egyptian prison camp, while Judea and Samaria were well integrated into Transjordan.[385] Since 2005, Gazans have lived without any Israeli presence—military or civilian—and since a year later in a Hamas-run terror state on the Mediterranean. And since the Oslo Accords of 1993, the Arabs of Judea and Samaria have experienced a tense but real relationship between the PA and the government of Israel.

It is hard to see how this diversity of experiences could forge a true national identity where decades chafing beneath the dictatorships of Iraq's Saddam and Syria's Assad or participating in a confessional parliamentary Lebanon have failed. The mythical "Palestinian" nation should not outlive the other attempted artificial post-Ottoman nations.

The collapse of the post-Ottoman order and the myth of distinct nationalisms within the Sunni Arab world lays bare the truth about Palestinianism: Its entire self-definition, and its entire *raison d'être*, is the negation of the Zionist dream for an independent Jewish state in the historic Jewish homeland. To this day, Palestinianism combines the inner workings of a hate group with the outer trappings of a nationalist movement. The statements of Palestinian leaders, the Palestinian press, the Palestinian educational systems, and Palestinian entertainment are replete with demonization of the Jews, incitement, calls for violence, even advocacy of genocide.[386] Palestinians raise their children to hate Jews and to glory in those who kill Jews.[387] Palestinian society, from top to bottom, allocates greater resources to ensuring that their people despise Jews than to encouraging their people to help themselves. Palestinianism on the ground today remains far, far more concerned with destroying Israel than it does with building Palestine; hatred of the reviled other is far more important than love of self.

This duality is unique. No other movement features such a complete misalignment of inner functioning with outwardly stated goals. No other allegedly nationalist movement has focused so little on nation building and so much on fostering hatred. Understanding this dual nature of Palestinianism is critical to appreciating why all attempts to extract reasonable and expected behavior from Palestinian leaders ultimately fail: When it comes to representation in international organizations or diplomatic negotiations, the movement is fully equipped to function as expected. But at the end of the day, at the point of agreement, compromise, and implementation, it lacks any of the necessary tools. The rare Palestinian leader—like former PA Prime Minister Salam Fayyad—who actually sets out to build the institutions necessary for a functioning state, must operate in a vacuum with little popular support.[388] The duality also explains why the line between opposition to Israel and Jew hatred in the world today is so thin: the dominant force in the anti-Israel movement is a century-old, virulent, anti-Jewish hate group. When it comes to questions of peace and security, it is nearly impossible to stand against Zionism without standing in favor of Palestinianism. And the core element of Palestinianism remains what it has always been—unreconstructed Jew hatred.

The permanent crisis in which both Israel and the "Palestine refugees" live is thus the intentional and necessary consequence of Palestinianism's success as an expression of inchoate imperialism. The movement has gained widespread acceptance of its foundational lie: that the "Palestinians" constitute a distinct people, fundamentally different from neighboring Sunni Arabs, rather than simply a hate group directed against the Jews in the service of the Empire. The global diplomatic emphasis on promoting regional stability by creating a new "State of Palestine" is thus doomed to fail; acceptance of oft-repeated mantra "two states living side by side in peace and security"[389] would represent the failure of Palestinianism—and without Palestinianism, there is neither need nor justification for a state of "Palestine." There can be no "Two State Solution" to the Arab/Israeli conflict because there is no stateless nation in waiting; there are only Arabs living in the historic Jewish homeland.

If the region is ever to know stability, the world must first dispense with the foundational lie of a distinct Palestinian nation. Palestine, like Andalusia or Rumelia, was an administrative region of relevance to those studying the history of Islamic (or Roman) Empires; it has never defined a state and has no place in the modern nation-state system. "Palestinian" Arabs are not a distinct people, but rather a powerful weapon in the arsenal of those seeking to recreate such an empire. The permanent immiseration of the people unfortunate enough to bear the "Palestinian" designation—promulgated by their Sunni Arab kin with the support of the international community—guarantees that even if some Sunni Arabs develop a temporary tactical accommodation with Israel, Israel can never integrate fully into the region.

The consequent permanent crisis will thus exist as long as the Sunni Arab taste for unification and empire remains. If and or when the Sunni Arab states begin to act like true nation-states, they will absorb their own ethnic kinsmen, defuse the Palestinianist hate movement, and accept the validity of ethnic self-determination for many of the region's ethnic minorities—including its Jews. Much to Israel's regret, such revolutionary thinking can come only from within the Sunni Arabs; there is nothing that Israel can do to hasten it. From an American—and Western—perspective, the elimination of this foundational lie from discourse, debate, and policy consideration is critical. "Palestine" is the weapon of choice of supremacist, imperialist Arabs and Muslims. Israel may be first in the crosshairs, but the attacks will not stop until the West dismantles the weapon—or succumbs to defeat.

The West cannot extinguish the desire for a Caliphate that the Islamic State has ignited until it depletes the imperial arsenal—even if the Islamic State itself falls beneath Western guns.[390] Disarmament, in turn, requires working towards the self-determination rights of the region's various minorities—and rejecting the spurious claims of the weaponized portions of the region's Sunni Arab majority. The end of Palestinianism and the recognition of Israel's claims to the historic Jewish heartland are the critical first steps towards that goal.

Lebanon

Life in permanent crisis mode is endemic to minorities living within the vast territory that Sunni Arabs claim as their rightful empire. Lebanon, like Israel, was supposed to have been an exercise in minority ethnic self-determination: France's gift to Maronite Christians.[391] This experiment in Christian self-determination has proved much less successful than the neighboring experiment in Jewish self-determination. Why? The answer lies in demographics. When the United Nations drew partition lines across the western sliver of Britain's Palestine Mandate, it sought to gerrymander Jews and Arabs into separate states. The refugee crises emanating from the subsequent Arab efforts to eradicate both the nascent Jewish state and the Jewish populations living within their own borders accelerated the sorting through a classic population exchange: Many Arabs left the Jewish State, while several much larger waves of Jewish refugees exiled from centuries-old communities throughout the Middle East found new homes in Israel.[392] As noted, the Jewish state welcomed its kinsmen; the numerous Sunni Arab states rejected theirs.

This two-pronged Arab strategy against Israel had a polarizing effect, precisely as the Lebanese scholar Palestine Studies, Sabri Jiryis, described in 1975:[393] It guaranteed perpetual Arab refugees and it stabilized Israel's demographics. Had the Arabs accepted the 1947 partition plan, the resultant Jewish state would have had a small Jewish majority—one that demographic trends might have dissipated by now, much as demographics have altered the balance in Lebanon.[394] By the time the dust settled on the refugee flows of the 1950s, however, Israel boasted a sizable Jewish majority.[395] These demographics allowed the country to stabilize and to thrive as a liberal democracy (albeit one with an initially statist economy), granting full citizenship rights to its non-Jewish Arab minority.[396] Lebanon, whose populations grew at different speeds rather than consolidating, became increasingly unstable.

When the French Mandatory authorities drew the lines around Lebanon, they gave the Maronites the largest state in which they would be a majority—albeit a small majority.[397] The resultant confessional state divided the spoils according to the size of the ethnic community at the moment of independence; as the majority, the Maronites retained the lion's share of those spoils.[398] At the same time, they chose to identify Lebanon as an Arab state (a perfectly reasonable choice under the circumstances) rather than as a Mediterranean state (which might have been an equally reasonable one). As Lebanese demographics shifted and as Sunni Arab Imperialism progressed from fighting European Mandatories to internal governance, Lebanon found itself increasingly isolated: a shrinking Christian plurality government holding down Shiite, Sunni, Druze, and other groups, ensconced in an Arab League designed to promote Sunni supremacy.

For decades, Lebanon's image reflected this duality—part European, part Arab—effectively precluding Western involvement when inter-Arab tension tore the country apart. Fouad Ajami described the downfall of his native land in macabre, tragicomic terms: "No one could really win in Beirut. In the mid-1970s, the combatants fought over beachfront hotels, over once-proud places. A decade later, they were fighting over shells of gutted buildings."[399] "By the early 1980s, in the city that had parodied Paris there was now a parody of Iran's theocratic revolution; parody had replaced parody."[400] The absence of a population exchange capable of strengthening Lebanon's Christian character had more-or-less doomed the country to a perpetual state of crisis.

This relationship between a population exchange and stability is hardly unexpected. Though it has fallen into disfavor in recent decades, intentional population exchanges helped to stabilize both Europe and large parts of the post-colonial world.[401] Unintentional exchanges, born of war and refugee flows, continue to reshape demographics around the globe—as current events originating in Syria demonstrate rather clearly.[402]   The international "human rights" community, however, accepts the utility of large-scale migration and demographic change only when unplanned, catastrophic, and crisis-driven; it mislabels preemptive population movements capable of preventing future genocides or stabilizing volatile regions as "human rights violations."[403]

The demographic paths that Israel and Lebanon have taken since independence provide a useful contrast.   The Arab states ethnically cleansed themselves of Jews, creating a crisis.   Israel provided humanitarian aid, resettlement, integration, and citizenship to the resultant Jewish refugees.   The international human rights community deems such a sequence of events acceptable.   Because neither Israel nor Lebanon have ever practiced ethnic cleansing, there are now numerous multi-generation Sunni Arab refugees destabilizing the region and Lebanon has lost much of the Mediterranean, European, and Christian character that made it unique.   Lebanon has instead collapsed into a loose confederation of confessional communities that the Syrian/Iranian Shiite shock troops of Hezbollah dominates.   The international human rights community would unquestionably deride—and attempt to criminalize—any planned demographic changes capable of ameliorating either situation.[404] Lebanon's permanent crisis persists to this day—though brutality and tragedy may soon intervene, as Islamism threatens to eradicate ancient Middle Eastern Christianity as surely as Arab nationalism and Islam conspired to eradicate ancient Middle Eastern Jewry.   The resulting flood of Middle Eastern Christian refugees in need of a new home may soon raise the question of Lebanon's identity once again.

Chapter 14. Revolution and Reaction

The unraveling of Iraq following the American decision to depose Saddam, disband its military, and de-Baathify the country provided clear and unmistakable proof of the weakness of Iraqi nationalism. Eighty-plus years as an independent state, eighty-plus years of shared experiences including monarchy, revolution, fascism, totalitarianism, war, and international sanctions were incapable of inculcating an assigned "Iraqi" identity among people who continued to see themselves, first and foremost, as Sunni Arabs, Shiites, or Kurds. Unsurprisingly, numerous voices—from then-Senator Joe Biden on down—began to clamor for the partition of Iraq into three distinct ethnic states. These suggestions found few takers among the region's leaders—the Sunni Arabs who control the Arab League.[405]

Given the imperial attitudes towards the strong Jewish and weak Christian "secessions," this opposition is hardly surprising. A Shiite state in the south and/or a Kurdish state in the north would reduce the imperial boundaries, marking the greatest affront to imperial integrity since Israel's birth in 1948. From the perspective of inchoate Sunni Arab imperialism, legitimate movements of ethnic self-determination like Zionism and Kurdish nationalism are necessarily Western implants. From the days of the Prophet through the fall of the Ottomans, the Islamic world was organized as a series of Empires, with a single elite group in charge and everyone else given lesser status. Minority rights and ethnic self-determination were ideals of the late European enlightenment.[406] They are alien to the Arab and Islamic worlds, and offensive to those who cling to supremacist and imperial objectives. Compounding the still-open wound of a Jewish state with the birth of a Kurdish one would emphasize the crumbling of the imperial dream.

For precisely those reasons, the birth of an independent Kurdistan would serve American and Western interests—and represent a defeat to those dreaming of a Caliphate reborn. In addition to serving the cause of justice in its own right, the insistence upon minority rights and ethnic self-determination that Israel and Kurdistan exemplify would strike a blow at the heart of all Sunni Arab imperialists. An American-led drive towards ethnic minority self-determination is thus a critical strategic imperative in the fight against the Islamic State and its reconstituted Caliphate.

Syria

The fear of imperial crumbling also explains the strange role of Syria. Like most Arab states, Syria is majority Sunni—though uniquely among Sunni-majority states, Syria's ruling elite is not. Hafez al-Assad consolidated his control of Syria in the early 1970s, nominally on behalf of the Baath Party, but actually on behalf of his Alawite kinsmen.[407] Relatively little is known about the Alawites; they are a secretive religion living along the Syrian coast of Latakia, where they form a majority and could reasonably claim the right to a small state paralleling Israel and Lebanon.[408] In fact, such an Alawite state appeared on many early maps of the French Mandate for Syria, only to disappear in the face of Sunni Arab demands.[409]

According to prominent Middle East scholar Daniel Pipes, "For many centuries, the 'Alawis were the weakest, poorest, most rural, most despised, and most backward people of Syria."[410] It was not until the 1970s that an Iranian cleric declared Alawism a form of Shiism, setting the stage for the warm relationship between Alawite-dominated Syria and the Islamic Republic of Iran.[411] Prior to that recent reclassification—still far from universally recognized—many considered Alawism a heretical offshoot of Islam, giving Alawites a social status even lower than that of *dhimmis*. It is thus hardly surprising that, like George Antonius and Michel Aflaq, (the staunchly secular Orthodox Christian founder of the Baath Party, whom Assad's faction chased from Syria to seize control of the local Baath),[412] Syria's Alawite leadership relished the ability to stand on equal footing with Muslims beneath the umbrella of Arabism. "Now, 'Alawis dominate the government, hold key military positions, enjoy a disproportionate share of the educational resources, and are becoming wealthy."[413]

The Alawite control of a Sunni country put the Syrian regime in a perpetually precarious position long before its current civil war erupted in 2011. Alawite-led Syria can neither trust any other member of the Arab League nor withdraw from that Sunni organization without facing significant repercussions. In a masterful move, the Assads finessed this situation for decades by combining strident pan-Arabist anti-Zionism and an alliance with the traditionally anti-Arab Shia of Iran.[414] These twin pillars sustain the regime, even today, when various Sunni factions have overtaken much of the country. It is hard to see how the Alawites could regain control of the country without significant outside assistance (primarily Iranian and Russian, though there are indications that American factions, including influential voices in the Obama Administration, have flirted with the idea of joining them).[415] Nor is it clear how a restored Alawite regime might retain control of a restive Sunni majority without taking an even harder line in defense of the inchoate empire. Taken together, the case for an independent Alawite states in Western Syria seems strong; the case for reuniting Syria's Sunnis, Alawites, and various minorities into a single dysfunctional state is weak.

Iran

Syria's alliance with Iran brings yet another of the region's significant philosophies into focus: Khomeinism. It is hard to underemphasize the truly revolutionary nature of Khomeini's work, or the effect that it has had on Shiism. The centerpiece of Khomeini's philosophy, *velayet-e faqih*, means "rule by (Islamic) jurist." It marks a sharp contrast from traditional Shiite thought; as a minority faith, Shiism unsurprisingly tended to favor a "quietist" division of clerical and temporal authority.[416] As the noted scholar of Islam Hillel Fradkin described it:

> Khomeini's success not only revolutionized the Iranian state. In fact, the capture of the state and its new organization amounted to a proposal to revolutionize Shiism itself. In a manner of speaking, the state and its requirements came to embody Shiism. As such, the rule of the jurist could entail and very often did require additional radical innovations....Khomeini declared that the survival of the state superseded all else—including even, if necessary, the various prescriptions of Shiite law. Khomeini's most general and important legacy was that the Islamic Republic and its requirements were to be definitive to Shiite Islamism's future....The net result of this is that Shiism—or rather, Shiite Islamism—is now, in principle, a function of Iran's politics, both domestic and foreign, and is somewhat indeterminate.[417]

Khomeinism was a truly radical philosophy, merging numerous Western ideas with those of Shiite Islam. Daniel Pipes, citing the work of political scientist Shahrough Akhavi, noted important structural parallels between the Islamic Republic of Iran and the Catholic Church—with Khomeini, of course, playing Pope:

> The centralization that has occurred in the religious institution in Iran is unprecedented, and actions have been taken that resemble patterns in the ecclesiastical church tradition familiar in the West. For example, in 1982, Khomeini encouraged the "defrocking" and "excommunication" of his chief rival, Ayatollah Muhammad Kazim Shari`atmadari (d. 1986), although no machinery for this has ever existed in Islam. Other trends, such as centralized control over budgets, appointments to the professoriate, curricula in the seminaries, the creation of religious militias, monopolizing the representation of interests, and mounting a Kulturkampf in the realm of the arts, the family, and other social issues tell of the growing tendency to create an "Islamic episcopacy" in Iran.[418]

> Khomeini's practice of issuing authoritative fatwas, obedience to which is made compulsory, comes close to endowing the top jurist with powers not dissimilar to those of the pope in the Catholic Church. After all, compliance with a particular cleric's fatwas in the past had not been mandatory.[419]

> In creating this faux Christian hierarchy, Islamists invented something more Western than Islamic. In similar fashion, Islamists have turned Friday into a Sabbath, something it had not previously been. Traditionally, Friday was a day of congregating for prayer, not a day of rest. Indeed, the whole idea of the Sabbath is alien to the vehemently monotheistic spirit of Islam, which deems the notion of God needing a day of rest falsely anthropomorphic....A day of rest so smacks of Jewish and Christian practice that some traditional Islamic authorities actually discouraged taking Friday off. In most places and times, Muslims did work on Fridays, interrupted only by the communal service. In modern times, Muslim states imitated Europe and adopted a day of rest.[420]

Pipes further saw Khomeinism, though a modern synthesis of Western and Islamic ideas, as fitting perfectly within the broad confines of Islamist thought that applies with equal ease to Sunni theorists like al-Bana and Qutb, and that refuses to recognize any debt to the West:

> One cannot emphasize too much the distinction between Islam - plain Islam - and its fundamentalist version.... Muslims have devised three political responses to modernity - secularism, reformism and Islamism. The first of these holds that Muslims can only advance by emulating the West.... Whereas secularism forthrightly calls for learning from the West, reformism selectively appropriates from it.... Islamism has three main features: a devotion to the sacred law, a rejection of Western influences, and the transformation of faith into ideology. Islamism holds that Muslims lag behind the West because they're not good Muslims....Contrary to its reputation, Islamism is not a way back; as a contemporary ideology it offers not a means to return to some old-fashioned way of life but a way of navigating the shoals of modernization....While Islamism is often seen as a form of traditional Islam, it is something profoundly different. Traditional Islam seeks to teach humans how to live in accord with God's will, whereas Islamism aspires to create a new order. The first is self-confident, the second deeply defensive. The one emphasizes individuals, the latter communities. The former is a personal credo, the latter a political ideology.[421]

Khomeinism hit the region like a bolt from the blue when it seized control of Iran in the 1979 revolution. Its potential for galvanizing the region's long downtrodden Shiites seemed obvious. After all, Zionism had managed to turn the world's politically flaccid Jewish community into a positive force for ethnic self-determination in the space of a few short decades—for the first time since 136.[422] Could Khomeinism do the same for the politics of Shiism? Given the sizable Shiite population scattered throughout the Sunni world—with a particular concentration in the oil-rich arc around the Persian Gulf—no sane Sunni leader wanted to risk learning the answer.[423]

The Arab League managed to coordinate its response with surprising speed—perhaps the closest thing to a unified Sunni Arab action that the world has yet seen. Within a year of the revolution's consolidation of power in Iran, Saddam Hussein had launched a brutal attack. His nominal reason—reclaiming rights to the Shatt-al-Arab waterway that he had relinquished under duress to the Shah—should have been of little interest to the other Arab countries.[424] Nevertheless, the Arab oil states shouldered the financial burden for this eight-year war, whose real objective was to serve as a bulwark against the spread of Khomeinism.[425] (Syria, as noted above, was Iran's sole Arab ally).[426] When the war finally ended, Saddam turned to the Arab League expecting payment for services rendered: control over OPEC policy and an *anschluss* with Kuwait.[427] Things didn't quite work out the way that he had planned.

Iraq

Iraq's August 1990 invasion of Kuwait was a watershed event that might have transformed the region. For only the second time (Nasser's early years were the first), a Sunni ruler had proposed a credible plan capable of making the putative empire a reality. Saddam's absorption of Kuwait would have doubled his capacity for oil production.[428] His control over OPEC policy, strengthened by his proximity to Saudi Arabia and the UAE, would have allowed him to cut overall supply—thereby doubling oil prices. This nearly instantaneous quadrupling of his revenues would have thrown the entire OECD into deep recession. Flush with cash and with a stranglehold over the global economy, Saddam could have invested in an army formidable enough to vanquish the Zionists and eliminate Israel. With that feather in his cap, he would have consolidated de facto control over West Asia and elevated his Baghdad-based Sunni Empire into a major world power. From the perspective of Sunni Arab Imperialism, it was not a bad plan.

Unfortunately for the imperial cause, most other Arab rulers had gotten used to ruling. Saddam's plan put them in an untenable position. It forced them to choose between the unspoken inchoate imperialism at the bedrock of all Sunni Arab movements and the state-centric benefits they had come to enjoy. The ruling families of Saudi Arabia, the smaller GCC countries, and Jordan all found themselves in a situation they shared with the Israelis: They had become potential targets of a putative Emperor's guns. In each of these states, the rulers found themselves in sudden need of a nationalist spirit, while many of their subjects felt greater affinity for the Empire. Which would they choose? Nation-state or Empire?

In a shocking display of status quo thinking, the American team of George H.W. Bush and James Baker worked deftly to alleviate the need for choice. Through the sheer force of foreign intervention, they defused the immediate crisis while locking in place all of its precursors and causes. They ensured that the Saudis and Kuwaitis could enjoy the security of the nation-state system without fully developing Saudi or Kuwaiti citizenries, without inculcating a nationalist sense distinct from Arabism and Islam, and without foregoing plans for an eventual unified empire. American policy under the Bush/Baker team thus preserved the Middle East's most dangerous Pan movement at precisely the moment that the movement's internal contradictions threatened to destroy it—and consequently to free its captive states and peoples to develop distinct national identities and promote their human capital development. As I wrote at the time:

> [The United States has] acceded to the convoluted notion that our Arab allies are doing us a favor by allowing us to stand up to Iraqi aggression. Were the coalition to fall apart tomorrow, the United States would suffer a loss of prestige on the world stage. The governments of Saudi Arabia, the United Arab Emirates, and Oman would probably not see New Year's Day; those of Egypt and Syria would be severely weakened. The United States should not bear primary responsibility for maintaining this coalition. Our Arab allies should be taking every measure possible to guarantee that we remain.
>
> We should be encouraging the Saudis to embrace some important Western ideas, such as the nation-state. Democracy has little hope of taking hold in the Arab world in the near future. Capitalism, on the other hand, holds great promise. The wealthy rulers in the Gulf have long enjoyed its benefits; they should be taught to accept its responsibilities, as well. The Saudis (and other Gulf leaders) should be encouraged to disavow their mythical positions as custodians of the great Arab resource (oil) by proclaiming their own national mineral rights. They should also be pushed to call for an end to terrorism and a need for long-term regional stability.
>
> The United States should encourage the Saudis to join the Camp David accords. Current political reality makes the Saudis and the Israelis natural allies. Recent Saudi statements about the danger of a well-armed Iraq and the affirmation of Palestinian rights without an acceptance of the PLO's leadership, all mirror long-held Israeli positions.
>
> A peace process begun along these lines would help the Saudis, the Israelis, the Egyptians, the United States, and all Palestinian Arabs willing to live in peace with Israel. It would hurt Iraq, the PLO, and their radical followers. There is no rational reason for the exclusion of Israel from the anti-Iraq coalition. Israel's exclusion is based on an ideology that is

deeply rooted in the Arabs' anti-Western myth system. If the Saudis are unwilling to negotiate with Israel during times of clear, common security concerns, no peaceful settlement can reasonably be expected.

The rest of the world should be as eager to embrace newly realistic Arab nations as they were to welcome Eastern Europe. The conditions for acceptance, however, must be absolute: a renunciation of anti-Western mythology, and a demonstrated commitment to peace, security, regional stability, and economic integration. If several Arab states accept these terms, history will record our current actions in the Gulf as a major success. If, on the other hand, we allow our Arab allies to cling to their myths and their hatred, we are simply wasting American time, money, and lives. The Arab world will remain unstable, bloody, and hopelessly biased against the West.[429]

Over the next decade, a combination of military force, diplomacy, sanctions, and inspections, kept these regional tensions bottled up, with no attempt to address the inherent internal conflicts or the underlying tension. After 9/11, the U.S. shifted strategies. Unfortunately—and fatally for the new strategy—George W. Bush never explained to the American or global public why his father's prolonged stalemate strategy had been such a disaster. To the contrary, he and his team implied that the strategy he had inherited had been appropriate for a pre-9/11 world.[430]

The American and global publics thus watched George W. Bush invade Iraq in 2003 without understanding why the invasion had "suddenly" become necessary. That left them unprepared for the dramatic consequences of the shift in strategy. By toppling Saddam's regime, the George W. Bush administration allowed myriad pent up forces to explode simultaneously.

The repercussions of that explosion continue to reverberate. Though early positive returns on the 2003 invasion included an end to Libya's nuclear program[431] and the Cedar Revolution in Lebanon[432]—as the Administration's understanding of the prevailing false narrative had predicted—the effects soon deviated from those rosy predictions. Iraqi stability proved unsustainable without long-term American military support—a seemingly endless commitment for which Bush had not prepared the American people, and that ran strongly counter to the vision of his twice-elected successor. The de facto American policy of the past decade-and-a-half, combining George W. Bush's unleashing of pent-up forces and Barack Obama's abandonment of those forces to their own trajectories, whipsawed the region's vaunted sclerosis into levels of instability not seen in fifty years. In the badly misnamed "Arab Spring" of 2010/11, longstanding regimes fell in Tunisia, Libya, Egypt, and Yemen; Syria and Iraq tumbled into instability, and at least four civil wars and one military coup soon followed.[433]

Not surprisingly, the two biggest winners of the early twenty-first century have been Revolutionary Khomeinism and Sunni Arab Imperialism—the philosophies dominating the region's two largest ethnic groups. President Bush freed these movements when he altered the regional order without a viable plan for a successful reordering. President Obama then assisted their ascendance. His military withdrawal from the region removed an impediment to their rise. His downplaying of America's relationship with the forces most likely to oppose them—the Arab states, the Egyptian military, and Israel—reduced the benefits accruing to pro-American Middle Easterners. And his diplomatic engagement of both Sunni Islamists (in Erdoğan's Turkey, Qatar, and among the Muslim Brotherhood)[434] and the Revolutionary Khomeinists (in Iran),[435] empowered and strengthened both groups—as well as numerous other groups who share their basic philosophies but differ on tactics and leadership.

Any fair reading of the Obama foreign policy suggests that the President understands the benefits he has conferred on the imperialists and the revolutionaries, but he believes that they can be coopted into the world of responsible state actors.[436] To date, this strategy has led to the effective dissolution of four Arab states: Libya, Iraq, Syria, and Yemen. It has allowed the Islamic State to seize sizable swathes of territory in the first three;[437] given the Iranians a toehold in which to foment Khomeinist revolution in the last three (along with Lebanon);[438] returned Iran fully to the international commercial and diplomatic communities;[439] set the Islamic Republic on a glide path to nuclearization;[440] started a regional arms race;[441] allowed Hamas to rearm amidst growing international respectability;[442] strained relations with pro-American forces in Egypt;[443] and invited Russia back into the region.[444] The only open question at this late stage of the Obama Administration is whether he will avail himself of his lame duck status to savage Israel at the UN, act against long-term American interests, and recognize an independent Palestine—as many of his supporters would like him to do.[445] At the end of the day, President Obama's Middle East policy has been a gift to revolutionaries and imperialists throughout the region. Quite a legacy, indeed.

Chapter 15. The New Narrative

Our journey through the past is nearing its end. We have repositioned ourselves to look to the future. Our quick review of empirical evidence has given us the core of a new narrative—one that, unlike conventional wisdom, actually explains both what has happened to the Middle East since the dissolution of the Ottoman Empire and what is happening there today. A proper perspective on the Middle East—and thus the appropriate basis for American policy—must recognize that the region's dominant forces have been the supremacist beliefs of its largest ethnic groups and the reactions of the many minorities with whom they share a home.

Stated simply, the Middle East is, and for at least the past century has been, a region beset by frustrated imperialism, revolution, and the quest for minority self-determination. The Sunni Arabs, as the region's the largest ethnic group, set the tone. They are torn between an abstract desire for a unified empire and tribal or local affiliations that defy such unification. Their rulers, who must never speak the truth, have no intention of relinquishing their thrones to a putative unifier—should a viable candidate arise. Nevertheless, the Sunni Arabs view all forms of minority ethnic self-determination as secession from their inchoate empire, and thus remain irretrievably opposed to it. They have deemed an entire segment of their own Sunni Arab population expendable, trapped in a hate group that may someday achieve statehood in name but can never emerge as a nation—for the sole purpose of thwarting the Zionist dream of Jewish self-determination in the historic Jewish homeland.

The Shiite revolutionary Khomeinists, representing the region's second largest group, seek to export their glorious theocratic revolution—simultaneously bringing the world one step closer to messianic deliverance and elevating the status of their long-suffering co-religionists. Like all revolutionary movements, Khomeinism thrives on chaos. Someday soon it is likely to place itself, its friends, and its allies beneath a nuclear umbrella as it pursues its eschatological dream.

Meanwhile, the region's smaller ethnic groups either push for ethnic self-determination or face likely extermination. On this count, the Jews have been successful; the Maronites less so; the Kurds seem poised to make the leap; the Druze have reportedly begun to consider the question; and the Alawites may find sanctuary in self-determination when the Syrian rupture is complete. The prospects currently look less bright for the region's many other ethnicities, including but not exclusively those grounded in Christianity.

American Strategy and Policy

Chapter 16. Geopolitics

Objectives

Understanding recent Middle Eastern history is one thing. Charting a course for American policy is another—and the terrain is unlikely to prove static. By the time our next President has settled into office, the region could boast an entrenched and growing Caliphate, a deepening and permanent Russian military presence, and an internationally recognized if still nonexistent terrorist State of Palestine. The genocidal razing of ancient Christian and other minority faith communities across the region is likely to continue apace. Iran will almost certainly reinvest its sanctions-relief windfall in ways that heighten Sunni-Shia tensions. A conventional arms race will likely be accelerating. Several countries could be on the brink of nuclearization. And those are just the known unknowns.

The new administration could enter eager to follow the course that President Obama has set. The key to that strategy has been recasting the U.S. as a detached neutral in the region's various disputes, with the goal of minimizing military engagement. Toward those ends, the U.S., during the Obama years, has alienated its traditional allies in Israel, Egypt, Jordan, and the GCC (particularly Saudi Arabia). American diplomatic overtures under Secretaries Clinton and Kerry have capitulated to Iranian and Russian demands, while reaching out to the Muslim Brotherhood and other Sunni Islamists. The Obama team—and former Secretary Clinton on the campaign trail—have praised European efforts to address the widespread and growing problem of dislocation and refugee flows by resettling Middle Eastern refugees in Western countries. Most leading Democrats have echoed that preference, and by all indication appear to favor Sunni Muslim immigrants over the Christians, Yazidis, and other minority faiths who face genocide as well as dislocation.

These Obama Administration policies have proved controversial among Americans, but the dispute is largely partisan. To the extent that the Obama foreign policy has invited criticism from within the Democratic caucus, it has more often been for remaining overly aggressive and engaged rather than for withdrawing precipitously and abandoning traditional allies. The many voices raising the latter set of points skew heavily Republican; foreign policy has become subject to the same partisan polarization that has long characterized social and economic policy. That split will complicate the next President's task of selling a Middle Eastern strategy to the American public.

In approaching that challenge, however, the recent European experience may prove instructive—and helpful. German Chancellor Angela Merkel, who led the drive to admit a flood of refugees into the EU and labeled the idea's opponents heartless or racist, has now conceded that her policy failed.[446] Unintegrated Muslim refugees are changing the social fabric of Europe.[447] As is all too often the case with societies in the early stages of unraveling, a dangerous wave of anti-Semitism is roiling the continent.[448] The situation has become so dire—and so blatant—that French Prime Minister Manual Valls has recognized the fight against anti-Semitism cum anti-Zionism as a critical front in the fight for the Fifth Republic's survival.[449] Many observers recognize Merkel's refugee policy as the critical factor in pushing Great Britain's decision to leave the EU.[450]

Perhaps even worse than the direct damage that the refugees are inflicting on the EU, they are accelerating the radicalization of the Muslim communities already resident in Europe.[451] The Islamic State has not been bashful about seeding the refugee flows with sympathizers.[452] Though Western journalists seem obsessed with proving that few if any refugees are fighters, such reporting overlooks the obvious: the most useful sympathizers for the Caliph to send into Europe are recruiters, not terrorists. Islamic State activists savvy enough to pass as peaceful around EU officials while radicalizing Muslim citizens of their host states would wreak far more damage on the continent than a few bombs.

Should the EU continue on its present course, its people would do well to study one of the pivotal dates of European history. In 732, Charles Martel halted the Islamic conquest at the Pyrenees;[453] in the 122 years since Mohammed's first prophesy, the Caliphate had spread from the Arabian Peninsula's Red Sea coast, through the

Middle East and North Africa, to include the entire Iberian Peninsula. Martel's victory at the Battle of Tours preserved Europe for Christendom. Though few Westerners spend much time dwelling on eighth century battles, there is little doubt that the defeat still rankles Islamists. The Islamic State's Caliphate seeks to reclaim all territory that Islam has ever held and lost—then reengage in the battles that the revered leaders of the first Caliphates met with defeat. Should the U.S. follow Europe's disastrous lead—as President Obama, Hillary Clinton, John Kerry, and many leading Democrats advocate[454]—the entire West would likely slide inexorably into *dhimmitude*, as its political, academic, media, and opinion elite noted at each juncture—with increasing accuracy—that the alternative to capitulation is war.

President Obama has done his best to ensure that his successor follows the path he has set; his military budgets, and his tension with top Generals and Admirals, have left the U.S. military at its weakest point in decades. A successor seeking to reverse many of the Obama policies would have to begin with a serious military buildup that may prove unpopular given the weak economy and enormous debts he is also leaving behind. Still, the new administration could choose a starkly different course. The next national security team could choose to learn not only from the Obama failures, but from the varying failures of each of our four post-Cold War Presidents:

George H.W. Bush's mistakes should teach them the importance of forcing Arab/Islamic leaders seeking American support to make difficult choices *as a precondition* for that support. Bill Clinton's mistakes should teach them that all attempts to conciliate the Jew-hating, genocidal Palestinian movement are contributors to regional instability, not solutions to it—and that any polity this hate movement governed would become, at best, another dysfunctional Arab/Islamic autocracy, and far more likely a safe haven for terror. George W. Bush's mistakes should teach them that ample resources, time, and patience are needed to build the infrastructure of a liberal society before one can plausibly emerge, and that democratic elections held prior to securing minority rights are more likely to foster factional fighting than to squelch it.

Ironically, though Barack Obama repeated the mistakes of George H.W. Bush and Bill Clinton while adding more than a few of his own, he created an opening for innovative strategic thinking. By inverting decades of bipartisan American policy in the region, and by personalizing new key relationships as non-binding Executive Agreements rather than vesting them in American law,[455] President Obama has cleared the decks. His successor will have greater latitude to approach the region with a clear vision and a fresh perspective than has any President since at least Harry Truman. The critical task facing the next President will thus be to move from a fresh understanding of the Middle East to a strategic vision consistent with that understanding, and to enact policies that serve American short-term interests and long-term values.

Appropriate policies must combine idealism and pragmatism. From the idealistic perspective, certain core liberal values should guide American foreign policy. U.S. policy has always been—and should remain—anti-imperialist, anti-revolutionary, and pluralist. The classic liberalism at the heart of American idealism begins with individual rights and the recognition that a functioning liberal society must strike a balance between institutional integrity and individual self-expression. It acts to ensure that every individual has the right to live in a society respectful of his or her basic identity—ethnicity, faith, gender, race, etc. It accepts that all people may own and trade property, deserve at least a significant portion of the benefits of their labors, and bear at least primary responsibility for their own decisions and actions. Admittedly, the American record in supporting these ideals has been human rather than perfect, but they remain core beliefs that should guide long-term policy considerations. In the specific context of the Middle East, they translate into some clear long-term strategic objectives requiring a concerted, directed combination of American military, diplomatic, commercial, and cultural inputs.

From a geopolitical perspective, President Obama's successor will have to begin by aligning American military *and humanitarian* activity in the region with the local rules of engagement. That shift will enable U.S. military planners and diplomatic personnel to approach several already-identifiable imperatives:

- Countering the Khomeinist revolution;
- Defusing the inchoate imperialist movement currently operating as the Islamic State's Caliphate;
- Recalibrating American and international attitudes toward refugees;
- Promoting ethnic self-determination; and
- Assembling an international coalition large enough to move any positive developments beyond unilateral American action and into broad acceptance.

The Rules of Engagement

Much has been written about the tepid response to the attacks in Fallujah in the spring of 2004, when the world awoke to see front-page photos of charred American bodies dangling from a bridge.[456] Relatively few of the discussions, however, have noted the implicit message that this scene sent to the locals: America will not avenge even its own. Who could believe that America would avenge its friends? This message creates perverse incentives. The U.S. has invested (heavily if inadequately) in "hearts and minds" campaigns designed to preach the benefits of pro-American liberalism while ignoring a basic tenet of that liberalism: rational decision-making nets costs and benefits.

The American insistence upon following Western-defined civilized standards in setting its rules of engagement ensures that the costs of being anti-American will always be lower than the costs of being anti-Islamist, anti-revolutionary, or even generically anti-radical. In an environment focused on minimizing costs rather than on maximizing benefits (as most crisis zones are), rational thinkers will gravitate towards anti-Americanism. The only way to reverse this trend is to increase the costs of anti-Americanism.

The 2007 surge that George W. Bush and General Petraeus enacted against the near-universal advice of America's elder statesmen was a small step in the right direction. The surge combined a significant increase in American power inflicting massive damage on anti-American forces with increased incentives to those who allied with the U.S. It succeeded precisely as long as it kept rational thinkers capable of concluding that pro-American positions conferred net benefits upon them, their families, their villages, their tribes, and their ethnoreligious groups. The success collapsed, however, when the rational calculus changed. President Bush lacked the time, and President Obama lacked the inclination, to sustain the proper incentives.

The 2011 withdrawal of American troops from Iraq doomed those who had incurred the risk of pro-Americanism to brutal retaliation—against themselves and all they hold dear. Few in the Arab/Islamic world are likely to forget the lesson. And even among those few, President Obama's antipathy towards Israel provided little reassurance. Far from making the U.S. appear more attractive to Arabs, those caught in the cross-currents saw it as further proof that the U.S. is not worth befriending.

Taken together, for any American policy to have any positive effect in the region, those who speak for America must respect the rationality of the people who live in anarchic, crisis-torn war zones. A small number will always be our friends. A larger number, possessing values antithetical to our own, will always be our enemies. The majority, however, will be persuadable one way or the other. An America unwilling to learn, internalize, and play by the local rules will prove singularly unpersuasive.

Containing Revolutionary Shiism

The U.S. must lead an international effort to contain the Khomeinist revolution either until it falls under its own weight or until its nuclearization appears imminent. That means returning to an explicit policy of regime change in Iran, employing American diplomatic efforts wherever possible to effect economic, information, and education campaigns directed against the regime. The Islamic Republic may moderate its tone from time to time, but it will never moderate its behavior. It will continue deploying the strategies is has used since its birth in 1979: It will sponsor and export terror, foment tension with its Sunni neighbors, spread virulent, genocidal anti-Semitism, and threaten everyone within reach with conventional and soon nuclear war. Regime change is critical if Persia—and the rest of the world—is ever to emerge from the cloud cast by this messianic band of murderers.

There is little doubt that President Obama succeeded in his efforts to invert longstanding American policy vis-à-vis Iran; he touts it as one of his singular successes.[457] Nor is there any doubt that his Executive Agreement with Iran has strengthened and enriched the regime while weakening its domestic opponents. (Even the Obama team concedes these points; the debate is whether these gifts to the regime will turn Iran into a responsible state actor).[458] Russia's reemergence as a regional player is likely to strengthen Teheran's hand even further—and that's in addition to the country's likely nuclearization and reintegration into international commerce. Furthermore, the Obama years witnessed two possible wedges with which to push regime change—the Green Movement arising in the wake of the stolen 2009 election, and the internal crisis destabilizing Iran's most important ally, Syria's Assad regime—whose like may not recur soon. Should a third such opportunity appear, the U.S. must be prepared to seize it.

If anything, the Iranian Mullahcracy appears further entrenched today than at almost any time since 1979. Yet the U.S. can never reconcile its values or interests with those of the Islamic Republic; stability is impossible in a region hosting a powerful revolutionary state intent upon exporting its revolution. The Islamic Republic is fulfilling the fear that motivated the eight-year Iran/Iraq war—it is galvanizing Shiite communities across the region. Iran's recent successes in supporting Shiite insurgencies in Bahrain and in Yemen have seeped into the eastern provinces of Saudi Arabia—home to most of Saudi Arabia's oil fields as well as most of its Shia.[459]

In the post-Obama years, the U.S. must redouble its efforts to topple the Iranian regime in favor of leaders exhibiting the traditional quietist Shiite acceptance of a division between clerical and temporal authority. The sanctions-relief windfall, Iran's imminent reintegration into the global commercial arena, and its ongoing unverifiable nuclear program make regime change more critical than ever—and increase the likelihood that American military involvement will be necessary to achieve or to secure it. As a result, President Obama's successor must prepare the American public and regional allies for the possibility of armed conflict, while nevertheless restricting significant military intervention to escalations (i.e., further, and now inevitable, movements toward WMD) or expansions (i.e., continued or ongoing exports of irregular international terror forces) of the Khomeinist revolution.

Defeating the Islamic State

The overriding American goal in the Middle East must be defusing the inchoate pan-Sunni Arab imperial movement. Because that movement's current manifestation is the Islamic State's Caliphate, American and allied militaries must crush the Caliphate by whatever means necessary. While military analysts must determine just how much of an effort is required—and how much collateral damage is likely—it is clear that a fully committed engagement is a prerequisite for a decisive victory. U.S. policy must refuse all attempts to accommodate the imperial impulse in any form, whether through a breakaway "moderate" faction of the Islamic State, the far better established Muslim Brotherhood (properly recognized as the terrorist organization it is), or under the auspices of any other group. It must also promote the assertion of individual national identities, and foster a concept of citizenry among the subjects of the remaining Sunni Arab states.

American theorists and strategists should recognize that this reorientation of Sunni Arab thought away from its imperial aspirations is likely to constitute their greatest geopolitical challenge. In particular, American policy must sideline the Arab League as an artifact of vestigial imperialism. Among the various incomprehensible blunders following the American ouster of Saddam, the rush to get Iraq back into the Arab League stands out— both for its misreading of regional dynamics and for the lack of criticism it received.[460] The Arab League is a tool of Sunni Arab Imperialism. As a toothless mechanism of an inchoate empire, its ability to achieve anything positive is severely constrained. Its record at preventing positive developments, on the other hand, is impressive. Because almost all positive developments in the region operate against imperial goals, any hardline appeal to imperial ideals generates immediate broad sympathy. The elimination of the Arab League is a critical concrete step toward defusing the Sunni Arab world's inchoate imperialism. The U.S. must take the lead in replacing it with alternative regional organizations attuned to the needs of military cooperation, economic development, and regional integration.

Rethinking Refugees

The U.S. must lead an international effort to recalibrate the treatment of refugees. Large numbers of stateless people, while indicative of a grave past injustice, are also guarantors of future instability and cascading future injustices. Where possible, the U.S. should create and enforce distinct safe-haven regions for each ethnic group. These safe havens, in turn, should lead to an arc of ethnonational states consolidating and housing minority populations. The preferred approach to refugees should involve resettlement among ethnic kinsmen in culturally similar environments—and the allocation of ample resources to aid in the resettlement. The U.S. must lead the world in divorcing the concepts of refugee resettlement (critical for stability, peace, and individual liberty) and refugee compensation (important for longer-term notions of justice). In particular, the U.S. must spearhead an international drive to build a compensation fund, beginning with the assets expropriated from or abandoned by previous waves of Middle Eastern refugees and exiles dating back to the post-WWII period, for administration and disbursal to those who fled or were resettled. Governments—whether existing or emergent—representing the various ethnic groups should take the lead in that disbursal. The U.S. should generally oppose the movement of large refugee flows out of the region and into Europe or the Americas.

Promoting Self-Determination

American policy must promote ethnic self-determination and stability through the consolidation and creation of ethnonational safe-haven states. The U.S. must emphasize the need for responsible self-determination. Given the overlap among historic homelands, no ethnic group anywhere can sustain a state across its entire historic homeland without disenfranchising another (neighboring) ethnic group. American policy should promulgate the notion that a modern ethnonational state in part of a historic homeland is a complete realization of ethnic self-determination, and establish a relinquishment of all political claims beyond state boundaries as a quid pro quo for integration into the international community. In assessing claims of ethnic identity, the U.S. should lead an international effort to consider the historically unique nature of any group making such a claim; the longer the group has differentiated itself from its neighbors, the more weight the international community should give to the claim. In the Middle Eastern context, religious affiliation is likely to define most distinctly recognizable ethnicities, with linguistic commonality playing a secondary role—an artifact, most recently, of the region's Ottoman legacy and the millet system. As the past few decades have shown, postcolonial national labels of recent vintage do not play a major role in defining either individual or communal identity. They are thus effectively useless in defining Middle Eastern nations.

These principles are hardly new, and the willingness of ethnic leadership to accept them provides a good indication of a nation sufficiently mature and confident to direct its newfound state toward internal development rather than residual animosity. The pre-state Zionist relinquishment of all claims east of the Jordan river and the willingness to partition even the remaining sliver of the Jewish homeland, along with Israel's actual and proffered withdrawals from further parts of that same historic homeland, illustrate these principles nicely in a regional context.[461] The consolidation of the Greek state between the 1820s and the 1970s,[462] and the movement of ethnic Germans out of Czechoslovakia and Poland following the Second World War[463] provide additional excellent examples in a European context.

To the extent that American or international troops liberate territory from the Islamic State or other terror-driven, anarchic, or revolutionary forces, the victors should not be bashful about redrawing international borders, or about effecting population exchanges, where necessary to consolidate safe-haven states and to promote regional stability.

At a bare minimum, American strategists should conceive an arc of ethnonational states from Jewish Israel, north through an increasingly Christian Lebanon, Jabal Druze, and Alawite/Shiite Latakia, then east through Kurdistan—largely reviving and expanding upon some stillborn ideas from the immediate post-Ottoman period.[464] American policy should explicitly reject any pretense that the proven stillborn labels that the European imperialists assigned to various primarily Sunni groups living throughout the Levant—Syrian, Iraqi, Lebanese, Jordanian, Palestinian—constitute distinct nations worthy of independent states. The evidence is overwhelming that these labels have failed to inculcate distinctness along the lines that the imperialists considered useful.

As we noted at the start of our journey, we must have enough respect for the region's people to accept them as they see themselves, not as the international community would like to see them. Their actions, over the course of decades, have made it clear how they see themselves. Sunni Arabs, Kurds, Shiites, Druze, Jews, and Christians are meaningful identities in the Middle East; Syrians, Iraqis, Palestinians, Lebanese, and Jordanians are not. Within the former grouping, people stand side-by-side fighting to preserve their shared identities. Within the latter, they are just as likely to fire on themselves as on those who have been assigned different labels.

Building Coalitions

While American leadership will prove critical in defeating the supremacist movements of inchoate Sunni imperialism and Shiite revolutionary Khomeinism, and in establishing safe-haven states for the region's minority ethnicities, the U.S. cannot go it alone. Redrawn maps and new regional orders cannot move forward without international recognition. The U.S. must assemble a sufficiently broad swathe of the international community eager to secure stability—even if their role in shaping it is negligible. The key to assembling such a coalition, as always, is a focus on the self-interest of putative members.

In the Middle East, oil is the factor most often determinative of a nation's geostrategic preferences. The split begins within OPEC itself, and in particular among the OPEC members touching the Persian Gulf. These countries have always split into two camps, the "Price Hawks" and the "Demand Hawks."[465] Price Hawks—notably Iran and Iraq—need significant short-term revenues to support their sizable populations. Demand Hawks—notably Saudi Arabia, Kuwait, Qatar, and the UAE—seek to ensure that demand for their oil continues throughout the foreseeable future. These strategic postures are not ideological; population, revenue needs, and reserve levels play far greater roles in determining which countries pursue which strategies than does the nature of the regime (e.g., Iran remained a Price Hawk when the Shah's governance gave way to that of the Mullahs).[466]

This strategic split has a significant effect on regional politics. The Demand Hawk preference for moderate oil prices requires stability and predictability, with supply levels set to generate reasonable profits without motivating investments in alternative fuel sources (including oil exploration outside the region). A Price Hawk's revenue needs, on the other hand, require supply levels tight enough to elevate prices—but not tight enough to constrain the Price Hawk's own sales. Effecting a Price Hawk strategy thus requires "persuading" other producers to produce far below their capacities— or, even better, taking competing capacity off line. As a result, regional stability tends to favor Demand Hawks over Price Hawks; instability often has the opposite effect. In a similar vein, the precipitous drop in oil prices between 2014 and 2016 arose largely as an economic weapon that Saudi Arabia deployed against Iran.

For countries outside the region, the preference between the strategies hinges on whether they too are oil producers (in which case, high prices help them) or consumers (whose citizens need low oil prices). Again, these positions derive from resources, populations, and economic structures, not ideologies. Russia—a petrostate with a weak non-resource economy—stands to benefit from crises capable of reducing Middle Eastern oil capacity and production, even as it takes a hard line against the Islamic State, Islamist terror, and other forms of Sunni Arab imperialism. This combination of Russian interests suggests that the emerging alignment of Russia, Iran, the Assads in Syria, and a Shiite-led central government in Iraq, is likely robust. All four share an interest in defeating the Islamic State while driving oil prices upward. US diplomatic maneuvering seeking support for its regional agenda is likely to meet its greatest challenges within this group.

On the flip side, however, the EU, China, India, Japan, South Korea, and many others need to keep oil prices relatively low and thus stand to benefit from anything increasing the stability and security of supply. Among the region's non-OPEC members, Jordan and Egypt share the consumer interest in stable, low oil prices, while Israel's sophisticated, export-driven, technology-heavy economy— not to mention its security interests—benefits greatly from regional stability and global growth.

The U.S. should leverage this widespread economic imperative of protecting the flow of Middle Eastern oil when seeking support for its policies, particularly those related to the refugee flows, population exchanges, and ethnonational states necessary to secure the region. The U.S. should also continue the expansion of its own oil industry, through traditional exploration, hydrofracking, and other new extraction technologies, to move beyond energy self-sufficiency and into exporter status. Such a conversion of the U.S. from a significant oil importer to a significant oil exporter will increase American diplomatic strength. It will also likely enable significant international support for redrawing the map of the Middle East in ways that enshrine minority rights, enable the human capital development of both Sunni Arabs and ethnic minorities, and protect the integrity of the global oil trade.

Chapter 17. Soft Power

Hard power, whether military, diplomatic, or economic, is rarely sufficient to effect positive regional change. Though hard power may win wars, soft power—the promotion of new ideas and opportunities through education and ideological warfare—is at least as important when it comes to winning the peace. For the Middle East to join the rule-based global international order, it must incorporate at least the concepts of nation-states and the rule of law into the regional gestalt—not as rhetorical devices but as ingrained realities. The inculcation of these ideas must form the basis of America's soft-power campaign.

Once again, several key objectives are readily identifiable:
- Restoring American honor and credibility;
- Promoting bilateral diplomacy;
- Strengthening the "nation" aspects of the nation-state system throughout the region;
- Promoting the growth of civil society outside the Mosque;
- Supporting a reformist agenda capable of winning "hearts and minds" at home throughout the Middle East;
- Identifying, cultivating, and rewarding regional actors eager to become part of the solution.

American Credibility

President Obama set exactly the wrong tone for the region in his 2009 Cairo speech.[467] By addressing Muslims as Muslims rather than as citizens of their respective states, he fed the agendas of both inchoate imperialism and global *jihad*. His attempt to relate to that audience on a personal level was more likely to offend than to engage: "I am a Christian, but my father came from a Kenyan family that includes generations of Muslims."[468] Even a cursory knowledge of *sharia* (Islamic law) should have reminded him that the child of a Muslim father is a Muslim, that a Muslim who renounces his faith is an apostate, and that the penalty for apostasy is death.[469] Obama thus asked an audience that he explicitly addressed as Muslims to accept the religious identity that he had adopted under Western conventions in direct contravention of *sharia*.

He then compounded his elevation of Western sensibilities above those culturally appropriate to his audience when he criticized and apologized for past American actions, (specifically though hardly exclusively those of the Bush Administration).[470] In a confidential 1964 article for the CIA's in-house journal—declassified thirty years after its initial publication pursuant to the Freedom of Information Act—Peter Naffsinger warned diplomats and case officers working in the Arab world about precisely this error:

> The American can apologize for revealed shortcomings and gain respect and prestige with an honest effort to correct his own errors. In our culturally determined scale of values the achieving of impersonal objectivity with regard to facts and truth is thus more important than preserving a man's personal dignity before the world at large....The Arab in his society is likewise expected to show personal integrity in order to be socially acceptable. He, however, manifests his honor and integrity by making a public, outward impression of dignity derived from an ostensible lack of guilt. Even if facts and conditions speak to the contrary, the social veneer of non-guilt must be maintained evident and dominant if he is to achieve the socially demanded face. Dignity and stature are granted only to those who show themselves as flawless; the society of the Arab world has no place or respect for one whose faults or errors come to public knowledge. Blame, fault, or error accruing to an Arab personally brings his immediate fall from social grace and a loss of dignity or face. He therefore feels revulsion and bitterness for anything that tends to compromise him in this way.[471]

Naffsinger's contemporary critics complain that his language is patronizing and politically incorrect—and then concede that he is substantively correct: When speaking to an Arab or Islamic audience, it is critical to exhibit honor and dignity as they see it, not as an American might see it (a rule we adopted as a prerequisite for this journey).[472] While Presidents Bush and Obama may have been rivals within the American political system, and while Obama may have been correct about Bush's unpopularity in the Arab/Islamic world, his critique of Bush's behavior in the Arab world was misplaced in Cairo; he spoke for America and defamed the previous leadership of his own tribe.

President Obama reinforced that impression of dishonor throughout his Presidency: His repeated public excoriations of Israel made the U.S. appear less reliable as an ally.[473] His refusal to enforce his own red lines in Syria made it less likely that anyone would take his future threats seriously.[474] His constant prevarications about the Iranian nuclear negotiations proved that he was willing to lie to allies.[475] Obama did himself no favors by leaving America's erstwhile allies in Iraq and Afghanistan unprotected;[476] by showing greater sympathy for Hamas in its wars against Israel than did even Egypt, Saudi Arabia, and Jordan;[477] or by handing over a longstanding American ally, Egyptian President Hosni Mubarak, to the Tahrir Square protestors.[478] Each of those abandonments simultaneously reduced the benefits and increased the costs of allying with the U.S. Obama's actions favoring the supremacist Muslim Brotherhood over the relatively pro-American Egyptian military;[479] opposing Egyptian military moves against Islamic State fighters in Libya;[480] and leaking Israeli intelligence necessary to contain the Syrian civil war;[481] reduced the likelihood that anyone would want to coordinate military or intelligence activities with the U.S. And he added insult to injury by ignoring Mahmoud Abbas's rejection of every American proposal forwarded in the name of peace while placing the blame on Binyamin Netanyahu who accepted many but not all of them;[482] and by refusing to support Saudi encounters with Iranian forces in Bahrain and Iranian proxies in its own Eastern Provinces.[483] In each of these cases, Obama stood with his nation's enemies against its friends—hardly the behavior of an honorable man.

President Obama demonstrated particularly bad faith in the P5+1 negotiations that led to his Iran deal. By insisting from early on that he was negotiating an Executive Agreement over which Congress would have little (if any) say, the Obama negotiating team announced to the world that it had no intentions of altering U.S. law to align with its negotiated commitments. From day one, the American negotiators thus offered only executive action, binding (if at all) only on the executive negotiating them, and likely subject to unilateral American amendment or abandonment within eighteen months. It is not hard to see why the Iranians may have been skeptical of American offers—or why they were adamant about immediate relief. It is hard to think of a less honorable negotiating position (for any organization) than that of an executive unwilling to commit any part of his organization beyond his lame-duck executive team—a stance that may explain, in part, why the American team was unable to achieve *any* of the goals that President Obama laid out upon entering the negotiations.[484]

The Cairo speech and the Iran deal thus bookend the Obama years nicely. By engaging an honor culture in a consistently dishonorable manner, Obama's behavior is likely to have a longstanding negative effect on Arab/Islamic perceptions of American honor and American credibility. Future Presidents will have to work hard to rebuild them.

Bilateral Diplomacy

American policy should favor immediate, unconditional, bilateral diplomatic recognition among all pairs of states in the region, followed by an exchange of ambassadors. Independent states rise to the fore when empires crumble—and the crumbling of the inchoate Sunni Arab empire is no exception. The perpetual linkage of unrelated problems—almost inevitable in multilateral negotiations—guarantees permanent instability. Bilateral relations among neighboring states is necessary for peace and stability.

Saudi Arabia holds the key to this diplomatic initiative. It has been clear for decades that Saudi Arabia should recognize Israel not as part of some grand bargain, but rather because they are neighbors sharing many concerns along with the obvious sources of tension. These two states have been reliable U.S. allies for more than sixty years for a simple reason: their *strategic* interests are nearly identical, and fully compatible with those of the U.S.[485]

Granted, Israeli Zionism and Saudi Wahhabism are *ideologically* incompatible; the former is an expression of minority self-determination and the latter a form of divinely guided imperialism whose claims encompass the entire Jewish homeland. Still, an expression of Saudi nationalism that downplayed the importance of imperial expansion would go far toward alleviating the ideological tension and opening the way to strategic collaboration. In a region whose recent history has featured numerous crises, Saudi and Israeli strategic interests have *never* fallen on opposing sides—the constant anti-Israel rhetoric emanating from Saudi Arabia notwithstanding. In many ways, the Saudi reliance on tribal affiliation and royal bloodlines is as antithetical to the emergence of a unified Sunni Arab empire as is the introduction of minority ethnonational states like Israel, and the threat from Shiite Iran is just as existential. It is hardly a coincidence that the two greatest putative unifiers of the twentieth century Arab world—Nasser and Saddam—were both virulently anti-Saudi during their expansionist, unification stages.

Recent events have highlighted the strategic overlap between Israel and Saudi Arabia and laid the groundwork for their cooperation.[486] The vacuum that President Obama created by reducing America's commitment to its longstanding allies has pushed both states to recognize the importance of direct coordination. Obama's successor should encourage that recognition and usher it to fruition. American shepherding of the fledgling relationship is critical. Though an overwhelming majority of Israelis would welcome closer—and official—ties with the Saudis, a majority of Saudis and non-Saudi Arabs would see it as a betrayal. It is hard to see how the Saudi leadership could steel itself against that sort of opposition without significant American assistance. The establishment of full Saudi recognition of Israel, and the exchange of ambassadors between the two neighbors, will spill over to the rest of the region. It will strengthen the acceptance of further ethnonational safe-haven states, serve the cause of national identity throughout the Sunni world, and improve the prospects for regional integration, stability, and peace.

Nationalism

The U.S. should undertake efforts to strengthen the "nation" aspects of the nation-state system throughout the Middle East. American diplomatic and commercial overtures in the region must emphasize the relationship between trustworthy institutions and economic development, and the relationship between individual dignity and human capital development. That means that the U.S. must seek ways to guarantee that investments and debts will outlive rulers or regimes. We must encourage each of the emerging states to extend offers of citizenship to the majority of the people already living there—including those happy to live as an ethnic minority in a different ethnicity's national homeland. We must do everything in our power to ensure that those unwilling to live as part of a peaceful, loyal minority relocate to emerging states better suited to their own tastes. We must work with the emerging states—those representing both the small nations and the Sunni majority—to help their citizens develop a strong affinity for their specific state distinct from any affinity that they may also feel for ethnic, religious, spiritual, or philosophical kinsmen who are not co-nationals.

Finally—in a twist that may prove to be the most challenging of all—we must inculcate throughout the region at least some of the fundamental liberal values currently present only in Israel. Specifically, we must help ensure that women throughout the region gain educational opportunities, empowerment, and full legal rights.

And we must urge the emerging nations to allow their individual citizens to retain broad latitude for self-expression within their national identity. More broadly, we must oversee the development the institutions of civil society.

If we are to effect such sweeping philosophical changes, there is only one way forward. The U.S. must support local rulers who appreciate the careful balance between enabling the emergence of a healthy policy-driven opposition loyal to the nation-state and crushing the cancerous imperial, revolutionary, anarchic, or terrorist movements seeking to topple the nation-state. And the U.S. must then "trust but verify" that those allies are striking an appropriate balance.

Civil Society

Civil society outside the Mosque is critical for the region to liberalize and modernize. The U.S. should exert efforts whenever and wherever possible to promote new liberal national institutions, particularly though not exclusively in the Sunni Arab world where they have been most sorely lacking. The Secretary of State should assign diplomatic personnel the permanent task of reviewing and grading each regime's progression toward liberalism—bearing in mind, of course, that liberal societies require a level of personal security unachievable beneath a terrorist umbrella. As American allies have demonstrated in Latin America (as well as elsewhere), it is possible to apply illiberal security measures while increasing the liberality of other parts of society.[487] American efforts in this respect must be mindful of the balance between freedom and security; the long-term objective is the emergence of *sustainable* open societies that respect individual dignity and promote economic welfare. A blind focus on ideals that renders basic security impossible cannot serve that long-term goal. These liberal institutions of civil society are important in their own right, critical for individual and economic development, and steps toward peace and stability.

Hearts and Minds

The U.S. must work overtime identifying, cultivating, and rewarding regional actors eager to become parts of the solution. American policymakers must recognize that no attempt to reformulate—or to reform—the Middle East is possible without local leadership, and that leaders who join the effort will incur significant risks. As a result, one primary task for those policymakers will involve discerning which key institutions, movements, and leaders that have long been parts of the problem may choose instead to become parts of the solution. Long-term political stability, cross-border and inter-ethnic cooperation, human development, and prosperity are impossible without philosophical change. Only Arab and/or Islamic institutions eager to develop and spread philosophies shorn of the imperial, supremacist, militant, anarchic, and conspiratorially anti-Semitic elements that define many of the most important contemporary movements in those worlds are worthy of American support. The U.S. and its allies must fight and degrade all Arab/Islamic institutions that promulgate and extol the centrality of those elements of Islam that are most clearly antithetical to regional stability and human capital development. As a result, the U.S. must cultivate, promote, fund, and—above all—protect locals willing to challenge the many currently popular movements falling into this latter category.

Finding such locals will prove challenging; it appears to have been challenging even in the West. Yet the identification of Muslim allies at home is likely a critical first step in bridging the divide with the Muslim mainstream. American efforts at such identification have been uniformly disappointing. In the United States, where Muslims possessing genuinely liberal voices can speak clearly and in relative safety, American leadership typically seeks guidance instead from soft-spoken apologists for radical Islam.[488] It remains entirely unclear whether this preference for smooth radicalism over true reform represents the broad American Muslim community, or stems from laziness among American political leaders most comfortable with well-funded lobbyists.

While there is a nascent Muslim Reform Movement that places a primacy on peace, human rights, and secular governance, it is tiny, entirely Western, and apparently disfavored by Western governments as inauthentic and non-representative.[489] Its membership appears to be limited to a handful of Western intellectuals, it has yet to demonstrate any influence even among Western Muslims, and there is no indication that it has penetrated the Muslim-majority world. In fact, it appears likely that under present circumstances, anyone attempting to take such a reform agenda into any member state of the Organization of Islamic Cooperation[490] would do so at the risk of grave harm, likely death.

Ayaan Hirsi Ali, the courageous Muslim reformer born in Somalia, elected to the Dutch Parliament, and now living in the United States for her own safety,[491] divides the Muslim world into three ideological groups: Medina Muslims, Mecca Muslims, and dissidents. The names of the first two groups reflect distinct phases in the life of the Prophet. As we noted, Mohammed began building the *ummah* as a peaceful preacher in Mecca before gaining the strength and following necessary to become the conquering warrior of Medina. His teachings reflected this shift in strategy. Most of the Koran's passages preaching tolerance and coexistence come from the Prophet's days in Mecca; those extolling supremacy and conquest derive from his days in Medina.[492] Unfortunately for those who prefer the Meccan message, traditional Islamic jurisprudence has adopted the sensible interpretive rule of "abrogation:" when two passages conflict, the latter supersedes the former—creating a general exegetic preference for many of the belligerent Medina passages.[493] Stated simply, though Mohammed may have said many things that are music to liberal Western ears, he later changed his mind about most of them.

Nevertheless, Hirsi Ali contends that the Mecca Muslims constitute the Islamic mainstream. They "are loyal to the core creed and worship devoutly but are not inclined to practice violence."

> Like devout Christians or Jews who attend religious services every day and abide by religious rules in what they eat and wear, Mecca Muslims focus on religious observance....Yet the Mecca Muslims have a problem: Their religious beliefs exist in an uneasy tension with modernity... The rational, secular and individualistic values of modernity are fundamentally corrosive of traditional societies, especially hierarchies based on gender, age and inherited status.[494]

As we have seen, Daniel Pipes has divided Muslim responses to modernity into three categories: secularist, reformist, or Islamist. Within that framework, the Mecca Muslims remain traditionalists, grappling with modernity uneasily at best.[495] Hirsi Ali believes— likely correctly—that the only reasonable hope for a stabilizing transformation of the Islamic world is for the Mecca Muslims to embrace reform. The strength of the Medina Muslims at pressing their case under the principle of abrogation, however, complicates any movement toward such a reformation. Even the peaceful Mecca Muslims who might like to dismiss the Islamist arguments cannot do so easily.

Pipes's Islamists are Hirsi Ali's Medina Muslims, who seek to "emulate [Muhammad's] warlike conduct after his move to Medina." They are

> the fundamentalists who...envision a regime based on Shariah, Islamic religious law. ... they see the forcible imposition of Shariah as their religious duty.... Even if they do not themselves engage in violence, they do not hesitate to condone it. It is Medina Muslims who call Jews and Christians "pigs and monkeys." It is Medina Muslims who prescribe

death for the crime of apostasy, death by stoning for adultery and hanging for homosexuality. It is Medina Muslims who put women in burqas and beat them if they leave their homes alone or if they are improperly veiled.... [I]t is the Medina Muslims who have captured the world's attention on the airwaves, over social media, in far too many mosques and, of course, on the battlefield. The Medina Muslims pose a threat not just to non-Muslims. They also undermine the position of those Mecca Muslims attempting to lead a quiet life in their cultural cocoons throughout the Western world.[496]

Hirsi Ali sees herself as part of the third, dissident group that includes all of Pipes's secularists and many of his reformers. Hirsi Ali describes Muslim dissidents as

a growing number of people born into Islam who have sought to think critically about the faith we were raised in...only a few of whom have left Islam altogether... A few of us have been forced by experience to conclude that we could not continue to be believers; yet we remain deeply engaged in the debate about Islam's future. The majority of dissidents are reforming believers—among them clerics who have come to realize that their religion must change if its followers are not to be condemned to an interminable cycle of political violence.[497]

These Muslim dissidents, and Western reformist thinkers in general, are unlikely to define the Muslim mainstream within the foreseeable future. The groups or movements they form are small, lack broad popularity, and have limited ability to represent or influence major trends in Islamic thought. Still, given time and a bit of assistance, they may be able to nudge mainstream Islamic thinking and scholarship in positive directions. For the most part, however, they have not received the assistance they need.

Even in the years since 9/11, when the importance of winning the hearts and minds of not-yet-radicalized Muslims has been a rare point of strong bipartisan consensus, the U.S. government has done nothing to promote reformist or dissident leadership. According to Hirsi Ali, "there are many dissidents who challenge Islam. Yet the West either ignores them or dismisses them as 'not representative.' This is a grave mistake...."[498] At a bare minimum, federal and local officials could elevate reformist thinkers to positions of prominence within the American Islamic community, inviting them to attend the White House *Iftar* dinners, sit on government advisory panels, and generally serve as the community spokespeople held up as examples of moderation—positioning them to become "as well known in the West as Solzhenitsyn, Sakharov and Havel were generations earlier."[499]

Instead, as both Daniel Pipes and terrorism expert Steven Emerson have documented, the Bush and Obama Administrations have turned to large, well-funded organizations whose Westernized airs of sophistication serve as thin veils for their work as apologists for—if not outright supporters of—the violent actions and pronouncements of Medina Muslims.[500] This error has been particularly acute in the mainstreaming of the Islamic Society of North America (ISNA) and the Council of American-Islamic Relations (CAIR), two organizations with significant histories as apologists and funding conduits for terror groups.[501] CAIR in particular has been heralded as a sort of "Muslim NAACP," despite complaints from moderate American Muslims who correctly see through CAIR's rhetoric to its Islamist agenda.[502] Ironically, when the United Arab Emirates designated CAIR an Islamist terror group, the Obama Administration pressured their government to drop the designation.[503]

These organizations have worked hard to blur the distinctions between peaceful Muslims seeking to live as equals in Western society or to develop their home countries on the one hand, and violent, supremacist, Muslims seeking to terrorize, conquer, and diminish the lives of *dhimmis* and infidels on the other. The official bipartisan imprimatur accepting them as valid representatives of Western Islam complicates the effort to protect the sizable Western Muslim community in need of protection—mostly from Islamists attempting to radicalize their children and terrorize their communities, but also from the slow-but-steady drip of anti-Muslim hate crimes—and impedes the emergence of a truly liberal Islamic reform movement.

Though the overwhelming majority of religiously inspired hate crimes—in the U.S. and throughout the West—continue to target Jews, there are still too many targeting Muslims (and often Sikhs mistaken for Muslims).[504] Continued Western mainstreaming of groups— like CAIR and ISNA—committed to excusing radicalism abroad while promoting it in the U.S. seems like an almost intentional plan to invite the anti-Muslim backlash that Americans have avoided (at least as of late 2016). The longer American officials give credence to such groups, the longer American policy is likely to alternate between ineffective counter-terrorism measures and overbroad anti-Muslim measures; though nothing in the latter category has yet been effected, proposals abound and are likely to work their way into policy at some point. Furthermore, American refusal to announce the truth about such groups only feeds terror and *jihad* abroad, complicating the efforts of American allies throughout the Muslim-majority world.

The notion that mainstream Islam is impervious to dissident or reformist ideas is both demeaning and unwarranted; it violates one of the prerequisites for our journey, namely the requirement that we treat people with respect. Communists and fascists have shown the Islamic world's openness to some of the West's very worst ideas.[505] As Daniel Pipes discussed, Sabbath rest days, weekends, and clerical hierarchies demonstrate an openness to more benign concepts originating with Christianity or Judaism.[506] Perhaps with appropriate encouragement and promotion, the liberal Western ideas shaping the dissident and reformist Muslim agendas will similarly work their way into a mainstream movement. The key, as Hirsi Ali noted, is for Mecca Muslims to stop seeing all dissidents as apostates (for which, as noted, the penalty is death)[507] and to begin seeing them—or at the very least, those who have not renounced their faith—as heretics (with whom discussion and debate is permissible).[508] Once that happens, an Islamic reformation becomes thinkable.

In calling for precisely such a reformation, Hirsi Ali sees Islam "at a crossroads. Muslims need to make a conscious decision to confront, debate and ultimately reject the violent elements within their religion."[509] She contends that this rejection is possible—but only with Western help and support.

> [T]hose under the greatest threat [from Medina Muslims] are the dissidents and reformers within Islam, who face ostracism and rejection, who must brave all manner of insults, who must deal with the death threats—or face death itself. For the world at large, the only viable strategy for containing the threat posed by the Medina Muslims is to side with the dissidents and reformers and to help them to do two things: first, identify and repudiate those parts of Muhammad's legacy that summon Muslims to intolerance and war, and second, persuade the great majority of believers—the Mecca Muslims—to accept this change.[510]

The incursion of such dissident thinking—still rare among Western Muslims and almost non-existent in the Middle East—is critical if the twenty-first century is to avoid a cataclysmic battle between Medina Muslims and the West. American efforts in the Middle East are unlikely to find local allies—Sunni Arab reformers genuinely committed to the causes of regional stability, coexistence, and development—as long as the White House and State Department continue to inculcate an unreformed Islamic leadership at home. Yet the identification and promotion of genuine liberal allies among the Sunni Arabs of the region is likely the most important and the most difficult of the strategic challenges facing the U.S. in the Middle East in both the short- and the long-terms. As noted, enlisting *anyone* in the anti-Islamist, anti-imperial, or anti-revolutionary causes means adapting to the local rules of engagement. The costs of being anti-American in the Middle East have rarely been high, while the costs of opposing any of the popular, radical, Arab/Islamic movements are quite high indeed. No change is possible until the U.S., and the broader West, alter that part of the region's rational calculus.

Such an altered calculus is a necessary precondition for philosophical change, but it is hardly sufficient. Another critical prerequisite is a form of brutal honesty that has escaped most Western leaders to date. The capitulation to Saudi and UN coalition terms in 1990;[511] the unconditional restoration of an illiberal monarchy in Kuwait in 1991;[512] the reinsertion of post-Saddam Iraq into the Arab League in 2003;[513] the continued funding of UNRWA camps designed to keep their charges permanently stateless;[514] the funding of a Palestinian Authority that actively incites violence, terror, and genocide;[515] the insistence upon maintaining Iraqi and Syrian territorial integrity;[516] the incessant talk of a "two-state solution" reducing the scope of Israel's territorial control and security;[517] the refusal to recognize a unified Jerusalem as part of Israel, much less as Israel's undivided capital;[518] the constant harping on Jewish villages in Judea and Samaria as the primary source of regional instability;[519] the abandonment of Iraq in 2011;[520] the erasure of a crossed red line in Syria in 2013;[521] the intentional inattention to Iran's anti-Americanism while negotiating a nuclear agreement (and afterward);[522] and the abandonment of American goals in those negotiations for the sake of securing an agreement;[523] all feed the region's most destructive myths. And that's only a partial list of the most egregious lies that the U.S. (and to an even greater extent, the rest of the West) has been willing to abide.

Every one of these past and/or ongoing American policies suggests the impermanence and unimportance of liberal ideas in the region—including, most significantly, ethnic minority self-determination. Attempts to engage the Iranian Mullahcracy—both the unsuccessful attempts of the Clinton[524] and George W. Bush[525] Administrations and the successful Obama overture—speak to the permanence of the Khomeinist revolution. Future Presidents must work hard to reverse all of these misguided policies; even those cast as putative solutions are parts of the problem.

Nowhere has this brutal honesty been more lacking, however, than in the disrespectful approach to Islam manifest throughout the West—and in particular among the Western elite. Presidents Bush and Obama, along with many other Western leaders, have waxed eloquently about the benevolent nature of Islam, asserting "truths" that are—at a bare minimum—overbroad, and possibly entirely aspirational.[526] To pick but a few glaring examples: Immediately after 9/11, President Bush informed a shell-shocked nation that "Islam is peace."[527] In 2014, when announcing the expansion of his military campaign, President Obama explained that the Islamic State "is not Islamic."[528] Hillary Clinton, in a 2015 campaign speech urging Congress to authorize additional military action against the Islamic State, assured Americans that "Muslims are peaceful and tolerant people and have nothing whatsoever to do with terrorism."[529]

This semi-official Western view of Islam reflects an outsider's wishes about the meaning of Islamic faith rather than an objective exploration of one of history's most important civilizations. Future Presidents, and Westerners in general, should approach Islam with the far greater humility appropriate for any non-believer attempting to understand a great faith. President Obama in particular relinquished any right to speak for Islam when he told his audience in Cairo that he was the Christian son of a Muslim father. From that point forward, it was the height of hubris for him to attempt to speak for the *ummah* he had rejected explicitly—in direct and total disregard for the rules that the *ummah* uses to define itself. From an Islamic perspective, the Christian George W. Bush was a *dhimmi*; Barack Obama was an apostate. Both were outsiders—and it is emphatically not up to outsiders to decide what Islam is, or what it may become. That prerogative rests solely with the Islamic *ummah* and its theological leadership. Westerners, and American policymakers, should focus exclusively on how Muslims behave without delving into the theological implications or underpinnings of their behavior. The disrespect inherent in ignorant (if occasionally well-meaning) pronouncements about Islamic theology is a shockingly poor way to win Muslim hearts and minds.

Allies

The American—or Western—ability to attract genuine allies among the Sunni Arabs of the Middle East is contingent on an honest and respectful approach to the theological debate currently roiling Islam. Every faith, culture, and civilization has experienced periods of internal schism and debate, often lasting centuries. In the case of great faiths, the philosophy to emerge victorious typically becomes accepted as a timeless truth, while those that experience defeat become recognized as once-dangerous blasphemies. If the West is to avoid ever being "at war with Islam," Islamic leaders and institutions with credibility among the *ummah* must ensure that Islamic philosophies capable of accepting non-Muslims as equals emerge as part of Islam's timeless truths. For the most part, that means that at least some of the institutions that have long been parts of the problem must develop and promulgate different Islamic philosophies to become parts of the solution. Should they prove unable to do so, a massive bloody conflict between a supremacist Islam and the infidels it deems inferior seems inevitable.

To some extent, President Obama attempted this approach with his outreach to the Islamic Republic of Iran, the Muslim Brotherhood in Morsi's Egypt (and elsewhere), and the Erdoğan regime in Turkey. Yet these astoundingly poor choices speak more to a leftist preference for revolutionary and anti-Western forces than to a reasonable effort to identify potential philosophical allies.

In the case of Iran, it is precisely the Khomeinist fusion of theology onto the state that has turned Shiism into a force for genocidal intolerance.[530] Given its history as a minority faith, Shiism has typically been far more accepting of the quietist distinction between clerical and temporal authority than has Sunnism. The best way—likely the only way—to recover that longstanding Shiite tradition of quietism is through regime change in Iran (possibly the most important of the near-term geopolitical goals); as Hillel Fradkin noted, Shiism has become "a function of Iran's politics."[531] The conclusive defeat of Khomeinism at modern Shiism's center, and the consequent end to the Khomeinist revolution, will allow a more tolerant, open, and traditionally quietist Shiite leadership to emerge—as the Grand Ayatollah Ali Sistani demonstrated in post-Saddam Iraq.[532]

In the case of the Muslim Brotherhood, Obama chose a movement whose entire *raison-d'être* is the reemergence and expansion of the Sunni Arab Empire and the subjugation of infidels. As Barry Rubin has noted, "[w]hat is most important to understand about the Brotherhood is that, despite its religion-based ideology, it should be viewed in political, not theological terms. It is and has always been a revolutionary organization seeking to seize state power and then to transform thoroughly the societies where it operates."[533] And while Erdoğan has more-or-less worked within the confines of the state system, his attempt to re-Islamize Turkish society and politics has focused heavily on exporting his own authoritarian Islamist philosophy throughout the Arab/Islamic world.[534]

At the moment, the most promising potential leader of the sort of philosophical movement capable of defusing Sunni Islam's militant, imperial drive appears to be Egyptian President Abdel Fattah al-Sisi. Reportedly a devout Muslim himself, and positioned to influence Cairo's prestigious Al-Azhar University, al-Sisi has spoken forcefully about the need for precisely such a revolution from within Islamic thinking:

> It's inconceivable that the thinking that we hold most sacred should cause the entire *umma* [Islamic world] to be a source of anxiety, danger, killing and destruction for the rest of the world. Impossible! That thinking—I am not saying "religion" but "thinking"—that corpus of texts and ideas that we have sacralized over the centuries, to the point that departing from them has become almost impossible, is antagonizing the entire world. It's antagonizing the entire world! Is it possible that 1.6 billion people [Muslims] should want to kill the rest of the world's inhabitants—that is 7 billion—so that they themselves may live? Impossible! I am saying these words here at Al Azhar, before this assembly of scholars and *ulema*—Allah Almighty be witness to your truth on Judgment Day concerning that which I'm talking about now. All this that I am telling you, you cannot feel it if you remain trapped within this mindset. You need to step outside of yourselves to be able to observe it and reflect on it from a more enlightened perspective. I say and repeat again that we are in need of a religious revolution. You, imams, are responsible before Allah. The entire world, I say it again, the entire world is waiting for your next move... because this *umma* is being torn, it is being destroyed, it is being lost—and it is being lost by our own hands.[535]

Al-Sisi has backed his statements with action. He has worked to counter the Muslim Brotherhood at home, to challenge Hamas in Gaza and Islamic State fighters in Libya, and to cooperate warmly both with Israel and with his own Coptic citizens.[536] Failure to cultivate his promising first few years and the potential for turning Al Azhar into an important part of the solution would represent a disaster for the region's future prospects. Western response, to date, has been shockingly cool.[537]

A second potential source of leadership comes from King Abdullah II, Jordan's Hashemite ruler. As Hussein and McMahon understood during the First World War, the Hashemites, as direct descendants of the Prophet[538] and long the least extreme of the Arab leaders,[539] combine inherent credibility within the *ummah* and a history of cooperation with the forces of coexistence and development. As noted, during the immediate post-Ottoman period, while the House of Saud was consolidating its power across the Arabian Peninsula, the British helped the Meccan Hashemites move north to assume the thrones of Iraq and Jordan.[540] In 1951, Jordan's King Abdullah I, (like Egypt's President Anwar el-Sadat and Lebanon's President-elect Bashir Gemayel thirty years later), was assassinated precisely because he preferred developing his own people to excoriating the Jews.[541] Perhaps, given ample Western and Egyptian support and an expansion of the regime's own program to inculcate a sense of Jordanian nationalism among the Kingdom's citizens, the pragmatism that has long characterized Jordan's rulers will spread more readily throughout its population.[542]

The most tantalizing, if least likely, potential candidate for this philosophical transformation from problem to solution is the House of Saud. The Kingdom of Saudi Arabia was founded as a partnership between the ruling Saudis and the Wahhabi clerisy representing an extremely intolerant, violent, fundamentalist strain of Islam. Middle East scholar James Dorsey summarized the challenge nicely:

> [The future of the Saudi regime] will be determined by how the kingdom's rulers restructure their Faustian bargain with Wahhabism, the puritan interpretation of Islam in which the Al Saud cloak themselves but which increasingly looms as a prime obstacle to resolving their problems.
>
> Founded on an alliance between the Al Saud family and descendants of 18th century preacher Mohammed ibn Abdul Wahhab, modern Saudi Arabia adopted an interpretation of Islam that is in many respects not dissimilar from that of the self-styled Islamic State (IS), the jihadist group that controls a chunk of Syria and Iraq. The Wahhabis' jihadist and expansionist instincts have since dulled and its strict *ulama* or religious scholars class, has progressively compromised to accommodate the needs of the state and its rulers.
>
> The question arises whether clerical accommodation of Saudi Arabia's rulers will give the government sufficient leeway to tackle the multiple challenges it confronts or whether the Faustian bargain needs to be restructured to a degree that the very legitimacy of the Al Saud is called into question.

The Saudi rulers repeatedly bump into Wahhabism as they move to reform the economy, seek to differentiate Saud Arabia from IS, repair a tarnished international image, and ensure that the kingdom is not penalized for its four-decade old global funding of intolerant, anti-pluralistic Muslim communities in a bid to counter the revolutionary appeal of Iran. Moreover, the more the Saudi establishment *ulama* accommodates the state, the more it sparks militant critics who accuse it of deviating from the true path of Islam.[543]

Dorsey's reference to Saudi funding of radical Islamic communities across the globe is critical. Saudi oil money has established a global Wahhabist network, founding or taking over mosques and Islamic organizations in Europe, the Americas, and throughout the Islamic world; their support of the Muslim Brotherhood during its mid-century decades in exile was part of this pattern.[544] This fundamentalist network has done more than any other single source to radicalize Muslims, to preach supremacism, and to promote the cause of violent global *jihad*. According to Steve Emerson:

Using an elaborate network of mosques, schools, "charitable" and "humanitarian" organization, and even official diplomatic facilities, Saudi Arabia has for years fostered the growth and spread of a militant doctrinal interpretation of Islam. The ideology of Wahhabism has been exported not only throughout the Middle East but throughout the world resulting in the indoctrination of anti-American, anti-Christian, anti-Semitic and anti-western hatred among new generations of militant Islamic youth. Moderate and secular Muslims are also targeted. Indeed, in looking at the numbers of terrorist victims worldwide at the hands of Islamic extremists during the past decade, the largest number of victims have been fellow Muslims killed or wounded by militant Islamic groups. It is imperative to point out at the outset that the terrorism of Osama bin Laden and the extremism of Wahhabism do not equal Islam. The vast majority of Muslims are not tethered to terrorism or extremism but rather seek a peaceful co-existence like members of other religious denominations. Rather it is only a small Islamic extremist minority that seeks to impose its views on the rest of the Muslim world. But because of the vast financial resources generated by years of petrodollar sales by Saudi Arabia, extremists have been able to disproportionately exercise influence in Muslim communities. Coupled with its virtually unlimited financial resources, the Wahhabi *dawah* invariably leads to acts of terror against non-Muslims and moderate Muslims alike.[545]

As a result, al Qaeda, the Islamic State, and numerous smaller terrorist groups all bear Saudi fingerprints. But it is precisely the rise of such groups that may create an opening because they all—including the Muslim Brotherhood—seek to topple the House of Saud.[546] The Saudis are well aware that they have created and fostered the greatest threats to their own continued rule. As long as Saudi largesse continues to fund this global network, however, the royal family's influence—and consequent ability to nudge it in a different direction—will remain significant. The Saudis thus understand that they must find a new balance between the *jihad* they have been exporting and their own survival.

American policy toward the House of Saud should be clear: The U.S. will not protect it from the global threat it has created unless and until the Kingdom shifts its work to defuse that threat. As the U.S. moves closer to energy self-sufficiency, the credibility of American willingness to withdraw longstanding protection will increase. Until then, the U.S. should not be bashful about attempting to influence the Kingdom's succession squabbles.

Chapter 18. Pragmatic Action

Lessons of the Past

Philosophical shifts do not occur overnight; they are a project of decades, generations, or even centuries. There is no guarantee that popular Islamic thought will ever move in a direction that eschews a resurgent Sunni Arab empire or Islamic Caliphate; that values coexistence over dominance; or that accepts Jews and Christians—and perhaps even pagans, heretics, atheists, and apostates—as equals worthy of human dignity, respect, and self-determination. Nor, for that matter, is there any guarantee that Sunni Arab thinking will ever recognize the equal legitimacy of self-determination rights for non-Arabs or non-Sunnis living in their neighborhood, such as Shiites, Alawites, Kurds, or Druze. In the absence of concerted American leadership, the Islamic State and/or the Islamic Republic of Iran could emerge as the dominant players in the region's politics, philosophy, and theology—expanding their ideologies along with their territorial control.

Philosophic moderation is thus a prerequisite for the eventual emergence of a stable Middle East within which human development, prosperity, and ultimately peace is achievable. In its absence, the region's next century is almost certain to be far bloodier, and far more tragic, than its most recent one, with casualties far exceeding those that Europe experienced during the first half of the twentieth century. Without such developments in Arab/Islamic thinking, things will get worse before they get better—much worse.

In the meantime, the Middle East will continue to pose a number of daunting challenges: Crushing the Caliphate to retake the territory it has claimed will require a committed military effort. Navigating the growing influence of Iran and of Russia will require deft military and diplomatic coordination. Finding local allies truly committed to changing Arab and Islamic *thinking*—and supporting them as they take the considerable risks necessary to effect such changes—will require strength and fortitude, blood and treasure. Standing aside as those same allies make decisions weighing stability and security against civil liberties will prove painful to the American psyche. Redrawing international boundaries will require overcoming international resistance. Resettling refugees and effecting population exchanges to consolidate the region's ethnic groups will require ignoring or silencing the cries of numerous non-governmental organizations (NGOs) and predictable protestors claiming to care about human rights while advocating policies whose only possible outcomes are instability and genocide. And those are only the most obvious of the challenges.

An American policy designed to take charge of the situation must address each of these challenges, and more. Only an intentional, conscious, American-led Western strategy can provide any hope of: moving the volatile region towards a more stable future; defusing the world's most brutal totalitarian movements; making the humanitarian case for consolidating ethnic populations; and beginning the slow incorporation of liberal values and human rights into the Arab/Islamic world. Any policy that fails to do so is simply reactive. It may appear to be easier and cheaper than intentionality, but such appearances would be deceiving. Reactivity merely elevates the importance of immediate costs over the long-term costs that they render inevitable, while squandering any opportunity to achieve sustainable benefits. Future American leaders must strive to do better.

Yet ideals and strategic objectives become viable only in the long run. In a region beset by constant overlapping crises, who has time for long-term planning? In today's Middle East, anarchic safe havens for terror abound. Iran is marching happily toward both nuclear weapons and long-range missile delivery systems—and even President Obama and Secretary Kerry expect it to spend its sanctions-relief windfall exporting terror and the Khomeinist revolution.[547] The Islamic State has become a focal point for terror recruitment, and has already erased at least one national border.[548] The EU is misguidedly funding Hamas's reconstruction of Gaza as a bunker and a death trap.[549] The Saudi/Iranian cold war continues to pick up steam, with ongoing overt conflict in Yemen.[550] Islamists running Turkey and Qatar play both sides of the street with full Western knowledge and complicity.[551] The Palestinian leadership disclaims any sense of obligation as it preaches genocidal incitement.[552] Elections, where held, favor Islamist supremacists who eschew liberal values.[553] Does the U.S. really have time for idealism or for long-term thinking? Shouldn't pragmatic short-term concerns dictate strategy?

Pragmatism does indeed teach some important lessons. First and foremost, crises do require attention—but they require attention both to effect and to cause. Some of America's greatest recent crisis managers have described themselves as "realists" (Henry Kissinger, Caspar Weinberger, James Baker, Colin Powell, George H.W. Bush, Brent Scowcroft, and Zbigniew Brzezinski all come to mind). Their realism, however, typically extended only as far as was necessary to resolve the crisis at hand; they rarely showed any interest in defusing its underlying causes. The 1990/91 Iraq policy is perhaps the finest example of this approach. President Bush and Secretary Baker led the international community to defuse the crisis of the moment— Iraq's invasion of Kuwait—quite effectively. Without addressing the underlying causes of that invasion, however, the American-led coalition locked an unsustainable policy in place for more than a decade, making the inevitably bloody end game bloodier by the year. In a rather ironic twist of fate, the Clinton administration managed to dance nimbly through the minefield of Iraq, leaving it to explode on many of the same people who had laid the mines—or their progeny. Few cared to note this irony, however, preferring instead the facile read that Iraq had been out of the news for a decade, the U.S. changed policies in 2003, and shortly thereafter Iraq became a high-profile mess. A fairer read would be that George W. Bush inherited an untenable policy from his father, that 9/11 made such untenable policies a luxury the world could ill afford, that the U.S. changed policies in 2003, and that Iraq moved from a low-profile disaster to a high-profile disaster.

That observation highlights a second key element of pragmatism: when all of the options on the table are bad, success consists of selecting the least bad among them—a situation that defines nearly all encounters bringing liberals into conflict with anti-liberal societies. In assessing the George W. Bush record in Iraq, the question is not whether the 2003 move to topple Saddam was a good idea, but rather whether there were better ideas on the table. While many of Bush's critics claim that a maintenance of the status quo would have yielded less unfavorable results, they invariably omit recognition of the mid-game strategy that Bush inherited. The combination of a continued American military presence in the Arabian Desert, American-patrolled no-fly zones in northern and southern Iraq, a shaky and corrupt UN-led oil-for-food program, and a totalitarian running roughshod on the ground, could not be sustained forever.[554] At some point, the situation would have moved into one of three end games: either the U.S. would have gone in to topple Saddam (as it did under Bush); the U.S. would have packed up, gone home, and allowed Saddam to reintegrate his rogue state into the international community (parallel to what the U.S. did with Iran under Obama); or some exogenous event, not of American timing or choosing, would have forced some change of policy (as the Arab Spring did in Libya, Egypt, and Syria).

While it is certainly possible that an unforeseen, unplanned event might have landed Iraq, its neighbors, and the U.S., in better places than did the 2003 invasion, such an outcome seems unlikely; unforeseen and unplanned triggers are far more likely to be harmful than helpful (again, as the misnamed Arab Spring of 2010/11 demonstrates). In fact, it seems likely that Bush's decision to topple Saddam in 2003 may have been the least bad option available under the circumstances. Bush's critical error lay in underestimating—by a very wide margin—the complexity of building a decent Iraqi society and the resources needed to build it. He would have done far better to have heeded General Shinseki's testimony that a force far larger than the one contemplated was necessary, and to have prepared the American public for a decades-long engagement in the liberalization of the Arab world.[555]

That unforced error, in turn, highlights a third key pragmatic principle: incrementalism. Iraq entered 2003 as a state with zero individual liberties and overpowering Baathist institutions. It ended 2003 as a state with extreme individual autonomy and no indigenous institutions. As a result, it whipsawed from totalitarianism to anarchy.

Functioning liberal societies cannot develop overnight; they require significant institutional infrastructure. Capitalist markets cannot thrive in the absence of trustworthy courts capable of enforcing contracts and property rights. Democratic rotations of power cannot occur in the absence of confidence that future fair, free elections will follow. The imposition of majority rule prior to the embrace of secure and enforceable minority protections is but one more example of might making right—hardly a liberal ideal even when derived through the ballot box. In many cases, the pragmatic combination of incrementalism and the least-bad principle favor strongmen capable of imposing order while liberal institutions emerge, grow, and gain the respect of the citizenry—in the model of twentieth century successes like Taiwan, South Korea, and Chile.

American foreign policy must thus balance idealistic opposition to both empires and revolutions; an embrace of individualism; a recognition of minority rights and self-determination; operation within the nation-state system; and a general American sense of humanitarianism and justice; with short-term nods to crisis management, incrementalism, and the selection of least-bad alternatives.

The difference between the Bush and Obama approaches to the region is instructive. Whereas Bush attempted to hew closely to American ideals but paid insufficient heed to pragmatic concerns, Obama jettisoned American ideals in the name of pragmatism. To Obama, the relative stability of the Islamic Republic within the state system, and the Muslim Brotherhood's long history of internal restraint (a clear contrast to other Islamist groups), made them suitably pragmatic allies. Meanwhile Israel's pariah status suggested that the most virulently anti-Israel groups would welcome any American steps away from the Jewish State—as well as any reduction of American troops from the region—thereby convincing them to moderate their behavior. Yet these moves, which many may have seemed sensible to some taking a myopic if pragmatic perspective, all failed to promote American interests in the region. In fact, they all backfired. President Obama is leaving America's short-term position and long-term interests in the Middle East in far worse shape than they were when he assumed office.

Future American Presidents must do better. They must remember that above all, successful soft power campaigns require patience. An appropriate strategy must incorporate a balance of long-term interests and short-term pragmatism that has eluded the first four post-Cold War Presidents. The path to a broadly liberal, open, tolerant society is likely to be slow and uneven; the U.S. must usher it forward without hastening it to the point of undermining regional stability.

Regional stability, as noted repeatedly above, hinges heavily on the emergence of modern nation-states. The previous attempt to integrate the Middle East into the nation-state system has failed. While lines drawn on a map may create states, they cannot inculcate a sense of nationhood among people who do not feel like members of a single nation. The next attempt at a political map of the Middle East must incorporate the lessons of the post-Ottoman map's failure. It must begin by looking at the region to determine where ethnic commonality might lead easily into a unified, distinct, nationalist sentiment—then drawing state borders capable of accommodating those nations.

Demographic Movement

History has taught that the first steps towards creating such viable nation-states often involve the division and consolidation of minorities through programs of refugee resettlement and population exchange. In the wake of the Allied victory in World War II, Winston Churchill famously addressed the House of Commons—specifically on the topic of reconstituting and independent Poland, but more broadly on the steps that he believed were central to stabilizing the war-torn continent:

> There will be no mixture of populations to cause endless trouble, as has been the case in Alsace-Lorraine. A clean sweep will be made. I am not alarmed by the prospect of the disentanglement of populations, nor even by these large transferences, which are more possible in modern conditions than they ever were before. The disentanglement of populations which took place between Greece and Turkey after the last war...was in many ways a success, and has produced friendly relations between Greece and Turkey ever since. That disentanglement, which at first seemed impossible of achievement, and about which it was said that it would strip Turkish life in Anatolia of so many necessary services, and that the extra population could never be assimilated or sustained by Greece having regard to its own area and population—I say that disentanglement solved problems which had before been the causes of immense friction, of wars and of rumours of wars. Nor do I see why there should not be room in Germany for the German populations of East Prussia and of the other territories I have mentioned...In fact, I cannot see any doubt whatever that the Great Powers, if they agree, can effect the transference of population.[556]

Europe's postwar experience proves that Churchill was far more right than wrong. The "disentanglements" brought unprecedented stability to large parts of the continent. His confidence in the Great Powers' ability to effect the transfers calmly and humanely, however, proved overly optimistic—particularly when it came to the Soviet Union. Actual postwar European transfers reiterated the indisputable: Such programs can be brutal and unfair, uprooting families and communities from homes of long standing. They can also, however, be humanitarian responses to an antecedent injustice, resettling refugees who have already fled the destruction of their homes. But even in their most humane manifestations, replete with timely aid and compensation, they remain coercive and disruptive.

International Relations theorist Chaim Kaufmann "offer[ed] a theory of how ethnic wars end, and propose[d] an intervention strategy based on it:"

> Stable resolutions of ethnic civil wars are possible only when the opposing groups are demographically separated into defensible enclaves. Separation reduces both incentives and opportunity for further combat, and largely eliminates both reasons and chances for ethnic cleansing of civilians. While ethnic fighting can be stopped by other means, such as peace enforcement by international forces or by a conquering empire, such peaces last only as long as the enforcers remain... [T]o save lives threatened by genocide, the international community must abandon attempts to restore war-torn multi-ethnic states. Instead it must facilitate and protect population movements to create true national homelands....Once massacres have taken place, ethnic cleansing will occur.   The alternative is to let the [genocidaires] "cleanse" their enemies in their own way."[557]

Though the contemporary distaste for strategic population exchanges is understandable, the refusal to move populations locks in place animosities and tension, perpetuates conflicts, creates multiple waves of refugees, impedes human development, and renders peace all but impossible. The practice—whether intentional or reactive—thus poses an inherent ethical conundrum: it straddles the fault lines between those scandalized by its inherent coercion and unfairness and those who recognize that it is often a prerequisite for the formation of stable nation-states and the cessation of ongoing violence that is even more coercive, unfair, and deadly than the exchange.

The prominent Hungarian political theorist István Bibó attempted to square that ethical circle. Though he recognized that the practice is "potentially monstrous," he also noted that its results have been strongly positive often enough to tempt copying; "in a matter of a decade, it ended Greco-Turkish animosity, which had a centuries-long past and prospect." The monstrous side revealed itself under Hitler, "by settling [Germans] on the fringes of the German linguistic area and removing or exterminating the original population." Bibó concluded:

> Population exchange need not be ruled out completely, but if we do not want to turn Europe into a highway of displaced peoples, we must lay down definite principles for using it...[P]opulation exchange can be justified only when

ethnographic borders cannot be physically followed but the historical condition or the status quo cannot be maintained because of heightened tensions.[558]

A clear focus on context can thus inform the situation. In times of rampant instability already replete with genocidal atrocities, massive dislocations, and destabilizing refugee flows, Churchill, Kaufmann, and Bibó would all argue for setting stability as the goal, constrained to minimize coercion, dislocation, and inconvenience—rather than the other way around. Under such circumstances, relocation and resettlement represent a least-bad option—provided that they do not slide into extermination. The Middle East today is experiencing such circumstances—and they show no signs of abating soon.

Much as coercive relocations can indeed be monstrous, it is neither the only nor the worst monstrosity worth avoiding. The abandonment of minorities to a violent neighboring majority—as the world has abandoned the Yazidi and Christian victims of the Islamic State's genocidal drive—is far worse.[559] So too is the destabilizing insistence upon maintaining a violent regional majority within a minority-run region, as Sunni Arabs living in Judea and Samaria illustrates. Minorities spread thinly throughout the territory that a violent majority dominates are indefensible, and likely doing little more than waiting their turn to be marked for genocidal extermination. Members of the violent majority living in territory that a regional minority dominates are a forward force, awaiting instructions to turn fully against their hosts. In such cases, relocation—whether reactive or preemptive, voluntary or coercive, (though again, never eliminationist)—emerges as by far the lesser evil. As Kaufmann noted, the contrary approach, whose goal is to avoid coercion at all costs, would require permanent outside forces to protect the thinly spread minorities living in majority-dominated land, while ensuring permanent instability in enclaves where regional majorities lives as a local minority.

The emphasis on stability thus promises to create the minimal conditions necessary for a positive regional future focused on human capital development and the emergence of civil society. For decades, Judea, Samaria, Gaza, and Lebanon, where Sunni Arabs constitute local minorities, have been subject to internal unrest. The decline of centralized authoritarianism in Iraq and Syria exposed the Christian, Shiite, Kurdish, Druze, and Yazidi communities scattered throughout their territories to exterminationist campaigns. Contemporary realities suggest that relocation and resettlement—of longstanding refugees, of recent refugees, of the permanently stateless, of minorities spread throughout Sunni-dominated areas, and of Sunnis living as local minorities in areas that regional minorities dominate—into separate ethnic enclaves represents the best, and perhaps the only, path to regional stability. The next, post-post-Ottoman map of the Middle East must incorporate this conclusion.

Chapter 19. Redrawing the Map
Objectives

A practical agenda for drawing a new, more stable, Middle East map thus begins with the adoption of a new, consistent, humanitarian approach to the resettlement of refugees—including the region's multigenerational stateless people—among their ethnic kinsmen. The consequent consolidation of the region's sizable minority groups into ethnonational states harkens back to the views and maps of the enlightened anti-imperial, post-colonial Europeans of the immediate post-Ottoman period. As such, it will lead to a strengthening of Lebanon's Christian and Israel's Jewish character; the emergence of independent Kurdish, Alawite, and Druze states; the possible birth of a Shiite Arab state; and a rethinking of the vast Sunni Arab expanse comprising the entire Arabian Peninsula, all of Jordan, and most of Iraq and Syria. A practical reassessment of the region will also avail itself of the capabilities and desires of the region's current rulers—and in particular, of the promising first few years of the current regime in Egypt.

In terms of specifics, the exercise should:
- Align principled refugee resettlement with the long-term interest in regional stability;
- Recognize Kurdistan as an independent state;
- Consolidate the region's Christian refugees into Lebanon;
- Support the emergence of a Druze territory in southern Syria;
- Encourage the retreat of Syria's Alawites into their traditional coastal home in Latakia;
- Apply a consistent preference for stability, consolidation, and ethnic self-determination across the region;

- Consider the emergence of a Shiite Arab state;
- Explore alternative arrangements for stabilizing the Sunni Arab interior;
- Recognize and build upon Egypt's uniqueness.

While the mere exercise of rethinking international maps may smack of science fiction, it is clear that the current map has failed. The twenty-first century map of the Middle East will accommodate the current round of turmoil one way or another. It is thus not too early to think about movements—of peoples and of states—most likely to serve the cause of regional stability, and most likely to lay the groundwork for the slow liberalization and consequent human capital development of West Asia.

Refugees

Perhaps the most important element of a reconfigured Middle East is the alignment of principled refugee resettlement with the long-term interest in regional stability. The dismemberment of an empire, even an inchoate empire, is a messy thing. The self-determination of newly freed ethnic minorities in even parts of their historic homelands only increases the messiness. The refugee crisis roiling Europe and seeking to poke into the U.S. was entirely predictable. Yet its solution, though equally well known, runs counter to much contemporary thinking about refugees—and to some misguided contemporary views of justice and human rights. In point of fact, however, such thinking about refugees is responsible for perpetuating far greater injustices, and for encouraging far greater attacks on basic decency, than were at least some earlier approaches to the issue.

Future leaders must learn from history. The period between the mid-nineteenth and mid-twentieth centuries saw many dislocations arising as colonial empires gave way to ethnonational states. Those that consolidated ethnic groups and resettled refugees among ethnic kin enabled far greater stability than those that did not.[560] Unfortunately, a fundamentally flawed (and in many ways, inverted) theory of justice popular in the years following WWII led the world to adopt a new approach to refugees. In many cases, international organizations pen refugees like prisoners or animals until the war zone from which they fled stabilizes enough to send them back to perpetuate the instability—unless they are fortunate enough to travel great distances in enormous numbers, at which point humanitarian concerns push unrelated societies to embrace them.[561]

This prevailing approach damages refugees, unstable states, the regions that surround them, and unsuspecting distant host countries. It is morally unconscionable, and helps no one other than the theorists who call it "just," the bureaucrats who use it to earn their keep, and the activists who revel in conflating the consolidation of ethnic populations into safe spaces where they can flourish with the exterminationist practices of genocide and ethnic cleansing. American policy must invert it, and push for refugee integration near but outside the crisis zone, primarily but not exclusively among ethnic kinsmen—simultaneously improving survival prospects for individuals forced to move and the prospects for the formation of stable, coherent ethnonational states.

The U.S. should begin this inversion by defunding UNRWA, eliminating the concept of multi-generational refugees, and pushing for the integration of UNRWA's charges into the broader Sunni Arab world. A second concrete step in the right direction would be the use of U.S. forces to establish and/or secure safe havens capable of leading to ethnonational states, at a bare minimum for the Kurds and the Druze. The explicit adoption of these principles and actions will mark the start of a resolution of the larger refugee crises arising in the wake of the nascent Caliphate—as well as representing a blow against the Caliphate's imperial impulses.

Kurds

The U.S. should recognize Kurdistan as an independent state. The Kurds have spent over two decades developing the infrastructure of a functioning state, largely on their own—posing a stark contrast to the Palestinian hate movement that has squandered decades and billions in international aid. The Kurds have been reliably pro-Western, show every indication of cooperating with American allies in the region—including Israel—and claim a kinship to many of the smaller groups currently facing genocide at the hands of the Islamic State. The breakup of Syrian and Iraqi territorial integrity long cited as a reason to oppose an independent Kurdistan has already occurred. The restoration of either country as a unified entity along familiar boundaries seems unlikely without significant outside intervention, and there is no particular reason to find such an externally imposed reunification desirable.

American policy should be strongly pro-Kurdish, helping the Kurds to consolidate their own territory, defeat the Islamic State, and absorb related refugees. Kurdish reconciliation with Turkey will prove challenging, but it should be doable—even as Turkey's continued status as a NATO ally and EU applicant seems increasingly displaced given Erdoğan's slide into illiberal Islamist despotism. The future of Turkey and the future of Kurdistan are inextricably intertwined. U.S. policy should work hard to usher in a peaceful border separating two neighboring allied states.

Christians

The U.S. should lead an international effort to consolidate the region's Christian refugees into Lebanon. Once again, population exchanges and refugee resettlement may be the only ways to prevent genocide. Lebanon's demographics have never allowed the country to stabilize;[562] its history as an independent nation has oscillated between periods in which it teetered on the brink of instability and periods of full-fledged civil war. The genocidal campaigns and refugee flows roiling the region, and the particular brutality facing ancient Christian communities across Syria and Iraq, necessitate a safe homeland for the Middle East's Christians. While the destruction of these communities is tragic, the Islamic State's campaign against history is likely to render their reconstruction *in situ* impossible. Consolidation into a Christian state seems far preferable (on the assumption and hope that different Christian factions are able to coexist peacefully)—and Lebanon is the only viable candidate. While obviously disruptive, a policy preference for Christian resettlement in Lebanon, coupled with the relocation of Hezbollah-aligned Shiites to territory more congenial to Alawite or Shiite control, would serve two important goals: it would stabilize Lebanon, and it would create at least one safe homeland for the Christians of the Middle East— many of whom can trace their communities back to the earliest days of Christianity.

Druze

The U.S. should support the emergence of a Druze territory in southern Syria. Syria's Druze have also been targeted for genocide by radical terrorist forces operating in that country's civil war. They too will need a safe haven, most appropriately in their traditional southern Syrian mountain home. Israel's sizable Druze community has always served as the Jewish State's model loyal minority, and there are reports that some Syrian Druze leaders have reached out to Jerusalem through their Israeli co-religionists.[563] Lebanese Druze leaders have also reportedly made similar overtures. The emergence of an independent Jabal Druze was on the table during the early post-Ottoman period; it may be time to reconsider it.[564] By many accounts, Israel would support the emergence of such a safe haven, and might even accept the nascent state as a protectorate—particularly if a pledge of American and NATO support were forthcoming. If any of these reports prove accurate, American policy should encourage them.

Alawites

American policy should encourage Syria's Alawites to retreat into their traditional coastal home in Latakia and declare independence. There is little doubt that the introduction of Russian forces into Syria to prop up the Assad regime complicates American movements within the country, but the Russian presence already appears to be a permanent part of the region's future. Even Russia, however, is likely to prove unable to rebuild the Syria that was. Given that Russia's greatest single interest in Syria is its naval base on the Mediterranean,[565] and that that base falls within the traditional homeland of Russia's Alawite allies, deft American diplomatic maneuvering *might* be able to enact a successful partitioning of northern and western Syria into ethnic enclaves by acceding to Russian dominance of the emergent Alawite state. Though far from ideal, a deal that simply helped Russia consolidate the gains it has made during the Obama years, while simultaneously laying the groundwork for refugee resettlement in new safe-havens and nascent states and weakening Iran, the Islamic State, and the cause of Sunni Arab imperialism, could well qualify as a least-bad approach to the region.

Jews and Israel

The Jewish State, and to a disturbing extent, the Jewish people, stand on the front lines of the civilizational clash between the West and supremacist, imperial Islamism. Much of the world prefers to deny that Jews—of any belief, of any nationality, anywhere on the planet—are special targets. When Islamists terrorizing Mumbai included a tiny Jewish Community Center, the Nariman Chabad House, among their selected high value targets, the international press seemed puzzled as to their motives.[566] When Islamist terrorists included a kosher supermarket, on the eve of *Shabbat*, among their high value Parisian targets, President Obama famously called the victims "random folks in a deli."[567] (In a similar vein, when an American-born Islamic State recruit took the *jihad* into a gay nightclub in Orlando in June 2016, parts of the Western LGBT community understood that the tragedy was little more than Islamists targeting for extermination those whom they find most theologically offensive;[568] critical parts of the Western press seemed as perplexed as to the shooter's motives as they are when the Islamists target Jews.)[569]

The widespread refusal to acknowledge that Islamists have singled out Jews as terror targets—and the equally widespread pretense that terror directed towards Israel is categorically different from terror attacks elsewhere—strengthens the Islamist cause while weakening the West.[570] It is but one high-profile example of the double standards that—according to the U.S. State Department—marks a position as anti-Semitic, rather than merely critical of an Israeli policy.[571] This State Department imprimatur notwithstanding, the use of double standards when dealing with anti-Jewish terrorists continues to color U.S. Policy. In 2005, the Bush Administration encouraged Ariel Sharon to remove all Israeli military forces from Gaza, despite knowing that the overwhelming local support for Hamas made a terrorist takeover of the territory likely;[572] it seems unlikely that any other front-line ally (say, Pervez Musharraf in Pakistan) offering to abdicate responsibility for a terror-infested territory would have received similar encouragement. In 2013, President Obama and Secretary Kerry exerted enormous pressure on Benjamin Netanyahu to free large numbers of Arab terrorists from Israeli prisons—while excoriating Afghanistan's Hamid Karzai for doing the same thing several months later.[573]

The world's double standards manifest themselves most clearly, however, in the validation they provide for the Palestinianist hate movement—a movement that has devastated the people it claims to represent and infected the broader Islamic world with its virulent Jew hatred. The insistence upon normalizing the world's treatment of Israel is critical for the welfare not only of Israel and the Jews, but for that of Arabs and Muslims as well. Regional stability is impossible while Israel's legitimacy, security, Jewish character, and borders remain subject to special considerations.

When it comes to redrawing the map of the Middle East, the U.S.—and the world—must apply a consistent preference for stability, consolidation, and ethnic determination across the region, even when it applies to the Jews and Israel. Israel's record of extending citizenship rights, legal equality, and integration of minorities eager or willing to contribute to the country's growth compares favorably with that of other liberal democracies. But Israel has also faced a unique longstanding challenge in dealing with a minority population—overwhelmingly Sunni Arab—seeking to destabilize the country. As noted, foreign forces have worked hard, for decades, to immiserate this Sunni Arab population. The sole purpose of this inhuman mistreatment is to challenge Israel's legitimacy as an ethnonational state—and as the world's only safe haven for Jews, located appropriately within the historic Jewish homeland. American policy must stop pretending that the anti-Zionist hate movement might morph into a positive conception of

Palestinian nationhood—a positive development that has eluded the populations of Syria, Iraq, and Lebanon.

Ironically, as we noted at the outset, the subset of "Two-State Solution" proponents who are actually advocating in good faith recognize—as did Kaufmann, in his advocacy of population exchanges—the importance of separating the populations.[574] Their insistence upon coercing and dislocating only Jews,[575] however, has blinded them to two critical shortcomings of such a plan. First, as already noted, the Jews of the Middle East have already suffered massive dislocation and resettlement. To the extent that misplaced contemporary notions of justice might argue that every group must bear a burden to achieve stability, the burden that the Jews have already borne must factor into the equation. Second, and far more significantly, the minimal requirement for a "solution" (involving a new Sunni Arab state or otherwise) is that it must "solve" the Arab/Israeli conflict in a reasonably durable and sustainable fashion. Porous, indefensible Israeli borders invite incursions—from terrorists, rocket fire, and perhaps eventually armies—rendering any subdivision of the land west of the Jordan untenable. The only way to serve the goal of regional stability, constrained to minimize coercion, dislocation, and inconvenience, is to relocate those Sunni Arabs neither unwilling to live as loyal minority citizens of the Jewish State into comfortably Sunni-majority territory.

The population exchange that started when most Arab states ethnically cleansed themselves of Jews (and sometimes also of Christians) must be allowed to reach its logical conclusion.[576] Unlike the Palestinian Authority, which has worked hard to eliminate or degrade the Christian Arabs living in its midst[577] and has announced its plan to ethnically cleanse Jews from any territory it controls fully,[578] Israel has never insisted upon a quid-pro-quo. Israel has never engaged in ethnic cleansing, and has demonstrated convincingly that it has no interest in doing so in the future. Israel has always welcomed those Arabs living in its midst pleased to live as a free minority in a democratic Jewish State. As to the Arab majority unwilling to embrace this offer, however, primary responsibility for their resettlement and integration should fall upon the Arab States. Perhaps now that several of them—notably Egypt, Jordan, Saudi Arabia, and the UAE—appear to understand that they, like Israel, may need to take risks to ensure their own security, forward motion may become possible. The U.S. should help usher that population exchange to its obvious conclusion, working with Israel and the Arab states to ensure that any relocations necessary to achieve stability are as painless and as humane as possible.

The U.S. should encourage Israel to annex Judea, Samaria, the Golan Heights, and possibly Gaza, and to offer Israeli citizenship to all residents of those territories willing to become loyal citizens of Israel. The U.S. should also lead an international campaign to resettle in Sunni Arab territory those residents either incapable of or unwilling to serve as part of a loyal ethnic minority within the Jewish State. In short, the U.S. should simultaneously capitalize on Israel as the model of the ethnonational states necessary to stabilize the region and defuse the world's only multigenerational refugee crisis by applying a more appropriate and humane approach to refugees. From a policy perspective, that means helping Israel consolidate its hold on disputed territory, embrace new loyal minority citizens, and gain international legitimacy on both fronts.

Shiite Arabs

Given the need for an arc of ethnonational statelets in the region's west and north, the emergence of a Shiite Arab state in and around Basra seems both consistent and inevitable. As recent history has shown, however, such a state is likely to become an Iranian client, turning to its much larger and better-established Shiite neighbor for protection and support. The U.S. cannot endorse the emergence of an Iranian client state dominating Iraq's only port while the Islamic Republic persists. Should the U.S. and the international community see a need for a Shiite safe haven region prior to the achievement of regime change in Iran, the region will have to remain a (U.S. or NATO) protectorate until new Shiite leadership arises. Though dominance of such a state could provide the positive benefit of nurturing such an alternative leadership, it will also lead to almost certain overt conflict between the U.S. and Iran. The U.S. should be prepared to foster such a Shiite safe haven, then use it as a weapon against the current Iranian regime, while taking steps to minimize military conflicts unless and until some strategic imperative for all-out war with Iran arises. Meanwhile, the region's other sizable Shiite enclave, in Southern Lebanon, has long allied itself with Syria's Assad and the Alawites. Lebanese Hezbollah fighters form a critical component of Assad's forces in the Syrian civil war. Relocation of Lebanon's pro-Syrian Shiites into a new Alawite state would help to stabilize both countries. According to some reports, their militias have already begun to make the trek to Syria; it would serve the cause of regional stability if the communities who support those militias followed them into the territory of their Alawite allies.[579]

Sunni Arabs

American policymakers must work with Sunni Arab allies to

explore alternative arrangements for stabilizing the region's vast interior. The declaration of ethnonational safe haven states for Kurds, Christians, Jews, Druze, Alawites, and likely Shiite Arabs would leave the Sunni Arabs in control of a vast interior, including the entire Arabian Peninsula, all of Jordan, and most of Syria and Iraq—sweeping north from the holy cities of Mecca and Medina through the metropolises of Damascus and Baghdad. By reducing the scope of the territory that Sunni Arabs dominate and insisting on the formation of nation-states, it would strike a blow against inchoate imperialism in theory and reduce the attractiveness of the Islamic State as the embodiment of that theory. Coexistence and internal development will become possible only after the imperial drive is extinguished.

On the Peninsula, existing state lines seem reasonably stable. The great challenge facing U.S. policy in these areas is likely philosophical: pushing for both an expansion from tribal thinking to nationalist thinking and a stark turn away from violent, radical, supremacist Islam. As noted, these philosophical changes will prove painful. Yet the ruling families of the Gulf and in Jordan recognize that they are fully in the crosshairs of the threats they have created. Should the U.S. condition continued support and protection on appropriate philosophical (and theological) developments, there is at least some chance that the ruling families will respond appropriately. If not, the U.S. must recognize that its interests lie elsewhere, and look for alternative local leaders more worthy of American support.

Further north, the situation is likely to prove extremely unstable. The Islamic State has already made significant inroads into Syrian and Iraqi territory, and may seize even greater swathes of it in the future. Minorities (as well as Sunni Arabs whose interpretation of Islam the Islamic State deems inappropriate) are fleeing outward, as campaigns of genocide and destruction uproot communities from the lands they have called home for centuries. Neither the Syrian nor the Iraqi armies appear likely to liberate much (if any) of that territory without significant foreign support. If and or when the dust eventually settles, the region is likely to host numerous internal refugees, as well as Sunni Arabs relocated from the various minority homelands. The case for re-dividing the Sunni interior into multiple countries is unclear. The best bet may be to work with the best local leaders—the Hashemite rulers of Jordan—to develop a large nation-state capable of developing the full human potential of the Sunni Arabs. Such a proposal, however, is both premature and speculative. The region will experience considerable turmoil and trauma before any meaningful reconstruction of the map is possible.

Egypt

Egypt is unique in many ways. It is the only Sunni Arab state whose sense of nationhood predates the modern nation-state system. It boasts the largest Christian minority of any Sunni Arab-majority state—a minority that may be capable of remaining in its historic home without destabilizing the region. Cairo's Al-Azhar University is considered the most prestigious in all of Sunni Islam, and as such, it maintains an outsized voice in the development of Sunni thought. Most significantly for present purposes, however, it is the only part of the Sunni Arab world to turn back from the brink of Islamism, and it is the country in which pro-American forces are best positioned to deal radical Islamists a fatal blow. When the longstanding Mubarak government crumbled in the face of Tahrir Square protestors and the Obama Administration's abandonment in 2011, elections put the Muslim Brotherhood in place. During the one-year presidency of Mohammed Morsi, the Brotherhood moved to solidify power, launched numerous pogroms against Coptic Christians, downplayed security cooperation with Israel, aligned with Hamas, and attempted to reposition Egypt as part of the Middle East's growing Islamist bloc.[580]

General—now President—al Sisi halted this slide with a military coup in July 2013. In the years since, he has righted the country to support regional stability and oppose terrorism, claimed electoral legitimacy with a landslide victory, developed a reasonably warm relationship with Israel, and set out to reform the country's economic, political, and social systems in ways that promote growth without abandoning Egypt's huge, impoverished population.[581] He has deployed the Egyptian military to counter the growing terror threat in the Sinai, to cut off Hamas' supply lines to Gaza, and to attack Islamic State positions in Libya.[582] He has also called explicitly for new modes of Islamic thought along precisely the necessary lines—tolerant, open, non-violent, and anti-supremacist.[583] Disturbingly, and ostensibly because he has approached some of these objectives with a heavy hand, his support from the Obama Administration and other Western governments has been lukewarm, at best.[584] Yet such a distancing is terribly shortsighted; Obama's successor should correct it immediately upon assuming office. The steps that al Sisi has taken, and the even greater ones he has begun to broach, are critical for the stability of the region—and for the philosophical changes to Arab/Islamic thinking necessary for minimizing bloodshed throughout the twenty-first century.

The next President should embrace and support al Sisi's efforts, and expand Egypt's leadership role. Furthermore, given that the only two forces remotely capable of handling the now-anarchic Libya are NATO and the Egyptian military, while the only two forces remotely capable of handling Hamas in Gaza are the IDF and the Egyptian military, U.S. policymakers should consider supporting an expansion of the Egyptian role in both theaters, and with both populations. An Egyptian absorption of the parts of the Gazan population unwilling or unable to join the loyal minority in the Jewish State, along with Libya's territory, population, and oil wealth, may serve the cause of regional stability along with long-term U.S. interests and values. Finally, by collaborating with the al-Sisi government, the U.S. will position itself to help Egypt find the appropriate balance between quelling terror and promoting civil society.

Chapter 20. Regional Integration

The emergence of coherent nation-states on a redrawn map is only the beginning. A stable, secure platform for regional development is only that—a platform. The hard work of securing whatever peace may emerge, of fostering the institutional stability of new or reformulated states, and of promoting the liberal values of individual dignity and human capital development, is necessary to render that platform sustainable and the struggle to have built it worthwhile. The U.S. should take the lead in developing two key organizations of regional integration, one economic, the other military.

Economic Integration

The U.S. and its regional allies should develop an economic organization committed to regional development and economic integration, perhaps reviving and expanding the largely moribund 2003 U.S. proposal for a Middle East Free Trade Area.[585] Recognition and negotiation among states may be a good start, but it is hardly a guarantee of peace and stability (as the experience of Europe between 1648 and 1948 proves). Recent history has shown, however, that economic integration coupled with bilateral respect can work fairly well (as the European experience since about 1950 proves). The U.S. already has free trade deals with Israel and Jordan.[586] The next Administration should extend the Israeli deal to include joint Israel-Egypt ventures—along with crafting labeling laws and anti-boycott legislation designed to confound international attempts to boycott Israel. More broadly, future American Presidents should work to develop a Middle Eastern free trade area and an organizational structure capable of making it an effective tool for regional economic development and integration. Development goals should include the opening of markets (particularly those related to agriculture and energy), the adoption of sound fiscal policies, and the reduction of subsidies other than those needed to alleviate abject poverty. Economic development should focus on private sector led growth capable of benefiting entire populations, rather than simply entrenched ruling classes or oligarchies. Regional integration should acknowledge that considerable points of comparative advantage already exist: Israeli technology, Gulf energy, and Egyptian labor, to name but a few. The U.S. should position itself as a key player in the economic development of the region.

Security Coordination

The U.S. and its regional allies should also develop a military organization capable of promoting regional security cooperation and defense against cross-border terrorist movements. The Middle East's next few decades are likely to be quite bloody, regardless of American policy. The necessary redrawing of borders, movement of populations, and recalibration of thinking will not happen overnight. The best that American policy can do is to nudge them in desirable directions. In the meantime, cross-border threats will continue, civil wars will rage, and terrorist movements will persist. The U.S. should lead a military alliance capable of strengthening American allies, raising the costs of anti-Americanism, and coordinating the activities of states eager to move the region into a future of secure, independent, meaningful, and prosperous nation-states. Membership in this military alliance will carry both costs and benefits—coupling American security guarantees to embattled developing nation-states with commitment and visible movement on other parts of the agenda outlined above.

In an ideal configuration, the alliance's founding members would include Israel and the Kurds, two groups that have demonstrated an understanding of, and a commitment to, American interests. But it cannot succeed without at least one meaningful Arab member on board from the outset. At the moment, Egypt appears to be the clear choice to fill that role, with Jordan a definite possibility. Should their involvement preclude explicit Israeli or Kurdish charter membership, the organization should begin with Sunni Arab allies while coordinating with Israel and the Kurds—until the full integration of these two critical pillars becomes a political possibility. Ideally, Saudi Arabia and the other GCC countries would join promptly—as their own stability and security loom ever larger in their own thinking. And Turkey, currently torn between its EU application and NATO membership on the one hand and Erdoğan's Islamism on the other, may find such an affiliation enticing whenever it enters its post-Erdoğan phase.

This military alliance will serve as a counterweight to Iran's growing influence—and the recent emergence of an Iran-Russia-Syria-Iraq axis. In terms of the other ethnonational states, their emergence will likely feed both alliances. Jabal Druze should enter the pro-American alliance as soon as it is ready for independence. The Alawite state is likely to be in Russia's pocket from inception, whether it remains strictly Alawite or it absorbs large parts of Lebanon's Assad-aligned Shiite minority. The best that the U.S. can reasonably hope for there is that it becomes a full-fledged Russian client state, rather than a Russian-Iranian (or fully Iranian) one. Lebanon—particularly as an increasingly Christian safe-haven state—may find itself torn between Russia's championing of Eastern Christianity and the American preference for liberal pluralism. Americans should not presume that even a very Christian Lebanon will see itself as Western; many Middle Eastern Christians consider themselves proud Arabs, and many of the Middle Eastern Christian communities predate either Catholicism or Orthodoxy, (though over the centuries, some have affiliated with one or the other). There are very few Protestants in the Middle East.

Taken together, these two new pro-American regional organizations can help success emanate outward. In many ways, Israel provides the best regional model for a flourishing society that balances security concerns, civil liberties, economic growth, human development, and minority rights. Its neighbors must move beyond their ingrained Jew hatred to embrace the models that Israel has proven—a task that is likely to be far less challenging for the emerging ethnonational periphery than for the Sunni Arab core. Israel, in turn, should provide generous assistance, support, and guidance as its former enemies decide to serve their own populations rather than war against the Jewish State—or as Golda Meir famously quipped, when they "love their children more than they hate us."[587]

As recently as the early 1950s, development levels across the Middle East were comparable to those of East Asia (other than Japan). Today, South Korea's per capita GDP is roughly nine times that of Egypt. The difference has little to do with the activities or attitudes of outsiders, or with the relative injustices befalling different ethnic groups. Asian states, most of which can claim coherent ethnonational bases, have pursued reasonable development strategies, while Middle Eastern states have not. Should either the Sunni Arabs or the smaller ethnic groups with whom it shares North Africa and West Asia choose to follow the path that East Asia and South Asia have blazed over the past few decades, they too can experience "miracles." American policy should seize every opportunity to motivate them to do so—and to ensure their success when they do.

Conclusion

Chapter 21. The Way Forward

The challenges of crafting and implementing a coherent Middle East strategy are daunting. Redrawing borders, relocating populations, establishing protectorates, defending nascent states, and tolerating strongmen whose movements towards liberalism prove glacial all sound unappealing. In fact, they sound downright un-American. History's other global powers have engaged in such behavior, but never the United States.

Therein lies the great problem with the post-Cold War period: the sole remaining superpower has refused to enforce its own values. With the demise of the Soviet Union, American thinkers, strategists, politicians, and policy makers—even those of the Huntington school—have all behaved like disciples of Fukuyama. The baseline belief of the 1990s was that the benefits of liberal democracy and neoliberal economics were self-evident. The relatively easy conversion of Eastern Europe proved intoxicating. America led the drive toward global rule-based institutions without ever allocating the resources necessary for global education and enforcement. America's policy leaders acted upon the naïve belief that given a bit of freedom and some gentle outside encouragement, all of the world's peoples, nations, and states would move—some might say evolve— in the direction of liberal democracy.

That assumption suffered from a fatal flaw. Liberalism may be many wonderful things, but self-evident is not among them. American policy has long rested upon the conceit that "we all want the same things." We don't. In today's world, China seeks to combine control and growth; Russia seeks to restore its own greatness; Islamists seek to order the world as they believe God commanded; and revolutionaries of various stripes seek to plunge the world into anarchy as a stepping-stone toward their preferred social structures. None of these groups has much use for the freedom, individual dignity, or self-determination that lie at the heart of classical liberalism—though (as the UN demonstrates quite clearly) they often find lip service to these concepts cynically useful in the pursuit of their own objectives.

American—and Western—leaders continue to ignore the fundamental value differences shaping the twenty-first century. They happily proclaim that we are not at war with Islam, that Islam is a religion of peace, and that the violent brutality committed in the name of Islam is not Islam. Setting aside that as a trivial matter of international law only states may be at war (hence Islam, as a non-state, cannot be at war with anyone), both these assertions and the assurances they intend to convey are naïve and ignorant at best, dangerous lies at worst. It is undeniable that a philosophy underpinning numerous violent, brutal groups and movements draws upon Islamic history, sources, and thinking, and enjoys considerable popularity among Muslims. As to whether it is *a* legitimate expression of Islam, *the only* legitimate expression of Islam, or a dangerous heresy, is a question that Islamic theologians may debate for decades or centuries. Only those boasting expertise in and connection to Islamic theology may offer reasonable opinions on the matter. No Western politician comes close to qualifying.

This supremacist strain of Islamic thinking (available in both Sunni and Shiite variants), the Sunni Arab pan movement now manifesting itself as the Islamic State's Caliphate, and revolutionary Khomeinism, are incompatible with a rule-based system that might someday grow to become truly global. They are thus antithetical to American interests, Western interests, and the cause of liberalism. Yet the current configuration of the Middle East locks these dangerous ideologies in place. American policy for the remainder of the twenty-first century must move the region in the appropriate direction—even if slowly—or concede the failure of the entire rule-based global system. Establishing safe-haven states for the region's minorities is a critical first step. Replacing revolutionary Khomeinism with a pride in Persian culture and history, and a drive to develop it in a positive direction, is a second. Identifying and supporting Sunni Arab leaders willing to rethink recent trends in both Arab and Islamic philosophy may be the most important step of all.

The manifest failure of past American policies traces easily to the false narrative upon which they have all rested. The empirical evidence against conventional wisdom is overwhelming. The post-Ottoman Middle East has featured perpetual instability, brutal illiberalism, poverty among riches, widespread illiteracy, permanent underemployment, multi-generational refugees, numerous brutalized minorities, chattel slavery, the oppression of women, and nearly universal violence and rage. The only group fortunate enough to pull itself out of this morass—the Jews—remains a perpetual target of those mired within it. Westerners, and in particular Americans, are objects of envy, venom, and when possible, violence. Were there ever a case for peering beyond conventional wisdom to take a fresh look at recent history in the service of a new analysis, the post-Ottoman Middle East presents it. The emerging post-post-Ottoman order compels it.

For nearly a century, outsiders have attempted to impose short-term stability on this region. Despite their successes, the region itself seems to grow progressively worse in the intermediate- and long-terms. Why? One reason may be that its problems are endemic. If so, then short-term stability makes a disastrous climax inevitable. Stability in the face of endemic problems allows belligerents to avoid tough choices and reforms, stew in their own bile, and improve their armaments. If a broad regional war is inevitable, past impositions of short-term stability have only increased its bloodiness. It would be best to let the bloodletting commence immediately, before one final deferral pushes it into the realm of nuclear conflict.

Our journey has culminated with a proposal to reorient American policy in a very different direction. U.S. policy in the Middle East should support American interests in a manner consistent with American values. It must be anti-imperial and anti-revolutionary while promoting minority self-determination. Its military dimension must defeat radical Islam at the tactical level, while its combination of hard and soft power must undermine radical Islamic fundamentalism. On geopolitics, it must protect minorities and refugees by separating populations into coherent national blocs, then fostering the concepts of national citizenry necessary for stability and security. Its economic component must emphasize growth and human capital development, while its social dimension must promote institutions of civil society, individual dignity, and liberalism to as large a degree as is possible while combating supremacism, radicalism, and terrorism.

Above all, American policy must recognize that regional stability cannot arise unless many players and institutions that have long been part of the problem choose instead to become part of the solution. Those who lean in the pro-American direction, or even those who turn to the U.S. as the only source of their own salvation, will face numerous tough choices. Past American policy has been to spare allies the agony of choosing. Moving forward, American policy must instead force them to choose—and provide both the carrots and the sticks necessary to make the right choices rational.

This agenda departs from past American perspectives and policies in important ways. Its novel aspects may make it controversial—whether it is implemented as actual policy or merely added to the realm of discourse and debate. It's not hard to predict some sources of opposition: Advocates for the "authenticity" of terrorist groups like Hamas, Fatah, Hezbollah, and the Muslim Brotherhood; apologists for the numerous supremacist and/or terrorist organizations; those who accept the legitimacy of the Sunni Arab claim of right to the entire region; NGOs seeking to move large numbers of refugees out of the region or to entrench them where they guarantee instability; Iran's friends in the United States and in Europe; the sizable virulent anti-Israel lobby; and opponents of "nationalism" in all of its forms; will undoubtedly oppose most of it. Believers in the fiction of "Islamophobia"—an invention of the Muslim Brotherhood that the Organization of Islamic Cooperation has promulgated to equate any hint that their version of Islam may be something less than the ideal solution to all that ails the world— may see it at play here;[588] as we have seen, any expressed preference for reformist over supremacist Islam tends to earn their ire.[589] NGOs, academics, and media outlets vested in the centrality of the Arab/Israeli conflict, the imposition of double standards for Israel, and the fantasy that wedging yet another failed Sunni Arab state into the land west of the Jordan River would generate some sort of magical "solution" to the region's problems, will balk at the thought that the region's dominant story surrounds its largest ethnic group rather than a tiny minority. Such complaints are foreseeable and inevitable.

The false narrative has deep roots. Many professionals have staked careers on it, and anyone advocating the maintenance of the status quo can always plausibly argue: "it could be worse." Opponents of our proposed agenda will likely vilify it precisely because they have so much vested in the conventional wisdom that has brought so much misery to so many. A more accurate perspective, and an agenda that emerges from it, might demonstrate their own complicity in that suffering—as well as question the basis for their professional prestige. But such predictable vilification will only highlight how much a new perspective and agenda have to commend them. The new narrative centered on the supremacist leanings of Sunni Arabs is simple and sensible; it explains the past and provides a strong framework for understanding the present—

and thus for predicting the future. The policy agenda combines American values with American interests, and creates a platform for the eventual integration of the Middle East into the rule-based global system of nation-states, as a reasonably stable region whose countries commit greater resources to human capital development than they do to ideological vendettas.

Its implementation will not prove painless. People will die and others will suffer—though almost certainly in smaller numbers than those to which current trends seem destined to lead. The death and suffering that does arise, however, will bear at least some American fingerprints. It will take significant American blood and treasure to resettle refugees in a humane way; to relocate communities into contiguous blocs; to help the region's minorities found and sustain thriving ethnonational states; to eject the terror-supporting, genocidal, messianic regime from Teheran; to liberate land seized by the nascent Caliphate; and to effect philosophical changes in the ways that Sunni Arabs conceptualize both their own Arabism and their own Sunni Islam.

The alternative, however, is chilling. Any thinking person contemplating the American investment—in time, resources, prestige, blood, and treasure—necessary to effect positive change in the Middle East should balk at the cost. Critics will mislabel the effort "nation building in the Islamic world," attempting to discredit it as a reprise of past American misadventures in Somalia and Iraq, when it is in fact precisely the opposite: It begins with preexisting nations, and attempts to help them construct the far less difficult mechanics and institutions of statehood. Still, it is hard to miss the temptation of withdrawing—allowing this maddening region and its violent people to destroy each other from a safe distance—while Americans invest in building a better America. Yet such a withdrawal is inconsistent with the American character and antithetical to American interests. The humanitarian costs of standing aside, already staggering, are likely to grow exponentially. True containment would trap minorities with their oppressors, and require America to look the other way through the ensuing genocide. Attempts to alleviate the suffering by moving massive refugee flows out of the region would threaten to destabilize host countries throughout Europe and the Americas. True conquest would turn the U.S. into the new Rome, laying asunder the very land beneath recalcitrant locals. Any of these choices would effectively end the rule-based global order that raised such great hopes so recently, running counter to both American ideals and American interests.

Over time, American retreat, containment, or conquest would

each impose greater suffering throughout the region, and require greater sacrifices of American blood and treasure, than would thoughtful strategic commitment. And they would impose those costs while promising few of the benefits that thoughtful commitment might enable. The true choice is thus not between commitment and disengagement; it is between thoughtful proactive commitment and mindless reactive engagement. The Obama Administration's reentry into a crumbling Iraq only a few short years after withdrawing from a much more stable country illuminates the difference brightly.

America's two twenty-first century Presidents have combined to teach an important lesson: either play to win or stay out of the game. George W. Bush chose to confront the enemy, seeking to bring the fight to them rather than waiting for them to bring it to America. But he did so without mobilizing all of American society, without committing the resources necessary to win the peace, and without preparing the American public for an open-ended commitment. Barack Obama chose to withdraw, seeking to leave the fight to its primary combatants while focusing his attention domestically. But he did so without withdrawing fully, continuing drone strikes, bombing raids, and even ground troops, and while opening America's borders to refugees. Taken together, Bush and Obama have demonstrated the folly of both incomplete engagement and incomplete disengagement.

Playing to win remains, by far, the superior choice. Fukuyama noted correctly that the U.S. has benefitted greatly from the global international order that it has led for decades—as have the values of liberalism. Huntington noted correctly that the international order at any point in time will necessarily reflect the character of the leading power or powers. The choice is thus stark: Committed engagement is necessary to continue the rule-based liberal international order. Committed withdrawal will end that order, and move the world into its next stage—one that is certain to be less amenable to either American interests or liberal values. This essay outlined the basics of a full-commitment engagement strategy, beginning with a new perspective—a minimally necessary precondition for a new Middle East. New opportunities can become visible only through a new window. Future Presidents can either continue the policy of withdrawal and reaction or open that new window to see a new Middle East. For an American vision to become possible, America's leadership must first choose to see.

Notes

* All websites visited June-October 2016 except where otherwise noted.

1 Hillary Clinton, *U.S. Senate Hearings on the Benghazi Attack*, Jan. 23, 2013, https://www.c-span.org/video/?c4329984/clinton-blows-gop-senator-benghazi-hearing.

2 Winston Churchill, Address to the House of Commons, Dec. 15, 1944, http://hansard.millbanksystems.com/commons/1944/dec/15/poland.

3 *See e.g.*, Michael Rowlands, Mogens Larsen, and Kristian Krtiansen, (eds.), *Centre and Periphery in the Ancient World*, (Cambridge Univ. Press, 1987) at ch. 4.

4 *See e.g.*, Lawrence Schiffman, "The United Monarchy: Rereading the Bible and the Archaeological Evidence," http://cojs.org/united-monarchy-rereading-bible-archaeological-evidence/.

5 *See*, 1 Kings 12.

6 *See*, Lester Grabbe, Ancient Israel: What Do We Know and How Do We Know It? (Bloomsbury, 2008) at ch. 5.

7 *See e.g.*, Christopher Chase-Dunne and Bruce Lerro, *Social Change: Globalization from the Stone Age to the Present* (Paradigm, 2013) at ch. 11.

8 *See e.g.*, "The Persians," *Jewish Virtual Library*, http://www.jewishvirtuallibrary.org/jsource/History/Persians.html; Roger Price, "What if Cyrus had not Freed the Jews," *Jewish Journal*, Sept. 24, 2013, http://www.jewishjournal.com/judaismandscience/item/what_if_cyrus_had_not_freed_the_jews.

9 *See e.g.*, Joshua Mark, "The Hellenistic World: The World of Alexander the Great," *Ancient History Encyclopedia*, Jan. 18, 2012, http://www.ancient.eu/article/94/.

10 *See e.g.*, "The Maccabees/Hasmoneans," *Jewish Virtual Library*, http://www.jewishvirtuallibrary.org/jsource/History/Maccabees.html.

11 *See e.g.*, "The Bar-Kochba Revolt," *Jewish Virtual Library*, http://www.jewishvirtuallibrary.org/jsource/Judaism/revolt1.html.

12 *See e.g.*, "The Pre-Islamic Middle East," https://cmes.uchicago.edu/sites/cmes.uchicago.edu/files/uploads/Maps/Map%20-%20Byzantines%20%26%20Sasanians.pdf.

13 *See e.g.*, Daniel Pipes, "Uncovering Early Islam," *National Review*, May 16, 2012, http://www.danielpipes.org/11280/uncovering-early-

<u>islam</u>.

[14] Ignaz Goldziher, *Muhammedanische Studien*, (Halle a. S., M. Niemeyer, 1889-90) tr. S. M. Stern, (SUNY Press, 1967).

[15] *See e.g.*, PBS, "The Life of Muhammad," <u>http://www.pbs.org/muhammad/timeline_html.shtml</u>.

[16] See e.g., Ayaan Hirsi-Ali, Heretic: Why Islam Needs a Reformation Now, (Harper Collins, 2015).

[17] *See e.g.*, PBS, *supra* n. 15.

[18] *See e.g.*, Elizabeth Urban, "Rashidun Caliphate," in *Encyclopedia of Empire* (Wiley, 2016).

[19] *See e.g.*, Editors, "Fitna," *Encycolpaedia Brittanica*, <u>https://www.britannica.com/topic/fitnah</u>.

[20] See e.g., id.

[21] *See e.g.*, JVL, "Islam: Sunni Sect," <u>http://www.jewishvirtuallibrary.org/jsource/History/sunni.html</u>.

[22] *See e.g.*, Editors, "Battle of Karbala," *Encycolpaedia Brittanica*, <u>https://www.britannica.com/event/Battle-of-Karbala</u>; Ramzan Sabir, "Karbala: The Chain of Events," <u>https://www.al-islam.org/articles/karbala-the-chain-of-events-ramzan-sabir</u> (for an unapologetic Shiite perspective).

[23] *See e.g.*, Firas Alkhateeb, "The Abbasid Revolution," *Lost Islamic History*, Jul. 3, 2013, <u>http://lostislamichistory.com/the-abbasid-revolution/</u>.

[24] *See e.g.*, Benjamin Braude, ed. *Christians and Jews in the Ottoman Empire: The Abridged Edition* (Lynne Reinner, 2014) at ch. 1, <u>https://www.rienner.com/uploads/53e278dea4631.pdf</u>.

[25] *See e.g.*, Encyclopedia Judaica: Abbasids, <u>http://www.jewishvirtuallibrary.org/jsource/judaica/ejud_0002_0001_0_00087.html</u>.

[26] *See e.g.*, Majid Fakhri, *A History of Islamic Philosophy* (2nd ed.) (Columbia University Press, 1983) at Introduction; Weebly, "Islamic Civilization Timeline: Abbasid Caliphate," <u>http://islamiccivilizationtimeline.weebly.com/abbasid-caliphate.html</u>.

[27] *See e.g.*, Weebly, *id.*; Muslim Hope, "The Druze Faith," Apr. 2013, <u>http://www.muslimhope.com/Druze.htm</u>; Muslim Hope, "'Alawites in the Muslim World," May 2007, http://www.muslimhope.com/Alawites.htm.

28 See e.g., James Waterson, *The Knights of Islam: The Wars of the Mamluks*, (Greenhill Books, 2007).

29 *See e.g.*, Editors, "Ottoman Empire," *Encyclopaedia Brittanica*, https://www.britannica.com/place/Ottoman-Empire.

30 *See e.g.*, Ömer Faruk Bozkurt, "The Ottoman non-Muslim Communities under Millet System from the Conquest of Constantinople to the Beginning of Tanzimat Era," (Middle East Technical University, 2011), http://www.academia.edu/21736954/The_Ottoman_non-Muslim_Communities_under_Millet_System_from_the_Conquest_of_Constantinople_to_the_Beginning_of_Tanzimat_Era.

31 *See e.g.*, Firas Alkhateeb, "How Atatürk Made Turkey Secular," *Lost Islamic History*, Jun. 11, 2013, http://lostislamichistory.com/how-ataturk-made-turkey-secular/.

32 *See e.g.*, Lee Smith, "Zone Defense," *Weekly Standard*, May 23, 2016, http://www.weeklystandard.com/zone-defense/article/2002376.

33 *See e.g.*, Firas Alkhateeb, "How the British Divided Up the Arab World," *Lost Islamic History*, Dec. 26, 2012, http://lostislamichistory.com/how-the-british-divided-up-the-arab-world/; Daniel Pipes, "The 'Shocking Document' that Shaped the Middle East turns 100," *Washington Times,* May 9, 2016, http://www.danielpipes.org/16661/sykes-picot-at-100.

34 See e.g., Robert Olson, The Emergence of Kurdish Nationalism and the Sheikh Said Rebellion, (University of Texas Press, 1989).

35 *See e.g.*, Brilliant Maps, "French Mandate for Syria and The Lebanon In 1922," http://brilliantmaps.com/syria-1922/.

36 *See e.g.*, Firas Alkhateeb, "Who Invented Lebanon?" *Lost Islamic History*, Dec. 15, 2012, http://lostislamichistory.com/the_creation_of_lebanon/.

37 U.S. Dept. of State, "Saddam's Chemical Weapons Campaign: Halabja, March 16, 1988", Mar. 14, 2003, https://2001-2009.state.gov/r/pa/ei/rls/18714.htm.

38 *See e.g.*, Daniel Pipes, "Caliph Ibrahim's Brutal Moment," *Washington Times*, Aug. 5, 2014, http://www.danielpipes.org/14691/caliph-ibrahim.

39 *See e.g.*, Susanne Koelbl, Samiha Shafy and Bernhard Zand, "The Cold War of Islam," *Der Spiegel*, My 9, 2016, http://www.spiegel.de/international/world/saudia-arabia-iran-and-the-new-middle-eastern-cold-war-a-1090725.html.

40 *See e.g.*, Michael Doran, *Ike's Gamble*, (Simon & Schuster, 2016).

41 Francis Fukuyama, *The End of History and the Last Man*, (Free Press,

1992).

[42] Samuel Huntington, The Clash of Civilizations and the Remaking of World Order, (Simon & Schuster, 1996).

[43] Samuel Huntington, "The Clash of Civilizations?" *Foreign Affairs*, Jun. 1993, https://www.foreignaffairs.com/articles/united-states/1993-06-01/clash-civilizations.

[44] *See,* Francis Fukuyama, *America at the Crossroads*, (Yale University Press, 2006).

[45] *See e.g.,* Andrew Roberts, "1776: Would You Like to Reconsider?" *Wall Street Journal*, Oct. 28, 2016, http://www.wsj.com/articles/1776-would-you-like-to-reconsider-1477694968.

[46] Arch Puddington and Tyler Roylance, "Anxious Dictators, Wavering Democracies: Global Freedom under Pressure," *Freedom in the World 2016*, (Freedom House, 2016), https://freedomhouse.org/sites/default/files/FH_FITW_Report_2016.pdf.

[47] *See e.g.,* Steve Yetiv, *The Persian Gulf Crisis*, (Greenwood Press, 1997) at 21-23; Norman Kempster, "Baker Discusses 'What-Ifs' With Arabs," *Los Angeles Times*, Jan. 11, 1991, http://articles.latimes.com/1991-01-11/news/mn-8299_1_arab-allies.

[48] George Bush and Brent Scowcroft, "Why We Didn't Remove Saddam," *Time*, March 2, 1998, https://www.globalpolicy.org/component/content/article/169-history/36409.html.

[49] *See e.g.,* George de Lama, "Bush Aides Hint Hussein must Fall," *Chicago Tribune*, Feb. 25, 1991, http://articles.chicagotribune.com/1991-02-25/news/9101180263_1_saddam-hussein-iraqi-leader-middle-east.

[50] See e.g., id.

[51] James Baker, "Interview," *Frontline*, Mid-October 2001, http://www.pbs.org/wgbh/pages/frontline/shows/gunning/interviews/baker.html.

[52] *See,* Bush and Scowcroft, *supra* n. 48.

[53] *See e.g.,* Joel Brinkley, "War in the Gulf," *The New York Times*, Jan. 19, 1991, http://www.nytimes.com/1991/01/19/world/war-gulf-israel-iraq-fires-new-missle-attack-israel-allies-continue-bombing-seek.html?pagewanted=all.

[54] *See e.g.,* Hassan Krayem, "The Lebanese Civil War and the Taif Agreement," *American University of Beirut*, http://ddc.aub.edu.lb/projects/pspa/conflict-resolution.html. ("Part

of this re-expansion of Syrian power was with Arab and Western acquiescence. This acquiescence was partly to avoid inter-Arab conflicts and partly to curry Syrian favor in the Persian Gulf and the Arab-Israeli peace process.").

[55] *See e.g.,* Youssef Ibrahim, "Jordan a Grim Refuge for Kuwait Palestinians," *New York Times*, Oct. 3, 1991, http://www.nytimes.com/1991/10/03/world/jordan-a-grim-refuge-for-kuwait-palestinians.html?pagewanted=all.

[56] *See e.g.,* BBC, "No-fly Zones: The Legal Position," *BBC News*, Feb. 19, 2001, http://news.bbc.co.uk/2/hi/middle_east/1175950.stm.

[57] *See e.g.,* Andrew Sprung, "Did the U.S. 'Abandon' Afghanistan in 1989?" *The Atlantic*, Dec. 17, 2009, http://www.theatlantic.com/daily-dish/archive/2009/12/did-the-us-abandon-afghanistan-in-1989/192860/.

[58] *See e.g.,* RealClearPolitics, "8 Handshakes that Changed History," *RealClearPolitics*, May 22, 2012, http://www.realclearpolitics.com/lists/famous_political_handshakes/rabin_arafat.html?state=play.

[59] *See e.g.,* David Eliezre, "Listen to Arafat in Arabic, Not in English," *Los Angeles Times*, Feb. 27, 1996, http://articles.latimes.com/1996-02-27/local/me-40531_1_west-bank.

[60] Ephraim Karsh, "Arafat's War," *Middle East Forum*, Dec. 2, 2003, http://www.meforum.org/581/arafats-war.

[61] Gerald Steinberg, "Peace, Security, and Terror in the 1996 Elections," *Israel Affairs*, Fall 1997, http://nebula.wsimg.com/e54e12e052e4b35929c54b077f89d4bf?AccessKeyId=819C4344531C36A020F2&disposition=0&alloworigin=1.

[62] *See e.g.,* Dafna Linzer, "Netanyahu: Peres Exploiting Good Relations with Clinton," *AP News Archive*, May 1, 1996, http://www.apnewsarchive.com/1996/Netanyahu-Peres-Exploiting-Good-Relations-With-Clinton/id-bbbddccca71a9bd08f9d26fbc34192fa.

[63] *See e.g.,* Robert Satloff, "The Clinton/Albright Plan," *Washington Institute Policywatch 140*, Aug. 7, 1997, http://www.washingtoninstitute.org/policy-analysis/view/the-clinton-albright-plan-step-1-fight-terror-step-2-make-peace-fast.

[64] *See e.g.,* Tony Karron, "Clinton Saves Last Dance for Arafat," *Time*, Jan 2, 2001, http://content.time.com/time/world/article/0,8599,93339,00.html.

[65] Karsh, *supra* n. 60.

[66] PNC, "Political Programme," Adopted at the 12th Session of the Palestinian National Council, Cairo, Jun. 9, 1974, http://www.iris.org.il/plophase.htm.

[67] Mahmoud Abbas, "Address to the UN General Assembly," http://www.timesofisrael.com/full-text-of-abbas-2015-address-to-the-un-general-assembly/. ("We therefore declare that we cannot continue to be bound by these agreements…").

[68] *See e.g.*, Clyde Haberman, "Israel and Jordan Sign Peace Accord," *New York Times,* Oct. 26, 1994, http://www.nytimes.com/learning/general/onthisday/big/1026.html#article.

[69] *See e.g.*, Byron York, "The Facts about Clinton and Terrorism," *National Review,* Sept. 11, 2006, http://www.nationalreview.com/article/218683/facts-about-clinton-and-terrorism-byron-york.

[70] *See e.g.*, "1998 Missile Strikes on Bin Laden May Have Backfired," *National Security Archive,* Aug. 20, 2008. http://nsarchive.gwu.edu/NSAEBB/NSAEBB253/.

[71] *See e.g.*, "USS Cole Bombing," http://www.911memorial.org/uss-cole-bombing.

[72] 9/11 Commission, *The 9/11 Commission Report,* http://www.9-11commission.gov/report/911Report_Exec.htm.

[73] George W. Bush, Second Inaugural Address, Jan. 20, 2005, http://www.npr.org/templates/story/story.php?storyId=4460172.

[74] *See e.g.*, Eric Schmitt, "Army Chief Raises Estimate of G.I.'s needed in Postwar Iraq," *New York Times,* Feb. 25, 2003, http://www.nytimes.com/2003/02/25/international/middleeast/25CND-MILI.html.

[75] *See e.g.*, John McCain, "Our Exit Strategy in Iraq is Victory," *Speeches,* Nov. 5, 2003, http://www.mccain.senate.gov/public/index.cfm/speeches?ID=2d7dce5e-ff99-4a07-8436-36bf310fc60b.

[76] *See e.g.*, CNN, "Lieberman Lashes Left-Wing Democrats," *CNN.com*, Aug. 10, 2003, http://www.cnn.com/2003/ALLPOLITICS/08/10/dems.candidates/.

[77] AP, "Full Transcript: Democratic Presidential Candidates Debate," Sept. 5, 2003, http://www.washingtonpost.com/wp-srv/politics/transcripts/090403demsdebate.html.

78 *See e.g.*, "U.S. Troops Capture Saddam Hussein," *The Wall Street Journal*, Dec. 15, 2003, http://www.wsj.com/articles/SB10714006529014900.

79 *See e.g.*, Flynt Leverett, "Why Libya Gave Up on the Bomb," *Brookings Institution*, Jan. 23, 2004, http://www.brookings.edu/research/opinions/2004/01/23middleeast-leverett.

80 *See e.g.*, Jefferson Morley, "The Branding of Lebanon's 'Revolution,'" *Washington Post*, Mar. 3, 2005, http://www.washingtonpost.com/wp-dyn/articles/A1911-2005Mar2.html.

81 *See e.g.*, "Iran Gave U.S. Help on Al Qaeda After 9/11," *CBS News*, Oct. 7, 2008, http://www.cbsnews.com/news/iran-gave-us-help-on-al-qaeda-after-9-11/.

82 *See e.g.*, David Patten, "Is Iraq in a Civil War," *The Middle East Quarterly*, Summer 2007, http://www.meforum.org/1694/is-iraq-in-a-civil-war.

83 James Baker & Lee Hamilton, *The Iraq Study Group Report* (Vintage Books, 2006) at Executive Summary.

84 *Id.* at 9.

85 Robert Satloff, Dennis Ross, and Mehdi Khalaji, "The Iraq Study Group: Assessing its Regional Conclusions," *Washington Institute Policywatch 1180*, Dec. 21, 2006, http://www.washingtoninstitute.org/policy-analysis/view/the-iraq-study-group-assessing-its-regional-conclusions.

86 *See e.g.*, "Iraq Study Group: The Forgotten Men," *Newsweek*, Jan. 28, 2007, http://www.newsweek.com/iraq-study-group-forgotten-men-98685.

87 Anne Flaherty, "Reid: U.S. Can't Win the War in Iraq," *Washington Post*, Apr. 19, 2007, http://www.washingtonpost.com/wp-dyn/content/article/2007/04/19/AR2007041901150.html.

88 *See e.g.*, Peter Feaver, "Hillary Clinton and the Inconvenient Facts about the Rise of the Islamic State," *Foreign Policy*, Aug. 13, 2015, http://foreignpolicy.com/2015/08/13/clinton-surge-iraq-maliki-obama/; AP, "Iraqi Surge Exceeded Expectations, Obama Says," *NBC News*, Sept. 4, 2008, http://www.nbcnews.com/id/26550764/ns/politics-decision_08/t/iraqi-surge-exceeded-expectations-obama-says/#.V28ayWQrK34.

89 *See e.g.*, Fred W. Baker, "Surge Troops Stabilized Iraq, Chairman Tells Troops," *U.S. Dept. of Defense*, Jun. 19, 2008,

http://archive.defense.gov/news/newsarticle.aspx?id=50256.

90 *See e.g.*, Greg Hitt, "Bush Vows to be Evenhanded in Mideast," *Wall Street Journal*, May 10, 2004, http://www.wsj.com/articles/SB108387428101504267.

91 *See e.g.*, "Israel's Withdrawal from Gaza," *NPR*, http://www.npr.org/series/4797062/israel-s-withdrawal-from-gaza.

92 *See e.g.*, Jim VanderHei, "Bush Prods Sharon on Peace," *Washington Post*, Apr. 12, 2005, http://www.washingtonpost.com/wp-dyn/articles/A43682-2005Apr11.html.

93 *See e.g.*, AP, "Looters Strip Gaza Greenhouses," *Associated Press*, Sept. 13, 2005. http://www.nbcnews.com/id/9331863/ns/world_news-mideast_n_africa/t/looters-strip-gaza-greenhouses/.

94 *See e.g.*, Scott Wilson, "Hamas Sweeps Palestinian Elections, Complicating Peace Efforts in the Middle East," *Washington Post,* Jan. 27, 2006, http://www.washingtonpost.com/wp-dyn/content/article/2006/01/26/AR2006012600372.html.

95 *See e.g.*, Fares Akram and Isabel Kershner, "Hamas Finds Itself Aligned with Israel over Extremist Groups," *New York Times,* Oct. 19, 2012, http://www.nytimes.com/2012/10/20/world/middleeast/hamas-works-to-suppress-militant-groups-in-gaza.html?_r=0.

96 *See e.g.*, Ben Ariel, "Hamas Leader: We'll Respond to Egypt as We Do to Israel," *Arutz Sheva,* Mar. 3, 2015, http://www.israelnationalnews.com/News/News.aspx/192055#.Vzz LNfkrKUk.

97 *See e.g.*, Kristina Wong, "Obama's Unsettled Legacy on Iraq and Afghanistan," *The Hill,* Feb. 10, 2016, http://thehill.com/policy/defense/268854-obamas-unsettled-legacy-on-iraq-and-afghanistan.

98 Barack Obama, "Remarks by the President at Cairo University," Jun. 4, 2009, https://www.whitehouse.gov/the-press-office/remarks-president-cairo-university-6-04-09.

99 *See e.g.*, Michael Oren, "How Obama Abandoned Israel," *Wall Street Journal,* Jun. 16, 2015, http://www.wsj.com/articles/how-obama-abandoned-israel-1434409772.

100 *See e.g.*, Morton Klein and Daniel Mandel, "Obama's Outrageous Decision to Fund Hamas-Aligned Palestinian Regime," *The Algemeiner*, Jun. 8, 2014, http://www.algemeiner.com/2014/06/08/obamas-outrageous-decision-to-fund-hamas-aligned-palestinian-regime/; Caroline Glick, "Obama's New Plan for Hamas," *Jerusalem Post*, Aug. 7,

2014, http://www.jpost.com/Opinion/Columnists/COLUMN-ONE-Obamas-new-plan-for-Hamas-370422.

[101] *See e.g.*, Jeffrey Goldberg, "The Obama Doctrine," *The Atlantic*, April 2016, http://www.theatlantic.com/magazine/archive/2016/04/the-obama-doctrine/471525/.

[102] *See e.g.*, Deborah Amos, "Arab Leaders Feel U.S. Abandoned Egypt's Mubarak," *NPR*, Feb. 9, 2011, http://www.npr.org/2011/02/09/133614346/Egypt-Arab-Leaders.

[103] *See e.g.*, Caroline Glick, "Obama to the Rescue—of Hamas," *Jerusalem Post*, Jul. 22, 2014, http://www.jpost.com/Opinion/Columnists/Obama-to-the-rescue-of-Hamas-368508.

[104] *See e.g.*, The Economist, "Anarchy Looms," *The Economist*, Aug. 30, 2014, http://www.economist.com/news/middle-east-and-africa/21614231-foreign-involvement-and-reckless-militias-make-flammable-cocktail-anarchy-looms.

[105] *See e.g.*, Lee Smith, "Has the Obama Administration become Iran's Lawyer?" *Tablet*, Jul. 6, 2015, http://www.tabletmag.com/scroll/192045/has-the-obama-administration-become-irans-lawyer; Iran Daily, "Obama Says Iran's Reintegration into Global Economy to Take Time," *Iran Daily*, Apr. 1, 2016, http://www.iran-daily.com/News/138802.html.

[106] *See e.g.*, Andrew Tabler, "Syria's Collapse and How Washington Can Stop it," *Foreign Affairs*, Jul./Aug. 2013, http://www.washingtoninstitute.org/policy-analysis/view/syrias-collapse-and-how-washington-can-stop-it

[107] *See e.g.*, David Feith and Bari Weiss, "Denying the Green Revolution," *Wall Street Journal*, Oct. 23, 2009, http://www.wsj.com/articles/SB10001424052748704224004574489772874564430.

[108] *See e.g.*, Guy Taylor, "Obama Yields to Russia and Iran, Puts Bashar Assad Ouster on Back Burner," *Washington Times*, Dec. 21, 2015, http://www.washingtontimes.com/news/2015/dec/21/obama-yields-to-russia-and-iran-puts-bashar-assad-/?page=all.

[109] Barack Obama, "Osama bin Laden Dead," May 2, 2011, https://www.whitehouse.gov/blog/2011/05/02/osama-bin-laden-dead.

[110] *See e.g.*, Warren Beatty, "Al Qaeda is 'On the Run,'" *American Thinker*, Jan. 22, 2015,

http://www.americanthinker.com/articles/2015/01/al qaeda is on the run.html.

111 Patrick Howley, "Obamacare Architect: Lack of Transparency Was Key Because 'Stupidity Of The American Voter' Would Have Killed Obamacare," *Daily Caller*, Nov. 9, 2014, http://dailycaller.com/2014/11/09/obamacare-architect-lack-of-transparency-was-key-because-stupidity-of-the-american-voter-would-have-killed-obamacare/#ixzz4OJj0gv00.

112 *See e.g.*, David Samuels, "The Aspiring Novelist Who Became Obama's Foreign-Policy Guru," *New York Times*, May 5, 2016, http://www.nytimes.com/2016/05/08/magazine/the-aspiring-novelist-who-became-obamas-foreign-policy-guru.html.

113 *See e.g.*, Oren, *supra* n. 99; Jennifer Rubin, "Why it's Correct to Label the Obama Administration 'Anti-Israel,'" *Washington Post*, Jan. 20, 2016, https://www.washingtonpost.com/blogs/right-turn/wp/2016/01/20/why-its-correct-to-label-the-obama-administration-anti-israel/; Ben Shapiro, "A Complete Timeline of Obama's Anti-Israel Hatred," *Breitbart*, Mar. 20, 2105, http://www.breitbart.com/national-security/2015/03/20/a-complete-timeline-of-obamas-anti-israel-hatred/; Daniel Halper, "Is Obama Pro-Israel;" *Weekly Standard*, Sept. 19, 2011, http://www.weeklystandard.com/is-obama-pro-israel/article/593694; Greg Rosenbaum, "Obama has a Stronger Record on Israel than you Might Have Been Led to Think," *Haaretz*, Jun. 23, 2015, http://www.haaretz.com/opinion/.premium-1.662588; Ian Schwartz, "Obama: I have been Called 'The First Jewish President," *RealClearPolitics*, May 22, 2015, http://www.realclearpolitics.com/video/2015/05/22/obama i have been called the first jewish president.html;

114 *See e.g.*, White House, "President Obama Speaks on the Recovery of Sgt. Bowe Bergdahl," May 31, 2014, https://www.whitehouse.gov/photos-and-video/video/2014/05/31/president-obama-speaks-recovery-sgt-bowe-bergdahl; Zachary Goldfarb and Ed O'Keefe, "Obama Defends Decision to Trade 5 Guantanamo Detainees for Bergdahl," *Washington Post*, Jun. 3, 2014, https://www.washingtonpost.com/world/national-security/obama-defends-decision-to-trade-5-guantanamo-detainees-for-bergdahl/2014/06/03/759151a8-eb10-11e3-b98c-72cef4a00499 story.html; Alex Quade, "Shock U.S. Army Admission: Obama Freed Taliban 'Psychopath' in Bergdahl Trade," *Washington*

Times, Aug. 4, 2014, http://www.washingtontimes.com/news/2014/aug/4/taliban-prisoner-traded-for-bowe-bergdahl-a-danger/; Fox News, "Gitmo Detainees Traded for Bergdahl Have Tried to Resume Terror Activities," *New York Post*, Mar. 26, 2015, http://nypost.com/2015/03/25/prisoners-swapped-for-accused-deserter-bergdahl-have-tried-to-rejoin-terror-networks/; Michael Crowley, "How the Bergdahl Story went from Victory to Controversy for Obama," *Time*, Jun. 3, 2014, http://time.com/2817830/bowe-bergdahl-obama/.

[115] *See e.g.*, Washington Wire, "Flashback: What Susan Rice Said About Benghazi," *Wall Street Journal*, Nov. 16, 2012, http://blogs.wsj.com/washwire/2012/11/16/flashback-what-susan-rice-said-about-benghazi/; Kimberly Strassel, "She Knew All Along," *Wall Street Journal*, Oct. 23, 2015, http://www.wsj.com/articles/she-knew-all-along-1445556778.

[116] Samuels, *supra* n. 111.

[117] Goldberg, *supra* n. 101.

[118] *See e.g.*, The Economist, "The New Face of Terror," *The Economist*, Sept. 28, 2013, http://www.economist.com/news/leaders/21586832-west-thought-it-was-winning-battle-against-jihadist-terrorism-it-should-think-again.

[119] *See e.g.*, Danny Romero, "ISIS, a Year of the Caliphate," *The Independent*, Jun. 28, 2015, http://www.independent.co.uk/news/world/middle-east/isis-a-year-of-the-caliphate-4-maps-that-show-how-far-and-fast-the-group-has-spread-10342191.html

[120] *See e.g.*, Natan Sachs, "US-Israel Relations have Reached a Dramatic Low Point," *Business Insider*, Jul. 21, 2015, http://www.businessinsider.co.id/us-israel-relations-have-reached-a-dramatic-low-point-2015-7/#.VzzaY_krKUk.

[121] *See e.g.*, Carol Lee, "U.S.-Saudi Tensions in Focus as Barack Obama Visits Mideast this Week," *Wall Street Journal*, Apr. 18, 2016, http://blogs.wsj.com/washwire/2016/04/18/u-s-saudi-tensions-in-focus-as-barack-obama-visits-mideast-this-week/

[122] *See e.g.*, Eric Trager, "Obama Wrecked U.S.-Egypt Ties," *The National Interest*, April 8, 2015, http://nationalinterest.org/feature/obama-wrecked-us-egypt-ties-12573.

123 *See e.g.*, Al-Ahram, "Russia in the Middle East," *Al-Ahram Weekly*, Jan. 7, 2016, http://weekly.ahram.org.eg/News/15179/21/Russia-in-the-Middle-East.aspx.

124 *See e.g.*, Aaron David Miller, "Saudi Arabia-Iran Crisis: Six Takeaways," *CNN*, Jan. 6, 2016, http://www.cnn.com/2016/01/05/opinions/miller-six-takeaways-saudi-arabia-iran-crisis/.

125 *See, e.g.*, Lucy Wescott, "ISIS is Committing Genocide Against Yazidis, Christians and Shiites: John Kerry," *Newsweek*, Mar. 17, 2016, http://www.newsweek.com/isis-genocide-kerry-yazidis-christians-shia-437944.

126 *See e.g.*, Carl Vick, "The Middle East Nuclear Race is Already Underway," *Time*, Mar. 23, 2015, http://time.com/3751676/iran-talks-nuclear-race-middle-east/.

127 *See e.g.*, Liz Shy, "As Tragedies Shock Europe, A Bigger Refugee Crisis Looms in the Middle East," *Washington Post*, Aug. 29, 2015, https://www.washingtonpost.com/world/middle_east/as-tragedies-shock-europe-a-bigger-refugee-crisis-looms-in-the-middle-east/2015/08/29/3858b284-9c15-11e4-86a3-1b56f64925f6_story.html

128 *See e.g.*, J. David Goodman, "Spate of Self-Immolations Reported in Tunisia," *New York Times*, Jan. 12, 2012, http://thelede.blogs.nytimes.com/2012/01/12/spate-of-self-immolations-reported-in-tunisia/?rref=collection%2Ftimestopic%2FBouazizi%2C%20Mohamed&action=click&contentCollection=timestopics®ion=stream&module=stream_unit&version=latest&contentPlacement=8&pgtype=collection

129 *See e.g.*, Paul Larkin, "The Role for Magna Carta in America in 2015," *Heritage Foundation*, Jul. 27, 2015, http://www.heritage.org/research/reports/2015/07/the-role-for-magna-carta-in-america-in-2015.

130 *See e.g.*, Domenico Montanaro, Lisa Desjardins, Rachel Wellford, and Simone Pathe, "Who Said it? Bush vs. Obama on Islam," *PBS NewsHour*, Feb. 19, 2015, http://www.pbs.org/newshour/updates/said-obama-vs-bush-islam/.

131 *See e.g.*, "Egypt Revolution Unfinished, Qaradawi Tells Tahrir Masses," *Christian Science Monitor*, Feb. 18, 2011, http://www.csmonitor.com/World/Middle-East/2011/0218/Egypt-

revolution-unfinished-Qaradawi-tells-Tahrir-masses.

[132] *See e.g.*, Paul Berman, *Flight of the Intellectuals*, (Melville House, 2011) at ch. 8.

[133] *See e.g.*, Sen. Ted Cruz, "America's Missed UNESCO Opportunity," *Washington Times*, Oct. 24, 2016, http://www.washingtontimes.com/news/2016/oct/24/americas-missed-unesco-opportunity/; Denis MacEoin, "Muslim Imperialsim Reaches the United Nations," *Gatestone Institute*, Oct. 29, 2016, https://www.gatestoneinstitute.org/9173/unesco-muslim-imperialism.

[134] Bernard Lewis, "The Return of Islam," *Commentary*, Jan. 1, 1976.

[135] *See e.g.*, Baker and Hamilton, *supra* n. 83 at 9.

[136] *See e.g.*, Elon Gilad, "What Israelis Call Palestinians and Why it Matters," *Haaretz*, Nov. 19, 2015, http://www.haaretz.com/israel-news/.premium-1.687147.

[137] *See e.g.*, David Newman, "The Myth of the Nation State in the Middle East," *Jerusalem Post*, Oct. 6, 2014, http://www.jpost.com/Opinion/Borderline-views-The-myth-of-the-nation-state-in-the-Middle-East-378210.

[138] *See e.g.*, Max Boot, "Don't Redraw the Map," *Commentary*, May 16, 2016, https://www.commentarymagazine.com/foreign-policy/middle-east/dont-redraw-map/.

[139] *See e.g.*, United Nations, "The Two-State Solution: A Key Prerequisite for Achieving Peace and Stability in the Middle East," Jun. 22, 2015, http://www.unrussia.ru/en/taxonomy/term/4/2015-06-22-0.

[140] *See e.g.*, Mansour Salsabili, "How Iran became the Middle East's Moderate Force," *National Interest*, Mar. 20, 2015, http://nationalinterest.org/feature/how-iran-became-the-middle-easts-moderate-force-12451.

[141] *See e.g.*, Council on Foreign Relations, "U.S.-Saudi Relations," *CFR Backgrounders*, Updated Apr. 21, 2016, http://www.cfr.org/saudi-arabia/us-saudi-relations/p36524. ("Differences on issues like the Palestinian-Israeli conflict, the 2011 Arab protest movements, and Iran have strained ties over the years, but officials on both sides have stressed the importance of the relationship and common interests.").

[142] *See e.g.*, Hilal Khashan, "Are the Arabs Ready for Peace with Israel?" *Middle East Quarterly*, Mar. 1994, http://www.meforum.org/214/are-the-arabs-ready-for-peace-with-israel#_ftn1. (Citing numerous sources opining that broad Arab opinions towards Israel were

favorable for peace).

[143] *See e.g.*, Explainer, "What are Hamas and Hezbollah," *Slate*, Oct. 17, 2000, http://www.slate.com/articles/news_and_politics/explainer/2000/10/what_are_hamas_and_hezbollah.html; Adam Serwer, "A Primer on the Muslim Brotherhood," *The American Prospect*, Feb. 9, 2011, http://prospect.org/article/primer-muslim-brotherhood-0.

[144] *See e.g.*, Barry Rubin, "'Moderate Islamism' Does it Exist?" *PJ Media*, Oct. 31, 2011, https://pjmedia.com/barryrubin/2011/10/31/moderate-islamism-does-it-exist/.

[145] *See e.g.*, P.J. Tobia, "Why Did Assad, Saddam, and Mubaraks Protect Christians?" PBS, Oct. 14, 2011, http://www.pbs.org/newshour/rundown/mid-easts-christians-intro/.

[146] *See e.g.*, Palash Ghosh, "Why do Black Americans Embrace Arabs and Reject Israel," *International Business Times*, Jun. 20, 2012, http://www.ibtimes.com/why-do-black-americans-embrace-arabs-reject-israel-705688. (Describing widely held beliefs about the Arab world).

[147] *See e.g.*, Serwer, *supra* n. 143.

[148] See e.g., Lee Harris, The Suicide of Reason: Radical Islam's Threat to the West, (Basic Books, 2007) at 32.

[149] *See e.g.*, Ariel Natan Pasko, "There they Go Again, those Arab Racists," *Islam Daily*, Jul. 19, 2004, http://www.islamdaily.org/en/world-issues/africa/1560.there-they-go-again-those-arab-racists.htm.

[150] *See e.g.*, Niall Ferguson, "History, Democracy, and Iraq," *Los Angeles Times*, Dec. 19, 2005, http://www.jewishworldreview.com/1205/nferguson.php3. ("Many glib commentators like to blame all the problems of the Middle East today on British and French imperial maneuvers to fashion dependencies out of the lost provinces of the Ottoman Empire...").

[151] *See*, Baker and Hamilton, *supra* n. 83.

[152] *Cf., e.g.*, Shadi Hamid, "Does ISIS Really have Nothing to do with Islam? Islamic Apologetics Carry Serious Risks," *Washington Post*, Nov. 18, 2015, https://www.washingtonpost.com/news/acts-of-faith/wp/2015/11/18/does-isis-really-have-nothing-to-do-with-islam-islamic-apologetics-carry-serious-risks/; Fareed Zakaria, "Saying 'Radical Islam' has Nothing to do with Defeating Terrorism,"

Washington Post, Dec. 17, 2015, https://www.washingtonpost.com/opinions/saying-radical-islam-has-nothing-to-do-with-defeating-terrorism/2015/12/17/d47cc82c-a4f6-11e5-9c4e-be37f66848bb_story.html.

[153] *See e.g.*, Michael Leigh, "Political Islam and the post-Cold War International Order," *German Marshall Fund*, Sept. 30, 2014, http://www.gmfus.org/blog/2014/09/30/political-islam-and-post-cold-war-international-order.

[154] *See e.g.*, George Jonas, "Thomas Friedman, the Arab Spring's Biggest Daydreamer," *National Post,* April 13, 2013, http://news.nationalpost.com/full-comment/george-jonas-2.

[155] *See e.g.*, Victor Davis Hanson, "The Israel Double Standard," *National Review*, Jan. 16, 2014, http://www.nationalreview.com/article/368563/israel-double-standard-victor-davis-hanson.

[156] *See e.g.*, Jean Francois Revel, *Anti-Americanism*, (Encounter Books, 2004).

[157] *See e.g.* Galit Shmueli, "To Explain or to Predict?" *Statistical Science* 25(3) 289-310, 2010, https://www.stat.berkeley.edu/~aldous/157/Papers/shmueli.pdf.

[158] *See e.g.*, Jack Khoury, "Abbas: Olmert Offered PA Land Equaling 100% of West Bank," *Haaretz*, Dec. 12, 2009, http://www.haaretz.com/news/abbas-olmert-offered-pa-land-equaling-100-of-west-bank-1.1747.

[159] *See e.g.*, Yousaf Butt, "How Saudi Wahhabism is the Fountainhead of Islamist Terrorism," *The World Post*, Jan. 20, 2015, http://www.huffingtonpost.com/dr-yousaf-butt-/saudi-wahhabism-islam-terrorism_b_6501916.html.

[160] *See e.g.*, Mitchell Prothero, "The 'Cedar Revolution' Meets Hezbollah," *Salon,* Mar. 5, 2005, http://www.salon.com/2005/03/05/hezbollah/.

[161] *See e.g.*, "Ahmadinejad says Holocaust Denial was His Major Achievement," *Times of Israel*, Jul. 6, 2013, http://www.timesofisrael.com/ahmadinejad-says-holocaust-denial-was-his-major-achievement/.

[162] *See e.g.*, Eric Reeves, "Genocide in Darfur – How the Horror Began," *Sudan Tribune*, Sept. 3, 2005, http://www.sudantribune.com/spip.php?article11445.

[163] *See e.g.*, Faiz Shakir, "Bush Ignored Warning of Iraqi Civil War," *ThinkProgress,* Feb. 23, 2006,

http://thinkprogress.org/politics/2006/02/23/3854/iraq-civil-war/.

[164] *See e.g.,* Editorial, "Underwriting Hamas," *The New York Times,* Mar. 4, 2006, http://www.nytimes.com/2006/03/04/opinion/04sat1.html?mtrref=www.google.com&gwh=8B6D079A5CB1FB97554A40F1E33633BA&gwt=pay&assetType=opinion; James Phillips, "Does U.S. Aid Subsidize Hamas Terrorism?" *The Daily Signal*, Jun. 14, 2010, http://dailysignal.com/2010/06/14/does-u-s-aid-subsidize-hamas-terrorism/.

[165] *See*, Baker and Hamilton, *supra* n. 83; Michelle Malkin, "Top Story of 2007: The Surge, The Military, and the Media," *Rasmussen Reports*, Dec. 27, 2007, http://www.rasmussenreports.com/public_content/political_commentary/commentary_by_michelle_malkin/top_story_of_2007_the_surge_the_military_and_the_media.

[166] *See e.g.,* Yasmine Ryan, "The Tragic Life of a Street Vendor," *Al Jazeera*, Jan. 20, 2011, http://www.aljazeera.com/indepth/features/2011/01/201111684242518839.html.

[167] *See e.g.,* Oren, *supra* n. 99.

[168] *See e.g.,* Bret Stephens, "Remember Bashar Assad, 'Reformer'?" *The Wall Street Journal*, Jul. 23, 2012, http://www.wsj.com/articles/SB100008723963904444025204577544891777555840; Max Fisher, "The Only Remaining Online Copy of Vogue's Asma al-Assad Profile," *The Atlantic*, Jan. 3, 2012, http://www.theatlantic.com/international/archive/2012/01/the-only-remaining-online-copy-of-vogues-asma-al-assad-profile/250753/; Asawin Suebsaeng, "Vogue's Puff Piece on the Assads is Back Online—for Now," *Mother Jones*, Sept. 10, 2013, http://www.motherjones.com/mojo/2013/09/asma-al-assad-vogue-profile-back-online-gawker. Joan Juliet Buck, "Asma al-Assad: A Rose in the Desert," *Vogue*, Feb. 2011, http://gawker.com/asma-al-assad-a-rose-in-the-desert-1265002284.

[169] *See e.g.,* Spencer Case, "How Obama Sided with the Muslim Brotherhood," *National Review*, Jul. 3, 2014, http://www.nationalreview.com/article/381947/how-obama-sided-muslim-brotherhood-spencer-case.

[170] See *id*; Smith, *supra* n. 105.

[171] *See e.g.*, Peter Baker, "Relief over U.S. Exit from Iraq Fades as Reality Overtakes Hope," *The New York Times,* Jun. 22, 2014, http://www.nytimes.com/2014/06/23/world/middleeast/relief-over-us-exit-from-iraq-fades-as-reality-overtakes-hope.html?mtrref=undefined&gwh=9D9FC4CC8857C166D5E947F68ADF350E&gwt=pay&assetType=nyt_now

[172] *See e.g.*, "Obama's 'Red Line' that Wasn't," *The Atlantic* (video), Mar. 10, 2016, http://www.theatlantic.com/video/index/473025/syria-red-line-that-wasnt/.

[173] *See e.g.*, AP, "Obama Administration Sharply Criticizes New Israeli Housing Projects," http://www.foxnews.com/politics/2014/10/01/obama-administration-sharply-criticizes-new-israeli-housing-projects.html ("The new 2,500 unit project that stoked U.S. anger is contentious because it would complete a band of Jewish areas that separate Jerusalem from nearby Bethlehem.").

[174] *See e.g.*, George Phillips, "Iran Deal: $150 Billion to Fund Obama's War," *Gatestone Institute*, Jul. 28, 2015, http://www.gatestoneinstitute.org/6225/iran-150-billion-dollars.

[175] *See e.g.*, Michael Sharnoff, "Arab Decline and Iran's Rising Influence," *The World Post*, Feb. 10, 2016, http://www.huffingtonpost.com/michael-sharnoff/arab-decline-and-irans-rising-influence_b_9179576.html.

[176] *See e.g.*, Con Coughlin, "Vladimir Putin is Calling the Shots over Syria—while Obama is Sidelined," *The Telegraph*, Sept. 29, 2015, http://www.telegraph.co.uk/news/worldnews/middleeast/syria/11900206/Vladimir-Putin-and-the-end-of-American-influence-in-the-Middle-East.html

[177] *See e.g.*, Lorenzo Ferrigno and Richard Roth, "ISIS Expands in post-Gadhafi Libya," *CNN*, Mar. 2, 2016, http://www.cnn.com/2016/03/02/world/isis-libya/.

[178] *See e.g.*, Jonas, *supra* n. 154.

[179] *See e.g.*, Brendan Bordelon, "Clinton Defends Obama's 'JV Team' Label for ISIS," *National Review*, Nov. 19, 2015, http://www.nationalreview.com/article/427355/clinton-defends-obamas-jv-team-label-isis-brendan-bordelon.

[180] *See e.g.*, Jonas, *supra* n. 154.

[181] *See e.g.*, Burak Sansal, "Treaties of Sèvres and Lausanne," *All About Turkey*, http://www.allaboutturkey.com/antlasma.htm.

[182] Urban Dictionary, "WTF," http://www.urbandictionary.com/define.php?page=2&term=WTF.

[183] Thomas Kuhn, *The Structure of Scientific Revolutions* (University of Chicago Press, 1962).

[184] Simon Cotte, "Pilgrims to the Islamic State," *The Atlantic*, Jul. 24, 2015, http://www.theatlantic.com/international/archive/2015/07/isis-foreign-fighters-political-pilgrims/399209/.

[185] Holly Yan, "Why is ISIS so Successful at Luring Westerners?" *CNN*, Oct. 7, 2014, http://www.cnn.com/2014/10/07/world/isis-western-draw/

[186] Francesca Trianni, "Why Westerners are Fighting for ISIS," *Time*, Sept. 5, 2014, http://time.com/3270896/isis-iraq-syria-western-fighters/.

[187] Cotte, *supra* n. 184.

[188] *See e.g.*, Jamie Glazov, "The Sexual Rage behind Islamic Terror," *FrontPage Mag*, Oct. 4, 2001, http://archive.frontpagemag.com/readArticle.aspx?ARTID=25196.

[189] Graeme Wood, "What ISIS Really Wants," *The Atlantic*, Mar. 2015, http://www.theatlantic.com/magazine/archive/2015/03/what-isis-really-wants/384980/.

[190] *Id.*

[191] *See*, Jeffrey Herf, *Nazi Propaganda for the Arab World*, (Yale University Press, 2009).

[192] *See e.g.*, Abu Yehuda, "How Western Ideology Empowers the Jihad," May 2, 2016, http://abuyehuda.com/2016/05/how-western-ideology-empowers-the-jihad/.

[193] Hannah Arendt, *The Origins of Totalitarianism*, (Schocken Books, 1951).

[194] Johann Gottlieb Fichte, "To the German Nation," (1806), https://legacy.fordham.edu/halsall/mod/1806fichte.asp.

[195] *See e.g.*, Eve Conant, "Ethnic Russians: Pretext for Putin's Ukraine Invasion?" *National Geographic*, May 24, 2014, http://news.nationalgeographic.com/news/2014/05/140502-russia-putin-ukraine-geography-crimea-language/.

[196] Leslie A. White, *The Evolution of Culture: The Development of Civilization to the Fall of Rome* (McGraw-Hill, 1959) at 321, (quoting Aristotle, *Politics*, book 5, ch. 9; book 8, chs. 1-2).

[197] Edward H. Reisner, *Nationalism and Education since 1789* (MacMillan, 1922) at 35., (quoting Napoleon Bonaparte).

¹⁹⁸ *See e.g.*, Roger Price, *A Concise History of France*, (Cambridge, 1997) at 197-8.

¹⁹⁹ *See e.g.*, Ashley Pettus, "End of the Melting Pot?" *Harvard Magazine*, May-Jun 2007, http://harvardmagazine.com/2007/05/end-of-the-melting-pot-html.

²⁰⁰ *See e.g.*, "Europe's Separatists," *The Economist,* Mar. 1, 2007, http://www.economist.com/node/8780153.

²⁰¹ Count Stanislas–Marie–Adélaide Clermont-Tonnerre, "Speech on Religious Minorities and Questionable Professions," Dec. 23, 1789, https://chnm.gmu.edu/revolution/d/284/.

²⁰² *See e.g.*, Émile Zola, "J'accuse!" *L'Aurore*, Jan. 13, 1898.

²⁰³ *See*, Theodor Herzl, *The Jewish State*, (Dover, 1988), originally published as *Der Judenstaat*, (1896), http://www.gutenberg.org/files/25282/25282-h/25282-h.htm.

²⁰⁴ *See* Fichte, *supra* n. 194.

²⁰⁵ *See e.g.*, Alkhateeb, *supra* n. 33; Pipes, *supra* n. 33.

²⁰⁶ His Majesty King Abdullah II Ibn Al Hussein, "Initiatives: Jordan First," http://kingabdullah.jo/index.php/en_US/initiatives/view/id/3.html.

²⁰⁷ *See e.g.*, Maurus Reinkowski, *National Identity in Lebanon since 1990*, file:///C:/Users/babramson/Downloads/Reinkowski_National_identity_in_Lebanon.pdf. (Originally appeared as: *Deutsche Zeitschrift für Politik und Wirtschaft des Orient* 39 (1997), S.493-515) at 503.

²⁰⁸ *See e.g.*, Martin Sherman, "Note to Newt (Part I): Uninventing Palestinians," *Jerusalem Post*, Dec. 16, 2011, http://www.jpost.com/Opinion/Columnists/Note-to-Newt-Part-I-Uninventing-Palestinians.

²⁰⁹ UNRWA, "Who We Are," http://www.unrwa.org/who-we-are.

²¹⁰ *See e.g.*, Shapour Ghasemi, "Safavid Empire 1502-1736," http://www.iranchamber.com/history/safavids/safavids.php.

²¹¹ *See e.g.*, Heba Saleh, "Sunni and Shia: Explaining the Divide," *Financial Times*, Jan. 6, 2016, http://www.ft.com/intl/cms/s/0/413ea2ea-b3df-11e5-8358-9a82b43f6b2f.html#axzz4AureM1EQ.

²¹² *See*, "Jews in Islamic Countries: The Treatment of Jews," *Jewish Virtual Library,* (updated Sept. 2011), http://www.jewishvirtuallibrary.org/jsource/anti-semitism/Jews_in_Arab_lands_(gen).html#N_2_. (Citing Bat Ye'or, *The Dhimmi,* (Fairleigh Dickinson University Press, 1985) at 56-57).

²¹³ H. E. W. Young, "Mosul in 1909," *Middle Eastern Studies*, 7(2):229-235

at 234 (Taylor & Francis, 1971).

214 *See e.g.*, Jamie Glazov, "Symposium: Convert or Die," *FrontPage Mag*, Oct. 20, 2006, http://archive.frontpagemag.com/Printable.aspx?ArtId=2009.

215 *See e.g.*, Alkhateeb, *supra* n. 31.

216 *See e.g.*, Caleb Lauer, "In Erdoğan's World, Two and Two may Well Equal Five," *The National*, Nov. 17, 2014, http://www.thenational.ae/opinion/in-erdogans-world-two-and-two-may-well-equal-five.

217 *See e.g.*, Osman Rifat Ibrahim, "AKP and the Great neo-Ottoman Travesty," *Al Jazeera*, May 23, 2014, http://www.aljazeera.com/indepth/opinion/2014/05/akp-great-neo-ottoman-travesty-201451974314589207.html; Ishaan Tharoor, "Why Turkey's President wants to Revive the Language of the Ottoman Empire," *Washington Post*, Dec. 12, 2014, https://www.washingtonpost.com/news/worldviews/wp/2014/12/12/why-turkeys-president-wants-to-revive-the-language-of-the-ottoman-empire/.

218 *See e.g.*, Joel Krieger, *The Oxford Companion to Politics of the World*, (Oxford University Press, 2nd. ed. 2001) at 37.

219 See e.g., id.

220 *See e.g.*, Editors, "Husayn-McMahon Correspondence," *Encyclopaedia Britannica*, https://www.britannica.com/topic/Husayn-McMahon-correspondence; Mitchell Bard, "The -McMahon Correspondence," *Jewish Virtual Library*, http://www.jewishvirtuallibrary.org/jsource/History/hussmac.html; ProCon, "What Was the Hussein-McMahon Correspondence?" http://israelipalestinian.procon.org/view.answers.php?questionID=498.

221 *See e.g.*, King Hussein, "The Hashemites," http://www.kinghussein.gov.jo/hash_intro.html.

222 See e.g., id.

223 See e.g., Howard Grief, The Legal Foundation and Borders of Israel Israel's Rights under International Law : A Treatise on Jewish Sovereignty over The Land of Israel, Nativ 2:2004, http://www.acpr.org.il/english-nativ/02-issue/grief-2.htm.

224 *See e.g.*, PSP, "The Palestinian People Intends to Sue the British Government over the Balfour Declaration—but What's the End Goal of it?" *Palestine Solidarity Project*, Sept. 30, 2016,

http://palestinesolidarityproject.org/2016/09/30/the-palestinian-people-intends-to-sue-the-british-government-over-the-balfour-declaration-but-whats-the-end-goal-of-it/.

225 *See e.g.*, Grief, *supra* n. 223.

226 *San Remo Resolution*, April 25, 1920. Available at http://www.cfr.org/israel/san-remo-resolution/p15248.

227 *Id.*

228 *See e.g.*, Frontline, "A Chronology: Saudi Arabia," http://www.pbs.org/wgbh/pages/frontline/shows/saud/cron/.

229 *See e.g.*, Frontline, "Analysis: Wahhabism," *PBS*, http://www.pbs.org/wgbh/pages/frontline/shows/saudi/analyses/wahhabism.html.

230 *See e.g.*, ISCA, "Islamic Radicalism: Its Wahhabi Roots and Current Representation," *Islamic Supreme Council of America*, http://www.islamicsupremecouncil.org/understanding-islam/anti-extremism/7-islamic-radicalism-its-wahhabi-roots-and-current-representation.html.

231 *See e.g.*, Economist, "Man of the Moment," *The Economist*, Feb. 8, 2014, http://www.economist.com/news/books-and-arts/21595880-revisionist-history-iraqi-king-man-moment.

232 *See e.g.*, Profile, "King Abdullah I of Jordan," *Al Jazeera*, Feb. 20, 2008, http://www.aljazeera.com/focus/arabunity/2008/02/20085251834 43732794.html.

233 *See e.g.*, Lewis, *supra* n. 134.

234 See, George Antonius, The Arab Awakening: The Story of the Arab National Movement, (H. Hamilton, 1938).

235 *See e.g.*, Martin Kramer, "Arab Nationalism: Mistaken Identity," *Daedelus*, Summer 1993: 171-206, http://martinkramer.org/sandbox/reader/archives/arab-nationalism-mistaken-identity/.

236 *See e.g.*, Arthur Hertzberg, "What Many Liberals Can't See," *Harvard Israel Review*, 2003, http://www.hcs.harvard.edu/~hireview/content.php?type=article&issue=spring04/&name=hertzberg.

237 *See*, San Remo, *supra* n. 226.

238 Antonius, *supra* n. 234 at ch. 13.

239 *See e.g.*, Editorial, "A Judenrein Palestine?" *Jerusalem Post*, Jan. 27, 2014, http://www.jpost.com/Opinion/Editorials/A-Judenrein-

Palestine-339549.

[240] *See e.g.*, Bernard Lewis, "Saddam's Regime is a European Import," *National Post*, Apr. 4, 2003, http://archive.frontpagemag.com/readArticle.aspx?ARTID=18889.

[241] Translated and quoted in William Cleveland, The Making of an Arab Nationalist: Ottomanism and Arabism in the Life and Thought of Sati' al-Husri, (Princeton University Press, 1971) at 127.

[242] *Id.* at 164.

[243] *See e.g.*, Lewis, *supra* n. 240.

[244] Constitution of the Baath Arab Socialist Party, approved 1947, Art. 7, http://www.baath-party.org/index.php?option=com_content&view=category&id=307&Itemid=327&lang=en&limitstart=0.

[245] *Id.* at First Principle.

[246] *Id.* at Art. 3.

[247] *Id.* at Art. 6.

[248] *See e.g.*, Kramer, *supra* n. 235

[249] *See e.g.*, Daniel Pipes, "The Alawi Capture of Power in Syria," *Middle Eastern Studies*, 1989, http://www.danielpipes.org/191/the-alawi-capture-of-power-in-syria.

[250] See e.g., Helen Chapin Metz, ed. *Iraq: A Country Study*. (GPO for the Library of Congress, 1988) at ch. 38, http://countrystudies.us/iraq/38.htm; Harith al-Qarawee, "The Rise of Sunni Identity in Iraq," *The National Interest*, Apr. 5, 2013, http://nationalinterest.org/commentary/sunni-identitys-rise-iraq-8314.

[251] Quoted in A. Sadi, "'Arab Socialism' and the National Movement," *International Socialist Review*, 24(2): 48-51, Spring 1963, https://www.marxists.org/history/etol/newspape/isr/vol24/no02/sadi.html.

[252] *See e.g.*, "Arab Unity: Nasser's Revolution," *Al Jazeera*, Jun. 20, 2008, http://www.aljazeera.com/focus/arabunity/2008/02/200852517252821627.html.

[253] *See e.g.*, Sarah Mousa, "Commemorating the United Arab Republic," *Al Jazeera*, Feb. 22, 2013, http://www.aljazeera.com/indepth/opinion/2013/02/20132198541 2606377.html.

[254] Max Weber, *The Theory of Social and Economic Organization*, trans.

A.M. Henderson and Talcott Parsons (Oxford University Press, 1947) at 358.

[255] Fouad Ajami, *The Arab Predicament: Arab Political Thought and Practice since 1967* (Cambridge University Press, 1981, updated 1992) at 98.

[256] *Id.* at 97.

[257] *See e.g.*, Adeed Dawisha, "Requiem for Arab Nationalism," *Middle East Quarterly*, Winter 2003, http://www.meforum.org/518/requiem-for-arab-nationalism#.

[258] *See e.g.*, Christian Porth, "The Two 'isms' of the Middle East," *Al Jazeera*, Feb. 4, 2008, http://www.aljazeera.com/focus/arabunity/2008/02/20085251853 4468346.html.

[259] *See e.g.*, Barry Rubin, "Understanding the Muslim Brotherhood," *Foreign Policy Research Institute*, July, 2012, http://www.fpri.org/article/2012/07/understanding-the-muslim-brotherhood/.

[260] *See e.g.*, *id.*; Herf, *supra* n. 191.

[261] *See e.g.*, *e.g.*, Al Jazeera, "Egypt's Coptic Pope Blasts Morsi 'Negligence,'" *Al Jazeera*, Apr. 9, 2013, http://www.aljazeera.com/news/middleeast/2013/04/2013499491 0991737.html; AFP, "Egypt's Morsi to Rethink Israel Peace Pact: Report," *Daily Nation*, Jun. 26, 2012, http://www.nation.co.ke/News/africa/Egypt+Copts+dismayed+but+ determined+after+Morsi+win+/-/1066/1435546/-/2cw1iu/- /index.html.

[262] *See,* Rubin, *supra* n. 259.

[263] See e.g., id.

[264] See e.g., id.

[265] Raymond Ibrahim, "The Muslim Brotherhood: Origins, Efficacy and Reach," *Frontpage Mag*, Aug. 27, 2013, http://www.frontpagemag.com/fpm/202247/muslim-brotherhood-origins-efficacy-and-reach-raymond-ibrahim.

[266] *See,* Barry Rubin, *Islamic Fundamentalism in Egyptian Politics*, (St. Martins Press, 1990) at 36.

[267] *See, id.* at 15.

[268] *See e.g.*, Ibrahim, *supra* n. 265.

[269] *See,* Rubin, *supra* n. 266 at 28.

270 *See e.g.*, Profile, "Egypt's Mohammed Morsi," *BBC*, Apr. 21, 2015, http://www.bbc.com/news/world-middle-east-18371427.

271 *See e.g.*, Jose Antonio Vargas, "Spring Awakening," *New York Times*, Feb. 17, 2012, http://www.nytimes.com/2012/02/19/books/review/how-an-egyptian-revolution-began-on-facebook.html?_r=0.

272 James Kirchick, "Interview: Barry Rubin Says Muslim Bortherhood 'Not a Moderate Group,'" *RFE/RL*, Feb. 14, 2011, http://www.rferl.org/content/interview_at_large_barry_rubin/2309 301.html.

273 *See e.g.*, Al Jazeera, *supra* n. 261; AFP, *supra* n. 261.

274 *See,* Ibrahim, *supra* n. 265.

275 *See e.g.*, Rubin, *supra* n. 259.

276 *See,* Ibrahim, *supra* n. 265.

277 *See* 9/11 Commission, *supra* n. 72.

278 *See,* Ali Hashem, The many names of Abu Bakr al-Baghdadi, *Al-Monitor*, Mar. 23, 2015, http://www.al-monitor.com/pulse/en/originals/2015/03/isis-baghdadi-islamic-state-caliph-many-names-al-qaeda.html.

279 *See e.g.*, Mshari Al-Zaydif, "The Muslim Brotherhood will Never Change," *Asharq Al-Awsat,* Feb. 15, 2015, http://english.aawsat.com/2015/02/article55341483/opinion-muslim-brotherhood-will-never-change.

280 *See* e.g., Cole Bunzel, "From Paper State to Caliphate: The Ideology of the Islamic State," *Brookings Institution*, Mar. 2015, http://www.brookings.edu/~/media/research/files/papers/2015/0 3/ideology-of-islamic-state-bunzel/the-ideology-of-the-islamic-state.pdf.

281 *See e.g.*, Paolo Lepori, "Saudi Arabia and the Muslim Brotherhood," *L'Indro*, Jan. 7, 2016, http://www.lindro.it/saudi-arabia-and-muslim-brotherhood/; Mordechai Kedar, "Why the Saudis and Muslim Brotherhood Hate Each Other," *Arutz Sheva*, May 13, 2014, http://www.israelnationalnews.com/Articles/Article.aspx/14994#.V 3eurTkrIy4.

282 *See e.g.*, Stéphane Lacroi, "Saudi Arabia's Muslim Brotherhood Predicament," *Washington Post,* Mar. 20, 2014, https://www.washingtonpost.com/news/monkey-cage/wp/2014/03/20/saudi-arabias-muslim-brotherhood-predicament/.

283 *See e.g.*, Bruce Reidel, "Saudi Arabia and the Third Gaza War," *Al-Monitor*, Aug. 6, 2014, http://www.al-monitor.com/pulse/originals/2014/08/saudi-arabia-gaza-war-egypt-quiet.html.

284 *See e.g.*, Ali Al-Arian, "Is Saudi Arabia Warming Up to the Muslim Brotherhood?" *Al Jazeera*, Jul. 29, 2015, http://www.aljazeera.com/news/2015/07/saudi-arabia-warming-muslim-brotherhood-150727121500912.html.

285 *See e.g.*, Hatem Ezz Eldin, "King Salman's Visit to Cairo," *Al-Ahram*, Apr. 7, 2016, http://weekly.ahram.org.eg/News/15988/31/King-Salman%E2%80%99s-visit-to-Cairo.aspx.

286 *See e.g.*, Mark Durie, "Salafis and the Muslim Brotherhood: What is the Difference?" *Middle East Forum*, Jun 6, 2013, http://www.meforum.org/3541/salafis-muslim-brotherhood.

287 *See e.g.*, Hassan Mneimneh, "Saudi Arabia," in Barry Rubin, ed., *Guide to Islamist Movements* (M.E. Sharpe, 2010) vol. 2 at 371.

288 *See, id.*

289 See e.g., Barry Rubin, The Middle East: A Guide to Politics, Economics, Society, and Culture, (Routledge, 2011) at ch. "Protectors of the Faith."

290 See e.g., id.

291 See e.g., id.

292 See e.g., id.

293 *See e.g.*, James Dorsey, "Creating Frankenstein: The Saudi Export of Wahhabism," *International Policy Digest*, Mar. 8, 2016, http://intpolicydigest.org/2016/03/08/creating-frankenstein-saudi-export-wahhabism/; Stephen Schwartz, "Saudis Announce a Turn Away from Wahhabi Cultural Vandalism," *Middle East Forum*, Jul. 19, 2016. http://www.meforum.org/6120/saudis-turn-away-from-wahhabi-cultural-vandalism.

294 See e.g., id.

295 *See*, Durie, *supra* n. 286.

296 See, id.

297 *See*, Clermont-Tonnerre, *supra* n. 201.

298 Fouad Ajami, "The End of Pan-Arabism," *Foreign Affairs*, Winter 1978/79, https://www.foreignaffairs.com/articles/yemen/1978-12-01/end-pan-arabism.

299 Walid Khalidi, "Thinking the Unthinkable: A Sovereign Palestinian State," *Foreign Affairs*, Jul. 1978,

https://www.foreignaffairs.com/articles/palestinian-authority/1978-07-01/thinking-unthinkable-sovereign-palestinian-state.

300 League of Arab States, *Charter of the Arab League*, Mar. 22, 1945, http://www.refworld.org/docid/3ae6b3ab18.html.

301 *See id.* at Art. VII.

302 *See e.g.*, Jonathan Masters and Mohammed A. Sergie, "The Arab League," Council on Foreign Relations, http://www.cfr.org/middle-east-and-north-africa/arab-league/p25967.

303 See id.

304 *See e.g.*, BBC, "Timeline: Arab League," *BBC News*, http://news.bbc.co.uk/2/hi/middle_east/country_profiles/1550977.stm.

305 *See e.g.*, Ishaan Tharoor, "How Yemen was once Egypt's Vietnam," *Washington Post,* Mar. 28, 2015, https://www.washingtonpost.com/news/worldviews/wp/2015/03/28/how-yemen-was-once-egypts-vietnam/.

306 *See e.g.*, Alex Danchev, "The Anschluss," *Review of International Studies,* 1994, http://journals.cambridge.org/action/displayAbstract?fromPage=online&aid=6301156; Daniel Pipes, *Damascus Courts the West,* (Washington Institute for Near East Policy, 1991) at 28.

307 *See e.g.*, Daniel Yergin, *The Prize*, (Simon & Schuster, 1990) at ch. 25.

308 *Id.*

309 MEES, "Can We Nationalize?," *Weekly Middle East Oil and Gas News,* Mar. 17, 1967.

310 *See e.g.*, Giuliano Garavini, "Completing Decolonization: The 1973 'Oil Shock' and the Struggle for Economic Rights," *The International History Review,* 33(3), Sept. 2011, 473-87.

311 *See e.g.*, Central Intelligence Agency, "Religions," *The World Factbook,* https://www.cia.gov/library/publications/the-world-factbook/fields/2122.html; Zvi Mazel, "Majority and Minorities in the Arab World: The Lack of a Unifying Narrative," *Jerusalem Center for Public Affairs*, Jan. 3, 2012, http://jcpa.org/article/majority-and-minorities-in-the-arab-world-the-lack-of-a-unifying-narrative/.

312 See e.g., id.

313 *See e.g.*, Ovie Farraday, "The Missing Black Populations of North Africa," Apr. 15, 2016, http://www.feelnubia.com/index.php/world-

view/mirror/121-the-missing-native-populations-of-north-africa.html; Nicholas Hanlon, "Genocide Against Black African Christians Continues in Sudan," Center for Security Policy, Apr. 10, 2015, http://www.centerforsecuritypolicy.org/2015/04/10/genocide-against-black-african-christians-continues-in-sudan/.

314 *See e.g.*, Mazel, *supra* n. 311; Jeffrey Tayler, "Among the Berbers," *National Geographic*, Jan. 2005, http://ngm.nationalgeographic.com/ngm/0501/feature4/fulltext.html; *The Amazigh*, http://phoenicia.org/berber.html.

315 *See e.g.*, Imad Boles, "Disappearing Christians of the Middle East," *Middle East Quarterly*, (2001), http://www.meforum.org/23/egypt-persecution.

316 *See e.g.*, Aharon Mor and Orly Rahimiyan, "The Jewish Exodus from Arab Lands: Toward Redressing Injustices on All Sides," *Jerusalem Issue Briefs* 11:21, Sept. 11, 2012, http://jcpa.org/article/the-jewish-exodus-from-arab-landstoward-redressing-injustices-on-all-sides/; William Dalrymple, "The End of Christianity in the Middle East could mean the Demise of Arab Secularism," *The Guardian*, Jul. 23, 2014, http://www.theguardian.com/commentisfree/2014/jul/23/arab-christians-secular-arabs-isis-middle-east-minorities.

317 *See e.g.*, JPost Editorial, "Christian Genocide," *Jerusalem Post*, Dec. 12, 2015, http://www.jpost.com/Opinion/Christian-genocide-437124; Tony Magliano, "Christian Genocide is Happening Now," *National Catholic Reporter*, Mar. 28, 2016, http://ncronline.org/blogs/making-difference/christian-genocide-happening-now; Raymond Ibrahim, "ISIS Massacre of Christians not 'Genocide,' Obama Administration Insists," *Gatestone Institute*, Mar. 17, 2016, http://ncronline.org/blogs/making-difference/christian-genocide-happening-now.

318 *See e.g.*, Shreeya Sinha, "Obama's Evolution on ISIS," *The New York Times*, Jun. 9, 2015, http://www.nytimes.com/interactive/2015/06/09/world/middleeast/obama-isis-strategy.html.

319 *See e.g.*, Frances Martel, "ISIS Releases Map of 5-Year Plan to Spread from Spain to China," *Breitbart*, Jul. 1, 2014, http://www.breitbart.com/national-security/2014/07/01/isis-releases-map-of-5-year-plan-to-spread-from-spain-to-china/.

320 The Arab Peace Initiative, 2002, http://www.al-

bab.com/arab/docs/league/peace02.htm.

321 *See e.g.*, MEMO, "Netanyahu: Moderate Arab Governments do not See Israel as an Enemy," *Middle East Monitor*, Dec. 8, 2014 (substituting the word "moderate" in the headline while quoting Netanyahu as saying "The collapse of the old order has made clear to pragmatic Arab governments that Israel is not the enemy."), https://www.middleeastmonitor.com/20141208-netanyahu-moderate-arab-governments-do-not-see-israel-as-an-enemy/.

322 *See e.g.*, Alex Fishman, "How IDF Intelligence Failed to Predict 'Hamastan' in Gaza Following Israeli Pullout," *YNet Magazine*, Jun. 27, 2015, http://www.ynetnews.com/articles/0,7340,L-4673208,00.html.

323 Evelyn Gordon, "The Two-State Solution is in Stalemate. Here's What Israel can do to Prevail," *Mosaic*, Sept. 1, 2015, http://mosaicmagazine.com/essay/2015/09/the-two-state-solution-is-in-stalemate-what-can-israel-do-to-prevail/.

324 *See e.g.*, Max Abrahms, "The 'Cycle of Violence' Fallacy," *National Review*, May 22, 2003, http://www.nationalreview.com/article/206983/cycle-violence-fallacy-max-abrahms.

325 *See* Ethan Bueno de Mesquita, "Conciliation, Counterterrorism, and Patterns of Terrorist Violence," *International Organization* 59 (Winter 2005): 145-76, http://home.uchicago.edu/bdm/PDF/adverseterrorcases.pdf.

326 *See* Ethan Bueno de Mesquita, "Conciliation, Counterterrorism, and Patterns of Terrorist Violence," *International Organization* 59 (Winter 2005): 145-76, http://home.uchicago.edu/bdm/PDF/adverseterrorcases.pdf.

327 *See*, Arab Peace Initiative, *supra* n. 320.

328 *See*, UNRWA, *supra* n. 209.

329 *See e.g.* Matti Friedman, "Mizrahi Nation," *Mosaic,* June 1, 2014. http://mosaicmagazine.com/essay/2014/06/mizrahi-nation/.

330 *See e.g.*, Ada Aharoni, "The Forced Migration of Jews from Arab Countries," *Peace Review*, 15(1): 53-60 (2003). http://www.tandfonline.com/doi/abs/10.1080/1040265032000059742?journalCode=cper20.

331 *See e.g.*, Shmuel Trigano, "The Expulsion of the Jews from Muslim Countries, 1920-1970: A History of Ongoing Cruelty and Discrimination," *Jewish Center for Public Affairs*, Nov. 4, 2010,

http://jcpa.org/article/the-expulsion-of-the-jews-from-muslim-countries-1920-1970-a-history-of-ongoing-cruelty-and-discrimination/.

332 *See e.g.*, Robert N. Rakowitz, "Exodus from the Babylonian Captivity: The Jews of Modern Iraq," *International Journal of Group Tensions*, 27(3): 177-191 (1997), http://www.academia.edu/3489988/Exodus_from_the_Babylonian_Captivity_The_Jews_of_Modern_Iraq.

333 *See*, Antonius, *supra* n. 234.

334 *See*, Cleveland, *supra* n. 241; Rakowitz, *supra* n. 332.

335 Ya'akov Meron, "Why Jews Fled the Arab Countries," *Middle East Quarterly*, Sept. 1995, (quoting U.N. General Assembly, Second Session, Official Records, Ad Hoc Committee on the Palestinian Question, Summary Records of Meetings, Lake Success, N.Y., Sept. 25-Nov. 15, 1947, p. 185, using Meron's translation of the official original French). http://www.meforum.org/263/why-jews-fled-the-arab-countries.

336 *Id.* (quoting U.N. General Assembly, Second Session, Official Records, Verbatim Record of the Plenary Meeting, p. 1391.)

337 Mallory Brown, "Jews in Grave Danger in all Moslem Lands," *New York Times*, May 16, 1948, http://zionism-israel.com/hdoc/Jewish_refugees_arab.htm.

338 *See e.g.*, Trigano, *supra* n. 331.

339 *See e.g.*, Meron, *supra* n. 335.

340 *Id.* (quoting An-Nahar, May 15, 1975).

341 *Id.*

342 *See e.g.*, Aris Tsifildis, "The Exchange of Populations between Greece and Turkey," http://pontosworld.com/index.php/pontus/history/articles/295-the-exchange-of-populations-greece-and-turkey.

343 See id.

344 *See e.g.*, Israeli Ministry of Foreign Affairs, "Jewish Refugees from Arab and Muslim Countries," Apr. 3, 2012, http://mfa.gov.il/MFA/ForeignPolicy/Peace/Guide/Pages/Jewish_refugees_from_Arab_and_Muslim_countries-Apr_2012.aspx.

345 *See e.g.*, Amrita Paul and Prithvish Nag, "Pattern of Post 1947 Refugee Resettlement in India," *Int. J. Geology, Agriculture, and Environmental Sciences* 3(1): 68-74 (2015).

346 *See e.g.*, Yaqoob Khan Bangash, "Refugee Resettlement in Pakistani Punjab, 1947-62," *Dissertation Reviews*, Apr. 4, 2016,

http://dissertationreviews.org/archives/13609.

[347] *See e.g.*, Bernard Wasserstein, "European Refugee Movements after World War Two," BBC, Feb. 17, 2011, http://www.bbc.co.uk/history/worldwars/wwtwo/refugees_01.shtml.

[348] *See e.g.*, Martha Gellhorn, "The Arabs of Palestine," *The Atlantic*, Oct. 1961, http://www.theatlantic.com/magazine/archive/1961/10/the-arabs-of-palestine/304203/; Judith Miller and David Samuels, "No Way Home: The Tragedy of the Palestinian Diaspora," *The Independent*, Oct. 21, 2009, http://www.independent.co.uk/news/world/middle-east/no-way-home-the-tragedy-of-the-palestinian-diaspora-1806790.html.

[349] UNRWA, *supra* n. 209.

[350] *See e.g.*, Alexandra Fielden, "Local Integration, An Under-Reported Solution to Protracted Refugee Situations," UNHCR, June 2008, http://www.unhcr.org/486cc99f2.pdf. ("The degree of linguistic, ethnic, and cultural similarities between the host and refugee population (sometimes referred to as 'psychological compatibility') is a significant factor in the initiation of a local integration process.").

[351] *See e.g.*, Martin Kramer, "Fouad Ajami Goes to Israel," *Mosaic*, Jan. 8, 2015, http://mosaicmagazine.com/observation/2015/01/fouad-ajami-goes-to-israel/.

[352] Fouad Ajami, "A Reality Check as Israel Turns 60," US News, May 7, 2008, http://www.usnews.com/opinion/fajami/articles/2008/05/07/a-reality-check-as-israel-turns-60.

[353] *See,* UNRWA, *supra* n. 209.

[354] *See e.g.*, Ya'akov Koran, "1939 Palestinian Flag. What does it Look Like? Surprised?" *FactualIsrael*, Nov. 14, 2014, http://www.factualisrael.com/1939-palestinian-flag-look-like-surprised/.

[355] *See,* Daniel Pipes, "Is Jordan Palestine?" *Commentary*, Oct. 1988, http://www.danielpipes.org/298/is-jordan-palestine.

[356] *See,* Palestine National Council, *The Palestinian National Charter* at Art. 2 (July 1-17, 1968), http://avalon.law.yale.edu/20th_century/plocov.asp.

[357] *See e.g.*, Gelhorn, *supra* n. 348.

[358] *See e.g.*, David Meir-Levi, "The Communist Roots of Palestinian Terror," *Frontpage Mag*, Dec. 14, 2007,

http://archive.frontpagemag.com/readArticle.aspx?ARTID=29207.

[359] *See e.g.*, Jewish Virtual Library, "Palestinian Maps Omitting Israel," http://www.jewishvirtuallibrary.org/jsource/History/palmatoc1.html#1.

[360] Palestine National Council, *supra* n. 356 at Art. 5.

[361] *See,* Moshe Aumann, *Land Ownership in Palestine* 1880–1948, (Jerusalem: Academic Committee on the Middle East, 1976), http://www.wordfromjerusalem.com/wp-content/uploads/2008/11/the-case-for-israel-appendix2.pdf.

[362] Id.

[363] Mark Twain, *Innocents Abroad,* (American Publishing Co., 1869), https://www.gutenberg.org/files/3176/3176-h/3176-h.htm#ch53

[364] Palestine National Council, *supra* n. 356 at Art. 4.

[365] *Id.* at Art. 7.

[366] *Id.* at Art. 20.

[367] *Id.* at Art. 14.

[368] *Id.* at Art. 12.

[369] *Id.* at Art. 13.

[370] *Id.* at Art. 15.

[371] *See e.g.*, Bruce Abramson and Jeff Ballabon, "The Lie of Palestine," *Jewish Press,* Jun. 7, 2016, http://www.jewishpress.com/indepth/opinions/the-palestinian-lie/2016/06/07/.

[372] *See,* Times of Israel Staff, "Full Official record: What the Mufti Said to Hitler," *Times of Israel,* Oct. 21, 2015. http://www.timesofisrael.com/full-official-record-what-the-mufti-said-to-hitler/.

[373] Palestine National Council, *supra* n. 356 at Art 19.

[374] *See e.g.*, "The Deception of Palestinian Nationalism," *Stanford Review,* Feb. 28 2008, http://www.stanfordreview.org/article/deception-palestinian-nationalism/.

[375] Palestine National Council, *supra* n. 356.

[376] Hamas Charter, "The Covenant of the Islamic Resistance Movement," Aug. 18, 1988 at Art. 11. http://avalon.law.yale.edu/20th_century/hamas.asp.

[377] *Id.* at Art. 15.

[378] *Id.* at Art. 14.

379 *Id.* at Art. 25.

380 *Id.* at Art. 27.

381 *See* UNRWA, *supra* n. 209.

382 Palestinian Central Bureau of Statistics, "Palestinians at the End of Year 2006," *Palestinian National Authority*, 2006. http://www.pcbs.gov.ps/Portals/_pcbs/PressRelease/end_year06e.pdf.

383 *See e.g.*, Yakov Faitelson, "The Politics of Palestinian Demography," *Middle East Quarterly*, Spring 2009, http://www.meforum.org/2124/the-politics-of-palestinian-demography#_ftnref31.

384 Palestinian Central Bureau of Statistics, *supra* n. 382 at 31, Tables 1 and 2.

385 *See e.g.*, Gelhorn, *supra* n. 348.

386 *See e.g.*, "Demonization of Jews/Israelis," *Palestinian Media Watch*, http://palwatch.org/main.aspx?fi=757.

387 *See e.g.*, "Violence and Terror," *Palestinian Media Watch*, http://palwatch.org/main.aspx?fi=448.

388 *See e.g.*, Khaled Abu Toameh, "Palestinians: Why Salam Fayyad Lacks Popular Support," *Gatestone Institute*, Jun. 30, 2015, http://www.gatestoneinstitute.org/6066/salam-fayyad-support.

389 *See e.g.* Quartet, "Our goal is two states, Israel and Palestine, living side by side in peace and security, says Obama," *Office of the Quartet*, http://www.quartetoffice.org/page.php?id=e5644y939588Ye5644.

390 *See e.g.*, Pipes, *supra* n. 38.

391 *See e.g.*, Kamal Salibi, *A House of Many Mansions – The History of Lebanon Reconsidered*, (I.B. Tauris & Co., 1993) at ch.1, http://almashriq.hiof.no/lebanon/900/902/Kamal-Salibi/.

392 *See e.g.*, Ya'akov Meron, "Why Jews Fled the Arab Countries," *Middle East Quarterly*, Sept. 1995, http://www.meforum.org/263/why-jews-fled-the-arab-countries; Mor and Rahimiyan, *supra* n. 316

393 *Id.* (quoting An-Nahar, May 15, 1975).

394 *See e.g.*, Monica D. Toft, "The State of the Field: Demography and War," *Woodrow Wilson Center*, ECSP Report 11 (2005), https://www.wilsoncenter.org/sites/default/files/Toft.pdf.

395 *See*, "Demographics of Israel," *Jewish Virtual Library*, http://www.jewishvirtuallibrary.org/jsource/Society_&_Culture/israel_palestine_pop.html

³⁹⁶ *See e.g.,* Mitchell Bard, "Israeli Arabs: Status of Arabs in Israel," *Jewish Virtual Library,* http://www.jewishvirtuallibrary.org/jsource/Society_&_Culture/arabstat.html.

³⁹⁷ *See e.g.,* Nelia Hyndman-Rizk, *My Mother's Table,* (Cambridge Scholars Publishing, 2011) at 39.

³⁹⁸ See, id.

³⁹⁹ Daniel Pipes, Reviewing and quoting Eli Reed and Fouad Ajami, *Beirut: City of Regrets* (Norton, 1988), http://www.danielpipes.org/11235/beirut-city-of-regrets.

⁴⁰⁰ Id.

⁴⁰¹ *See e.g.,* Globalsecurity, "Forced Population Transfers," http://www.globalsecurity.org/military/world/war/forced-population-transfers.htm; Mark Lewis, "Population Transfer as a Tool," http://www.middleeastpiece.com/expulsion_tool.html.

⁴⁰² *See e.g.,* Migration Policy Center, "Syrian Refugees," http://syrianrefugees.eu/.

⁴⁰³ *See e.g.,* Egidijus Vareikis (rapporteur), "Enforced population transfer as a human rights violation," Parliamentary Assembly, Council of Europe, Dec. 5, 2011, http://assembly.coe.int/CommitteeDocs/2011/ajdoc49_2011.pdf.

⁴⁰⁴ *See e.g.,* Timothy Waters, ""The Blessing of Departure: Acceptable and Unacceptable State Support for Demographic Transformation: The Lieberman Plan to Exchange Populated Territories in Cisjordan," *Law and Ethics of Human Rights,* 2(1): Article 9 (2008) at fn. 8.

⁴⁰⁵ *See e.g.,* Dan Senor, "Iraqi Leaders Opposed Biden's Partition Plan," *Wall Street Journal,* Sept. 9, 2008, http://www.wsj.com/articles/SB122092005533912759?cb=logged0.5841148311607094; Lionel Boehner, "Why Sunnis Don't Support Iraq's Constitution," *Council on Foreign Relations,* Oct. 12, 2005, http://www.cfr.org/iraq/why-sunnis-dont-support-iraqs-constitution/p9002.

⁴⁰⁶ *See e.g.,* André Lecours, "Balancing Self-Rule and Shared-Rule: Sources of Tensions and Political Responses in Contemporary Political Systems," in Alberto López and Basaguren, Leire Escajedo San Epifanio, eds., *The Ways of Federalism in Western Countries and the Horizons of Territorial Autonomy in Spain* (vol. 1), 103-114 at 104.

⁴⁰⁷ *See e.g.,* Pipes, *supra* n. 249.

⁴⁰⁸ *See e.g.,* Reuters, "Syria's Alawites, a Secretive and Persecuted Sect,"

Reuters, Feb. 2, 2012, http://www.reuters.com/article/us-syria-alawites-sect-idUSTRE80U1HK20120131.

409 *See e.g.*, Brilliant Maps, *supra* n. 35.

410 Pipes, *supra* n. 249.

411 *See e.g.*, Lawrence Franklin, "Iran's Commitment to Shia in the Region," *Gatestone Institute*, Jan. 17, 2016, http://www.gatestoneinstitute.org/7242/iran-shia-commitment.

412 *See e.g.*, Aaron Lund, "The Miserable Afterlife of Michel Aflaq," *Carnegie Endowment for International Peace,* Mar. 10, 2014, http://carnegieendowment.org/syriaincrisis/?fa=54844.

413 Pipes, *supra* n. 249.

414 *See e.g.*, Jubin Goodarzi, "Iran and Syria," *The Iran Primer*, U.S. Institute of Peace, http://iranprimer.usip.org/resource/iran-and-syria.

415 *See e.g.*, Nathan Hodge and Jay Solomon, "Kerry Softens Position on Syrian President Assad," *Wall Street Journal*, Dec. 15, 2015, http://www.wsj.com/articles/john-kerry-in-russia-in-effort-to-keep-syria-talks-on-course-1450183175.

416 *See e.g.*, Neil Shevlin, "*Velayet-E Faqih* in the Constitution of Iran: The Implementation of Theocracy," *University of Pennsylvania Journal of Constitutional Law*, Fall 1998, 358-82; Sharon Otterman, "Iraq: Grand Ayatollah Ali al-Sistani," *Council on Foreign Relations*, Sept. 1, 2004, http://www.cfr.org/iraq/iraq-grand-ayatollah-ali-al-sistani/p7636.

417 Hillel Fradkin, "The Paradoxes of Shiism," *Current Trends in Islamist Ideology* (Hudson Institute, 2009), http://www.hudson.org/research/9885-the-paradoxes-of-shiism.

418 Shahrough Akhavi, "Shīʿī ʿUlamāʿ," *Oxford Islamic Studies Online*, http://www.oxfordislamicstudies.com/article/opr/t236/e0814?_hi=0&_pos=8952.

419 *Id.*

420 Daniel Pipes, "The Western Mind of Radical Islam," *First Things*, Dec. 1995, http://www.firstthings.com/article/1995/12/001-the-western-mind-of-radical-islam

421 Daniel Pipes, "Islam and Islamism – Faith and Ideology," *National Interest*, Spring 2000, http://www.danielpipes.org/366/islam-and-islamism-faith-and-ideology.

422 *See e.g.*, Jona Lendering, "Simon ben Kosiba (130-136 CE)," http://www.livius.org/ja-jn/jewish_wars/jwar07.html.

423 *See e.g.*, Mike Shuster, "As Iran Exported its Shiite Revolution, Sunni

Arabs Resisted," *NPR,* Feb. 14, 2007, http://www.npr.org/2007/02/14/7392405/export-of-irans-revolution-spawns-violence.

424 *See e.g.,* Roger Hardy, "The Iran-Iraq War: 25 Years On," *BBC,* Sept. 22, 2005, http://news.bbc.co.uk/2/hi/middle_east/4260420.stm.

425 *See e.g.,* Daniel Pipes, "A Border Adrift: Origins of the Iraq-Iran War," in Shirin Tahir-Kheli, ed., *The Iran-Iraq War: New Weapons, Old Conflicts* (Praeger, 1983), http://www.danielpipes.org/164/a-border-adrift-origins-of-the-iraq-iran-war.

426 *See e.g.,* Goodarzi, *supra* n. 414.

427 *See e.g.,* "Saddam States Reasons for Kuwait Invasion," *Gulf News*, July 21, 2009, http://gulfnews.com/opinion/thinkers/saddam-states-reasons-for-kuwait-invasion-1.502105; Nick Williams, "Iraqi Leader Shakes OPEC with Threats Against Overproducers," *Los Angeles Times*, Jul. 20, 1990, http://articles.latimes.com/1990-07-20/news/mn-198_1_persian-gulf.

428 *See e.g.,* Bruce Abramson and Anthony Finizza, "Probabilistic Forecasts from Probabilistic Models: A Case Study in the World Oil Market," *International Journal of Forecasting,* 11:63-72 (1995); Bruce Abramson, "The Design of Belief Network-Based Systems," *Computers and Electrical Engineering,* 20:163-180 (1993).

429 *See e.g.,* Bruce Abramson, "Realpolitik, Not Myth, Will Help Saudis," *Los Angeles Daily News*, Nov. 15, 1990. Available from http://nl.newsbank.com/nl-search/we/Archives.

430 *See e.g.,* Linda Feldmann, "The Impact of Bush Linking 9/11 and Iraq," *Christian Science Monitor,* Mar. 14, 2003, http://www.csmonitor.com/2003/0314/p02s01-woiq.html.

431 *See e.g.,* "Bush, Blair: Libya to Dismantle WMD Programs," *CNN*, Dec. 20, 2003, http://www.cnn.com/2003/WORLD/africa/12/19/bush.libya/.

432 *See e.g.,* Editorial, "The Cedar Revolution," *New York Sun*, Mar. 1, 2005, http://www.nysun.com/editorials/cedar-revolution/9872/.

433 *See e.g.,* Lydia Smith, "Arab Spring 5 Years On: Timeline of the Major Events and Uprisings in the Middle East," *International Business Times,* Jan. 23, 2016, http://www.ibtimes.co.uk/arab-spring-5-years-timeline-major-events-uprisings-middle-east-1539085.

434 *See e.g.,* Jordan Schachtel, "Egyptian Pres. Says Qatar & Turkey Inciting Chaos in Middle East," *Breitbart*, Aug. 27, 2014, http://www.breitbart.com/national-security/2014/08/27/egyptian-

pres-says-qatar-turkey-inciting-chaos-in-middle-east/; James Lewis, "Obama is Openly Colluding with the Enemy," *American Thinker*, Feb. 2, 2015, http://www.americanthinker.com/articles/2015/02/obama_is_openly_colluding_with_the_enemy.html; Gamal Eassam El-Din, "V for Vindication," *Al-Ahram Weekly*, Oct. 2, 2014, http://weekly.ahram.org.eg/News/7434/17/V-for-vindication.aspx.

[435] See e.g., Samuels, *supra* n. 111.

[436] *See e.g.,* Goldberg, *supra* n. 101.

[437] *See e.g.,* Ariel Ben Solomon, "Libya Could Replace Syria and Iraq as Main Islamic State Hub," *Jerusalem Post*, Apr. 4, 2016, http://www.jpost.com/Middle-East/Libya-could-replace-Syria-and-Iraq-as-main-ISIS-hub-450150.

[438] *See e.g.,* Pam Key, "McCain: US Absence in Middle East Giving Iran Control of Iraq, Yemen, Syria, and Lebanon," *Breitbart*, May 18, 2005, http://www.breitbart.com/video/2015/05/18/mccain-us-absence-in-middle-east-giving-iran-control-of-iraq-yemen-syria-and-lebanon.

[439] *See e.g.,* Juan Cole, "Iran is Open for Business. What Does This Mean for the Global Economy?" *The Nation*, http://www.thenation.com/article/iran-is-open-for-business-what-does-this-mean-for-the-global-economy/.

[440] *See e.g.,* Jennifer Rubin, "Obama's Iran Scheme is Laid Bare," *Washington Post,* Mar. 13, 2015, https://www.washingtonpost.com/blogs/right-turn/wp/2015/03/13/obamas-iran-scheme-is-laid-bare/.

[441] *See e.g.,* Seth Mandel, "The Iran Deal Ensures a Mideast Arms Race— Nukes and All," *New York Post*, Aug. 21, 2015, http://nypost.com/2015/08/21/the-iran-deal-ensures-a-mideast-arms-race-nukes-and-all/.

[442] *See e.g.,* "EU Officials Warn: Hamas Siphoning Off Reconstruction Funds to Rearm, Despite Aid Projects," *The Algemeiner*, Nov. 17, 2014, https://www.algemeiner.com/2014/11/17/eu-officials-warn-hamas-siphoning-off-reconstruction-funds-to-rearm-despite-aid-projects/ and "EU Appeals Removal of Hamas from Terror List," *Al Jazeera,* http://www.aljazeera.com/news/europe/2015/01/eu-appeals-removal-hamas-from-terror-list-20151199455520670.html.

[443] *See e.g.,* El-Din, *supra* n. 434.

[444] *See e.g.,* Dennis Ross, "Why Middle Eastern Leaders are Talking to Putin, not Obama," *Politico,* May 8, 2016,

http://www.politico.com/magazine/story/2016/05/putin-obama-middle-east-leaders-213867; Paul Bonicelli, "Russia Capably Steps into Middle East's Void," *The Federalist*, Mar. 16, 2016, http://thefederalist.com/2016/03/16/russia-capably-steps-into-middle-easts-void/; Con Coughlin, "Vladimir Putin and the End of American Influence in the Middle East," *The Telegraph*, Sept. 29, 2015, http://www.telegraph.co.uk/news/worldnews/middleeast/syria/11900206/Vladimir-Putin-and-the-end-of-American-influence-in-the-Middle-East.html.

445 *See e.g.*, Editorial, "At the Boiling Point with Israel," *New York Times*, Oct. 6, 2016, http://www.nytimes.com/2016/10/07/opinion/a-way-to-keep-the-2-state-option-alive.html; Muhammad Shtayyeh, "How to Save Obama's Legacy in Palestine," *New York Times*, Oct. 26, 2016, http://www.nytimes.com/2016/10/27/opinion/how-to-save-obamas-legacy-in-palestine.html.

446 *See e.g.*, Erik Kirschbaum and Andrea Shalal, "Merkel Admits Mistakes Made in Germany, EU with Refugee Crisis," *Reuters*, Aug. 30, 2016, http://www.reuters.com/article/us-europe-migrants-germany-idUSKCN1152IU.

447 *See e.g.*, Barry Shaw, "Solving the European Migrant Problem," *Gatestone Institute*, Sept. 13, 2015, https://www.gatestoneinstitute.org/6491/european-migrant-problem.

448 *See e.g.*, Bruce Abramson and Jeff Ballabon, "For Whom they Came...First," *American Spectator*, Jan. 12, 2016, http://spectator.org/65153_whom-they-came-first/.

449 *See e.g.*, Denis MacShane, "France's Prime Minister is Right to Equate anti-Zionism with anti-Semitism," *Haaretz*, Mar. 11, 2016, http://www.haaretz.com/opinion/.premium-1.708264 .

450 Abi Wilkinson, "The Brexit Vote is Really About Just One Thing," *The New Republic*, Jun. 21, 2016, https://newrepublic.com/article/134507/brexit-vote-really-just-one-thing.

451 *See e.g.*, Devorah Halberstam and Bruce Abramson, "Are We Next?" *Jerusalem Post*, Oct. 5, 2016, http://www.jpost.com/Opinion/Are-we-next-469476.

452 *See e.g.*, Marc Theissen, "Poll: 13% of Syrian Refugees are ISIS Sympathizers," *AEIdeas*, Nov. 20, 2015, http://www.aei.org/publication/poll-13-of-syrian-refugees-are-isis-

sympathizers/.

453 *See e.g.*, Ret. Adm. James Lyons, "Tracing the Roots of Islamic Jihad," *Accuracy in Media*, Mar. 12, 2016, http://www.aim.org/guest-column/tracing-the-roots-of-islamic-jihad/.

454 *See e.g.*, Rebecca Kaplan, "Hillary Clinton: U.S. Should Take 65,000 Syrian Refugees," *CBS News*, Sept. 20, 2015, http://www.cbsnews.com/news/hillary-clinton-u-s-should-take-65000-syrian-refugees/.

455 *See e.g.*, Goldberg, *supra* n. 101.

456 *See e.g.*, Michael Meyer, "The 10th Anniversary of a Photo that Changed the Iraq War," *Columbia Journalism Review*, Mar. 30, 2014, http://www.cjr.org/feature/one_day_in_the_war_of_images.php?page=all.

457 *See e.g.*, Goldberg, *supra* n. 101.

458 *See e.g.*, *id.*; Samuels, *supra* n. 111.

459 *See e.g.*, Sohail Mahmood, "The United States and the Issue of Iran-Saudi Arabia Rivalry," *E-International Relations*, Jan. 20, 2016, http://www.e-ir.info/2016/01/20/the-united-states-and-the-issue-of-iran-saudi-arabia-rivalry/.

460 *See e.g.*, Roland Flamini, "Analysis: Arab League Admits 'New' Iraq," *UPI*, Sept. 10, 2003, http://www.upi.com/Business_News/Security-Industry/2003/09/10/Analysis-Arab-League-admits-new-Iraq/48081063237043/.

461 *See e.g.*, Pipes, *supra* n. 355.

462 *See e.g.*, Richard Clogg, *A Concise History of Greece*, (Cambridge U. Press, 2002).

463 *See e.g.*, R.M. Douglas, "The Expulsion of the Germans: The Largest Forced Migration in History," *Huffington Post*, Aug. 25, 2012, http://www.huffingtonpost.com/rm-douglas/expulsion-germans-forced-migration_b_1625437.html.

464 *See e.g.*, Brilliant Maps, *supra* n. 35.

465 *See e.g.*, Abramson and Finizza, *supra* n. 428.

466 See e.g., id.

467 Obama, *supra* n. 98.

468 *Id.*

469 *See e.g.*, Shireen Burki, "Barack Obama – Muslim Apostate?" *Christian Science Monitor*, May 19, 2008, http://www.csmonitor.com/Commentary/Opinion/2008/0519/p09s

02-coop.html.

470 *See e.g.,* Jayson Georges, "Honor and Shame Societies: 9 Keys to Working with Muslims," http://www.zwemercenter.com/guide/honor-and-shame-9-keys/.

471 Peter Naffsiger, "'Face' Among the Arabs," *Studies in Intelligence* 8(3) (1964) 44-54, https://www.cia.gov/library/center-for-the-study-of-intelligence/kent-csi/vol8no3.

472 *See e.g.,* Dina Rezk, "(W)Archives: CIA and the 'Arab Mind,'" Nov. 21, 2014, http://warontherocks.com/2014/11/warchives-cia-and-the-arab-mind/.

473 *See e.g.,* Rubin *supra* n. 113.

474 *See e.g.,* Patrice Taddonio, "'The President Blinked': Why Obama Changed Course on the 'Red Line' in Syria," *Frontline,* http://www.pbs.org/wgbh/frontline/article/the-president-blinked-why-obama-changed-course-on-the-red-line-in-syria/.

475 *See e.g.,* Samuels, *supra* n. 111.

476 *See e.g.,* Kristina Wong, "Obama's Unsettled Legacy on Iraq and Afghanistan," *The Hill,* Feb. 10, 206, http://thehill.com/policy/defense/268854-obamas-unsettled-legacy-on-iraq-and-afghanistan.

477 *See e.g.,* Caroline Glick, "Understanding the Israeli-Egyptian-Saudi Alliance," *Jerusalem Post,* Aug. 21, 2014, http://www.jpost.com/Opinion/COLUMN-ONE-Understanding-the-Israeli-Egyptian-Saudi-alliance-371891.

478 *See e.g.,* Deborah Amos, "Arab Leaders Feel U.S. Abandoned Egypt's Mubarak," *NPR,* Feb. 9, 2011, http://www.npr.org/2011/02/09/133614346/Egypt-Arab-Leaders.

479 *See e.g.,* Schachtel, *supra* n. 434; Lewis, *supra* n. 434; El-Din, *supra* n. 434.

480 *See e.g.,* Nancy Youssef, "U.S. Won't Back Egypt's Attacks on ISIS," *Daily Beast,* Feb. 19, 2015, http://www.thedailybeast.com/articles/2015/02/18/u-s-won-t-back-egypt-s-attacks-on-isis.html.

481 *See e.g.,* "Obama 'Leaking Info on Israeli Strikes in Syria,'" *Arutz Sheva,* Aug. 3, 2013, http://www.israelnationalnews.com/News/News.aspx/170547#.V15LTmQrIy4.

482 *See e.g.,* Matthew Continetti, "The Obama Intifada," *National Review,* Oct. 17, 2015,

http://www.nationalreview.com/article/425707/obama-intifada-matthew-continetti.

483 *See e.g.,* James Phillips, "Obama Needs to Mend Fences at Gulf Cooperation Council Summit," *Heritage Issue Brief #4549*, Apr. 20, 2016, http://www.heritage.org/research/reports/2016/04/obama-needs-to-mend-fences-at-gulf-cooperation-council-summit.

484 *See e.g.,* Editorial Board, "Obama's Iran Deal Falls Far Short of His Own Goals," *Washington Post,* April 2, 2015, https://www.washingtonpost.com/opinions/obamas-iran-deal-falls-well-short-of-his-own-goals/2015/04/02/7974413c-d95c-11e4-b3f2-607bd612aeac_story.html.

485 *See e.g.,* Abramson, *supra* n. 429.

486 *See e.g.,* Ruth Eglash, "How Two Red Sea Islands Shed Light on Secret Relations Between Israel and Saudi Arabia," *Washington Post,* April 13, 2016, https://www.washingtonpost.com/news/worldviews/wp/2016/04/13/how-two-red-sea-islands-shed-light-on-secret-relations-between-israel-and-saudi-arabia/.

487 *See e.g.,* Julie McCarthy, "A Dictator's Legacy of Economic Growth," *NPR,* Sept. 14, 2006, http://www.npr.org/templates/story/story.php?storyId=6069233.

488 *See e.g.,* Steve Emerson, "State Department Website Panders To Radical Islamists," *IPT News,* September 14, 2009, http://www.investigativeproject.org/1411/state-department-website-panders-to-radical.

489 Muslim Reform Movement, *Declaration,* Dec. 4, 2015, http://muslimreformmovement.org/declaration; *see also,* Ayaan Hirsi Ali, "The Islam Reformers vs. the Muslim Zealots," *Wall Street Journal,* Mar. 27, 2015, https://www.washingtonpost.com/opinions/the-islam-reformers-vs-the-muslim-zealots/2015/03/27/acf6de6c-d3ed-11e4-ab77-9646eea6a4c7_story.html.

490 *See,* "Member States," *Organization of Islamic Cooperation,* http://www.oic-oci.org/oicv3/states/?lan=en.

491 *See e.g.,* Sam Harris and Salman Rushdie, "Ayaan Hirsi Ali: Abandoned to Fanatics," *Los Angeles Times,* Oct. 9, 2007, http://www.latimes.com/news/la-oe-harris9oct09-story.html.

492 Ayaan Hirsi Ali, "Why Islam Needs a Reformation," *Wall Street Journal,* Mar. 20, 2015, http://www.wsj.com/articles/a-reformation-for-islam-

<u>1426859626</u>.

[493] *See e.g.,* David Bukay, "Peace or Jihad? Abrogation in Islam," *Middle East Quarterly,* Fall 2007, 3-11, http://www.meforum.org/1754/peace-or-jihad-abrogation-in-islam; Mark Durie, "Violence and Context in Islamic Texts," *Gatestone Institute,* Jun. 20, 2013, http://www.gatestoneinstitute.org/3771/violence-islamic-texts.

[494] Hirsi Ali, *supra* n. 492.

[495] Pipes, *supra* n. 421.

[496] Hirsi Ali, *supra* n. 492.

[497] Id.

[498] Hirsi Ali, *supra* n. 489.

[499] *Id..*

[500] *See e.g.,* Emerson, *supra* n. 488; Daniel Pipes, "The U.S. Government's Poor Record on Islamists," *Lion's Den,* Jun. 23, 2004, http://www.danielpipes.org/blog/2004/06/the-us-governments-poor-record-on-islamists.

[501] *See e.g.,* Sherrie Gossett, "Federal Money goes to Controversial Muslim Group," *Accuracy in Media,* Mar. 15, 2005, http://www.aim.org/aim-column/federal-money-goes-to-controversial-muslim-group/; IPT, "Islamic Society of North America," *Investigative Project,* http://www.investigativeproject.org/documents/misc/275.pdf; IPT, "CAIR Exposed," *Investigative Project,* http://www.investigativeproject.org/documents/misc/122.pdf; Joe Kaufman, "Sam ISNA, Same Terror," *Frontpage Mag,* Dec. 11, 2013, http://www.frontpagemag.com/fpm/212865/same-isna-same-terror-joe-kaufman.

[502] *See,* Daniel Pipes and Sharon Chadha, "CAIR: Islamists Fooling the Establishment," *Middle East Quarterly,* Spring 2006, http://www.meforum.org/916/cair-islamists-fooling-the-establishment.

[503] *See e.g.,* Daniel Pipes, "Is CAIR a Terror Group?" *National Review,* Nov. 28, 2014, http://www.nationalreview.com/article/393614/cair-terror-group-daniel-pipes.

[504] *See e.g.,* FBI, "2012 Hate Crime Statistics," FBI, https://ucr.fbi.gov/hate-crime/2012/topic-pages/victims/victims_final.

[505] *See e.g.,* Cleveland, *supra* n. 241 at 164.

506 *See e.g.,* Pipes, *supra* n. 420.

507 *See e.g.,* Burki, *supra* n. 469.

508 *See,* Hirsi Ali, *supra* n. 492.

509 *Id.*

510 *Id.*

511 *See e.g.,* Bush and Scowcroft, supra n. 48; Baker, *supra* n. 51.

512 *See e.g.,* "Freedom in the World: Kuwait," https://freedomhouse.org/report/freedom-world/2015/kuwait.

513 *See e.g.,* Flamini, *supra* n. 460.

514 *See e.g.,* UNRWA, "Overall Donor Ranking, 2015," http://www.unrwa.org/sites/default/files/2015_donors_ranking_ove rall.pdf.

515 *See e.g.,* Avi Issacharoff, "Palestinian Television StillGlorifies Terror Attacks Against Israel," *Haaretz,* Feb. 19, 2012, http://www.haaretz.com/israel-news/palestinian-television-still-glorifies-terror-attacks-against-israel-1.413485.

516 *See e.g.,* The White House, "Readout of the President's Phone Call with Prime Minister Haidar Al-Abadi of Iraq," Jan. 6, 2016, https://www.whitehouse.gov/the-press-office/2016/01/06/readout-presidents-phone-call-prime-minister-haidar-al-abadi-iraq; Henry Kissinger, "A Path Out of the Middle East Collapse," *Wall Street Journal,* Oct. 16, 2015, http://www.wsj.com/articles/a-path-out-of-the-middle-east-collapse-1445037513.

517 *See e.g.,* Reuters, "U.S. Clinging to Two-State Solution for Israel and Palestine," *Newsweek,* Mar. 9, 2016, http://www.newsweek.com/us-clinging-two-state-solution-israel-and-palestine-435342.

518 *See e.g., Zivotofsky v. Kerry,* 135 S.Ct. 2076 (2015).

519 *See e.g.,* Elliott Abrams, "The Settlement Obsession," *Foreign Affairs,* Jul./Aug. 2011, https://www.foreignaffairs.com/reviews/review-essay/settlement-obsession.

520 *See e.g.,* Wong, *supra* n. 476.

521 *See e.g.,* Taddonio, *supra* n. 474.

522 *See e.g.,* Guy Taylor and Ben Wolfgang, "Obama Downplays Iran 'Death to America' Remarks, Toes Hard Line on Benjamin Netanyahu, *Washington Times,* http://www.washingtontimes.com/news/2015/mar/23/obama-downplays-iran-death-to-america-remarks-toes/.

[523] *See e.g.*, Editorial, *supra* n. 484.

[524] *See e.g.*, Malcolm Byrne, "Secret U.S. Overture to Iran in 1999 Broke Down over Terrorism Allegiance," *National Security Archive Electronic Briefing Book No. 318*, May 30, 2010, http://nsarchive.gwu.edu/NSAEBB/NSAEBB318/.

[525] *See e.g.*, Geopolitical Diary, "Bush's Overtures to Iran and a Message to the American Public," *Stratfor*, April 11, 2008, https://www.stratfor.com/geopolitical-diary/geopolitical-diary-bushs-overtures-iran-and-message-american-public.

[526] *See e.g.*, Montanaro, *et. al.*, *supra* n. 130.

[527] George W. Bush, "'Islam is Peace,' says President," The White House, Sept. 17, 2001.

[528] *See e.g.*, Aaron Blake, "Obama says the Islamic State 'is not Islamic.' Americans Disagree." *Washington Post*, Sept. 11, 2014, https://www.washingtonpost.com/news/the-fix/wp/2014/09/11/obama-says-the-islamic-state-is-not-islamic-americans-are-inclined-to-disagree/.

[529] Hillary Clinton, "Transcript," *Time,* Nov. 9, 2015, http://time.com/4120295/hillary-clinton-foreign-policy-isis/.

[530] *See e.g.*, Fradkin, *supra* n. 417.

[531] *Id.*

[532] *See e.g.*, Otterman, *supra* n. 416.

[533] See e.g., Rubin, *supra* n. 259.

[534] *See e.g.*, Michael Rubin, "Is Erdoğan's End Game a Caliphate?" *AEIdeas*, Mar. 9, 2016, https://www.aei.org/publication/is-Erdoğans-end-goal-a-caliphate/.

[535] Raymond Ibrahim, "Egypt's Sisi: Islamic 'Thinking' is 'Antagonizing the Entire World," Jan. 1, 2015, http://www.raymondibrahim.com/2015/01/01/egypts-sisi-islamic-thinking-is-antagonizing-the-entire-world/.

[536] *See e.g.*, John Bolton, "Egypt's President is a Courageous Warrior who has the Guts to Confront Radical Islam," *New York Daily News,* Jan. 14, 2015, http://www.nydailynews.com/opinion/john-bolton-egypt-courageous-warrior-article-1.2076747.

[537] *See e.g.*, Jonah Goldberg, "Islam Reformer being Ignored," *USA Today*, Jan. 8, 2015, http://www.usatoday.com/wlna/opinion/2015/01/07/paris-terror-shooting-al-sisi-epochal-speech/21390881/.

538 *See e.g.,* King Hussein, *supra* n. 221.

539 *See e.g.,* King Abdullah II, "Speech before the Military Society of Norway," April 11, 2000, http://kingabdullah.jo/index.php/en_US/speeches/view/id/129/videoDisplay/0.html; Profile, *supra* n. 232.

540 *See e.g.,* Milton Viorst, *In the Shadow of the Prophet: The Struggle for the Soul of Islam,* (Basic Books, 2001), at ch. 10, "The Hashemite Option," (1998), available at http://www.kinghussein.gov.jo/98_viorst.html.

541 *See e.g.,* Marc Charney, "The Calculations of Strategic Assessment," *New York Times,* May 23, 2004, http://www.nytimes.com/2004/05/23/weekinreview/the-world-the-calculations-of-strategic-assassination.html?_r=0.

542 *See e.g.,* Counter-Extremism Project, "Jordan: Extremism & Counter-Extremism," http://www.counterextremism.com/countries/jordan.

543 James M. Dorsey, "Saudi Arabia's Future: Will Al Saud's Partnership with Wahhabism Hold?" *The World Post,* Feb. 26, 2016, http://www.huffingtonpost.com/james-dorsey/saudi-arabias-future-will_b_9324124.html.

544 *See e.g.,* Rubin, *supra* n. 259.

545 Steven Emerson and Jonathan Levin, "Terrorism Financing: Origination, Organization, and Prevention: Saudi Arabia, Terrorist Financing and the War on Terror." Testimony before the United States Senate Committee on Governmental Affairs, Jul. 21, 2003, http://www.investigativeproject.org/documents/testimony/17.pdf.

546 *See e.g.,* Scott MacLeod, "Osama Bin Laden vs. the House of Saud," *Time,* May 14, 2003, http://content.time.com/time/world/article/0,8599,451935,00.html.

547 *See e.g.,* Rebecca Kheel, "Kerry: Some Iran Sanctions Relief will go to Terrorists," *The Hill,* Jan. 21, 2016, http://thehill.com/policy/defense/266619-kerry-some-iran-sanctions-relief-will-go-to-terrorists.

548 *See e.g.,* Erika Solomon, "ISIS Aims to Erase Regional Borders," *Financial Times,* Jun. 23, 2014, http://www.ft.com/intl/cms/s/0/aa5dafc2-fae6-11e3-8959-00144feab7de.html#axzz4BZ77WwTM

549 *See e.g.,* Algemeiner, *supra* n. 442.

550 *See e.g.,* Susanne Koelbl,*et. al., supra* n. 39.

[551] *See e.g.*, Schachtel, *supra* n. 434.

[552] *See e.g.*, PMW, *supra* n. 386.

[553] *See e.g.*, Melani Cammett and Pauline J. Luong, "Is there an Islamist Political Advantage," *Annual Review of Political Science*, 17: 187-206 (May 2014), http://www.ncbi.nlm.nih.gov/pmc/articles/PMC4354680/.

[554] *See e.g.*, Sheila Carapico and Chris Toensing, "The Strategic Logic of the Iraq Blunder," *Middle East Research* 239 (Summer 2006), http://www.merip.org/mer/mer239/strategic-logic-iraq-blunder.

[555] *See e.g.*, Schmitt, *supra* n. 74.

[556] Churchill, *supra* n. 2.

[557] Chaim Kaufmann, "Possible and Impossible Solutions to Ethnic Civil Wars," *International Security*, 20(4): 136-175 (Spring 1996), http://www.columbia.edu/itc/sipa/U6800/readings-sm/Kaufmann_PossibleImpossibleSolns.pdf.

[558] István Bibó, The Art of Peacekeeping, (Yale University Press, 2015) at 173-74 (tr. Péter Pásztor).

[559] *See e.g.*, Editorial, "Genocide and the Islamic State," *New York Times*, Mar. 18, 2016, http://www.nytimes.com/2016/03/18/opinion/genocide-and-the-islamic-state.html.

[560] See e.g. id.

[561] *See e.g.*, UNRWA, *supra* n. 209; UNHCR, *supra* n. 350.

[562] *See e.g.*, Samya Kullab, "Trial by Fire: Can Lebanon's Fragile Stability Hold?" *World Politics Review*, Jun. 18, 2015, http://www.worldpoliticsreview.com/articles/16031/trial-by-fire-can-lebanon-s-fragile-stability-hold.

[563] *See e.g.*, Caroline Glick, "Israel's Great Opportunity," *Jerusalem Post*, Jun. 18, 2015, http://www.jpost.com/Opinion/Column-one-Israels-great-opportunity-406531.

[564] *See e.g.*, Ofir Haivry and Yoram Hazony, "The Druze fight for Israel: Should they now Fight Alone?" *Tablet*, Jul. 7, 2015, http://www.tabletmag.com/jewish-news-and-politics/191891/druze-israel-syria.

[565] *See e.g.*, Edward Delman, "The Link between Putin's Military Campaigns in Syria and Ukraine," *The Atlantic*, Oct. 2, 2015, http://www.theatlantic.com/international/archive/2015/10/navy-base-syria-crimea-putin/408694/.

566 *See e.g.*, Abraham Cooper and Harold Brackman, "Mumbai: Deadly Media Euphemisms," *Simon Wiesenthal Center*, http://www.wiesenthal.com/site/apps/nlnet/content2.aspx?c=lsKWLbPJLnF&b=4441467&ct=6426387#.V3EtPmQrIy4.

567 *See e.g.*, Daniel Greenfield, "Life for Jews in Muslim-Occupied France," *FrontPage Mag*, Jul. 11, 2015, http://www.frontpagemag.com/point/259404/life-jews-muslim-occupied-france-daniel-greenfield.

568 *See e.g.*, Log Cabin Republicans, "Statement on Orlando Shooting," *Log Cabin*, Jun. 12, 2016, http://www.logcabin.org/pressrelease/log-cabin-republicans-statement-on-orlando-shooting/; Anonymous, "I'm a Gay Activist, and After Orlando I have Switched my Vote to Trump," *PJ Media*, Jun. 12, 2016, https://pjmedia.com/trending/2016/06/12/gay-activist-after-orlando-trump-voter/. *See also*, Ayaan Hirsi Ali, "Islam's Jihad Against Homosexuals," *Wall Street Journal,* Jun. 13, 2016, http://www.wsj.com/articles/islams-jihad-against-homosexuals-1465859170.

569 *Cf. e.g.*, Max Fisher, "Gays, Guns and Jihad: Motives Blur on Closer Scrutiny," *New York Times*, Jun. 19, 2016, http://www.nytimes.com/2016/06/15/world/trying-to-know-the-unknowable-why-terrorists-attack.html and Editorial, "Jihad in Orlando," *Wall Street Journal*, Jun. 13, 2016, http://www.wsj.com/articles/jihad-in-orlando-1465772204.

570 *See e.g.*, Martin Peretz, "Why Won't Obama List Israelis among the Victims of Terrorism?" *The New Republic*, Sept. 8, 2011, http://www.wsj.com/articles/islams-jihad-against-homosexuals-1465859170.

571 *See*, U.S. Dept. of State, "Defining Anti-Semitism," Jun. 8, 2010, http://www.state.gov/j/drl/rls/fs/2010/122352.htm; Hannah Rosenthal, "Remarks at the 2011 B'nai B'rith International Policy Conference," *U.S. Dept. of State*, Dec. 5, 2011, http://www.state.gov/j/drl/rls/rm/2011/178448.htm.

572 *See e.g.*, VanderHei, *supra* n. 92.

573 *Cf.*, Jodi Rudoren, "Palestinian Prisoner Release is Critical Hurdle in Resuming Peace Talks," *New York Times,* Jul. 20, 2013, http://www.nytimes.com/2013/07/21/world/middleeast/palestinian-prisoner-release-is-critical-hurdle-in-resuming-peace-talks.html and Jawad Sukhanyar and Rod Nordland, "In Prison Release, Signs of Karzai's Rift with U.S.," *New York Times*, Feb. 13, 2014,

http://www.nytimes.com/2014/02/14/world/asia/afghanistan-releases-prisoners-over-us-objections.html.

574 *See e.g.,* Isaac Herzog, "Only Separation can Lead to a Two-State Solution," *New York Times,* Feb. 28, 2016, http://www.nytimes.com/2016/02/29/opinion/international/only-separation-can-lead-to-a-two-state-solution.html.

575 *See e.g.,* Editorial, *supra* n. 239.

576 *See e.g.,* Mor and Rahimiyan, *supra* n. 316.

577 *See e.g.,* Michael Curtis, "The Disquieting Treatment of Christians by the Palestinians," *Gatestone Institute,* Feb. 15, 2012, http://www.gatestoneinstitute.org/2838/palestinians-christians.

578 *See e.g.,* Morton Klein, "ZOA Condemns Dictator Abbas Reiterating Statement: 'No Jews in Future Palestinian State," *ZOA,* http://zoa.org/2013/07/10209533-zoa-condemns-dictator-abbas-reiterating-statement-no-jews-in-future-palestinianstate/.

579 *See e.g.,* Yalibnan, "Iran Backed Iraqi, Lebanese Shiite Militias Deploy to Syria's Aleppo," *Yalibnan,* Aug. 8, 2016, http://yalibnan.com/2016/08/08/iran-backed-iraqi-lebanese-shiite-militias-deploy-to-syrias-aleppo/.

580 *See e.g.,* Al Jazeera, *supra* n. 261; AFP, *supra* n. 261.

581 *See,* Abdel Fatah El Sisi, "Re-engineering Egypt's Economy," *Wall Street Journal,* Sept. 27, 2015, http://www.wsj.com/articles/re-engineering-egypts-economy-1443385766.

582 *See e.g.,* Erin Cunningham and Heba Habib, "Egypt Bombs Islamic State Targets in Libya after Beheading Video," *Washington Post,* Feb. 16, 2015, https://www.washingtonpost.com/world/egypt-bombs-islamic-state-targets-in-libya-after-brutal-beheading-video/2015/02/16/3b32c50c-b5b6-11e4-9423-f3d0a1ec335c_story.html.

583 *See* Ibrahim, *supra* n. 533.

584 *See e.g.,* Goldberg; *supra* n. 537; Yermi Brenner, "Germany Offers Two-Faced Welcome to Egypt's Sisi," *Al Jazeera,* Jun. 3, 2015, http://america.aljazeera.com/articles/2015/6/3/germany-welcomes-egyptian-president-sisi.html.

585 *See,* USTR, "Middle East Free Trade Area Initiative," https://ustr.gov/trade-agreements/other-initiatives/middle-east-free-trade-area-initiative-mefta.

586 *See,* USTR, "Israel Free Trade Agreement," https://ustr.gov/trade-agreements/free-trade-agreements/israel-fta; USTR, "Jordan Free

Trade Agreement," https://ustr.gov/trade-agreements/free-trade-agreements/jordan-fta.

587 Golda Meir, *A Land of Our Own: An Oral Autobiography* (1973) (ed. Marie Syrkin) at 242.

588 *See e.g.*, Claire Berlinski, "How the Term 'Islamophobia' got Shoved Down Your Throat," *Ricochet*, Nov. 24, 2010, https://ricochet.com/archives/moderate-muslim-watch-how-the-term-islamophobia-got-shoved-down-your-throat/.

589 *See e.g.*, Bina Shah, "The High-Risk Strategy of Muslim Reformers," *Al Jazeera*, Sept. 25, 2015, http://www.aljazeera.com/indepth/opinion/2015/09/cloneofhigh-risk-strategy-muslim-reformers-15092-150925074623115.html; Kashif Chaudhry, "Challenging the ISIS and Islamophobe Narrative on Islam," *Huffington Post*, Nov. 20, 2015, http://www.huffingtonpost.com/kashif-n-chaudhry/does-islam-really-need-re b 8602622.html; Robert Spencer, "Muslim Reformer Exposes Insidious Agenda of 'Islamophobia' Propagandist," *Jihad Watch*, Feb. 25, 2016, https://www.jihadwatch.org/2016/02/muslim-reformer-exposes-insidious-agenda-of-islamophobia-propagandist; Transcript, "Irshad Manji on Islamophobia," *Al Jazeera*, Feb. 8, 2016, http://www.aljazeera.com/programmes/headtohead/2016/01/transcript-irshad-manji-islamophobia-160123075229052.html.